Lincoln's

Devotional

LINCOLN'S

Introduction by

Carl Sandburg

CHANNEL PRESS

Channel Press, Inc. · Great Neck, N. Y.

Library of Congress Catalog Card Number: 57-13,471

First Edition

IN DECEMBER of the year 1849, Edward Baker Lincoln, the second of the Lincoln boys, was struck down with illness. It may have been diphtheria. No records of the exact nature of the sickness exist. After fifty-two days of waiting and fear, on the first day of February, Abraham Lincoln held in his arms the white still body of a child of his own. He could call the name of Eddie to his boy, and the boy had no ears to hear nor breath to answer.

This was his own kith and kin, who had come out of silence and gone back to silence, back where Nancy Hanks had gone the year he helped his father peg together a plank coffin. He tried to pierce through into regions of that silence, and find replies to questions that surged in him.

On the day that Eddie was buried, a funeral sermon was pronounced by the Reverend James Smith of the First Presbyterian Church of Springfield, Illinois, and a friendship developed between the Lincoln family and Mr. Smith. The minister had been a wild boy in his young days in Scotland, had been a scoffer at religion, and then had become a preacher in Kentucky. He could tell a story—he and Lincoln were good company. "A good story," said Lincoln, "is medicine to my bones."

It wasn't long after Eddie's death that the Lincolns rented a pew in the church. In 1852 Mrs. Lincoln took the sacrament and joined in membership. Pastor Smith presented Lincoln with a copy of his book, "The Christian's Defense," a reply to infidels and atheists. Lincoln read the book, said he was interested, later attended revival meetings held in the church, and served in several capacities, but when asked to join the church, said he "couldn't quite see it."

In the same year, the Religious Tract Society of London, England, published a daily devotional titled "The Believer's Daily Treasure; or, Texts of Scripture Arranged for Every Day in the Year." On the title page appeared this verse from Psalm cxix:72:

> *The law of thy mouth is better unto*
> *me than thousands of gold and silver*

How Abraham Lincoln acquired his copy of
the devotional we do not know. In 1852 he received as a gift at least one other book concerned with religion, but there is no word to be
found of "The Believer's Daily Treasure." It
could have been a gift from Mary Lincoln; sometime after 1847, Lincoln gave her a large family
Bible, and perhaps this handy, vest-pocket book
was a present from her in return, one he could
carry with him for occasional reading on the
Old Eighth Circuit. We do know that on the
inside cover of the tiny book of Scripture and
verse, Lincoln signed his name with typical
abbreviation. And from this we can surmise that
either the volume itself or the person who presented it to him was held in deep regard, for
throughout his life Lincoln was sparing in the
number of books in which he wrote his name.
His signature, it would seem, was inscribed
more as an expression of strong interest or affection than as a precaution against a book's be-
coming lost, strayed, stolen.

From his earliest reading days as a boy, Lincoln turned the pages of the Bible, and over all
the years of his life he went on with his reading

of it, often quoting from it in private conversations and public addresses. He and his family owned several Bibles. Writing to Mary, the sister of his best friend, Joshua Speed, he said, "Tell your mother that I have not got her present with me, but I intend to read it regularly when I return home." The gift was an Oxford Bible. In 1864 he received a beautiful Bible from a group of Negroes from Baltimore. In acknowledging the gift, Lincoln said, "In regard to this great book, I have but to say it is the best gift God has given to man."

Among universal possessions of the American people are certain speeches and letters of Lincoln that are colored and in part drenched with biblical references and learning. Why did Lincoln say "Four score and seven" instead of the plain figure "eighty-seven" at the opening of his Gettysburg speech? Probably, it has been suggested, because in the Old Testament it reads most often "two score" instead of "twenty," and "four score" instead of "eighty." In the Second Inaugural he spoke as an interpreter of the purposes of the Almighty, as a familiar of the pages of Holy Writ: "The Almighty has his own purposes. 'Woe unto the world because of offences: For it must needs be that offences come; but woe to that man by whom the offence cometh'."

In this Second Inaugural address, of biblical derivation is the expression, "Let us judge not, that we be not judged." As the end of the War came into sight, and the awesome tasks of reconstruction and reconciliation loomed, Lincoln's deep heart's desire was a minimum of hate. When Senator Charles Sumner of Massachusetts spoke of Jefferson Davis—"Do not allow him to escape the law—he must be hanged"—Lincoln replied calmly, "Judge not, that ye be not judged." Again, as Sumner later wrote of it, he pressed Lincoln with a remark that the sight of Libby Prison made it impossible to pardon the President of the Confederate States, and Lincoln repeated twice over the words, "Judge not, that ye be not judged."

In his message of December 1, 1862, Lincoln told Congress of the need for action by the present and living generation, the territory of a nation, its land, being the only part which is of certain durability; and quoting from Scripture, he said: "One generation passeth away, and another generation cometh, but the earth abideth forever."

In Springfield, in the year 1858, biblical in color was Lincoln's address which ever thereafter was known as The House Divided speech. He quoted, "A house divided against itself cannot stand," adding, "I believe this Government cannot endure permanently half slave and half free." The brevity and portent of a Bible verse was there in the opening sentence of that speech: "If we could first know where we are and whither we are tending, we could better judge what to do and how to do it."

The odor of true sanctity and an air of consecration past words saturates the letter of Lincoln to Mrs. Lydia Bixby of Boston, who had lost four sons in the war:

But I cannot refrain from tendering to you the consolation that may be found in the thanks of the Republic they died to save. I pray that our Heavenly Father may assuage the anguish of your bereavement, and leave you only the cherished memory of the loved and lost, and the solemn pride that must be yours to have laid so costly a sacrifice upon the altar of Freedom.

The secretaries Nicolay and Hay were amazed at one instance of Lincoln's familiarity with the Bible. In 1864 news had come of the Cleveland, Ohio, convention of a third party which nominated John C. Frémont for President. A friend drifted into the White House, gave Lincoln an account of the convention, and said that instead of the many thousands expected there were present at no time more than 400 people. The President, struck by the number mentioned, reached for the Bible on his desk, searched a moment, then read the words: "'And everyone that was in distress, and everyone that was in debt, and everyone that was discontented, gathered themselves unto him; and he became captain over them; and there were with him about four hundred men.'"

In proclamations, in recommendations of thanksgiving or of fasting and prayer, and in numerous references to God, Providence, the Almighty, the Common Father, Lincoln gave the impression to the multitude that he had a creed. A clergyman—William E. Barton—sought to formulate such a statement of faith from Lincoln's own words, changing the text merely to the extent of transposing pronouns from plural to singular, making other slight modifications, and prefixing the words, "I believe." The result was almost liturgical, containing expressions such as these:

I believe in penitential and pious sentiments, in devotional designs and purposes, in homages and confessions, in supplications to the Almighty, solemnly, earnestly, reverently.

I believe in blessings and comfort from the Father of Mercies to the sick, the wounded, the prisoners, and to the orphans and widows.

I believe it pleases Almighty God to prolong our national life, defending us with His guardian care.

I believe in His eternal truth and justice.

I believe the will of God prevails; without Him all human reliance is vain; without the assistance of that Divine Being I cannot succeed; with that assistance I cannot fail.

I believe I am a humble instrument in the hands of our Heavenly Father; I desire that all my works and acts may be according to

His will; and that it may be so, I give thanks
to the Almighty and seek His aid.

I believe in praise to Almighty God, the
beneficent Creator and Ruler of the Universe.

Henry C. Deming, Congressman from Connecticut, reported that when Lincoln was asked
why, with his obvious interest in religious matters and his familiarity with the Bible, he did
not join a church, Lincoln replied:

When any church will inscribe over its altars, as
its sole qualification for membership, the Savior's
condensed statement for the substance of both law
and gospel, "Thou shalt love the Lord thy God with
all thy heart, and with all thy soul, and with all thy
mind, and thy neighbor as thyself," that church will
I join with all my heart and soul.

And his law partner, William H. Herndon,
quotes Lincoln as saying that his religion was
like that of an old man he once heard speak at
a church meeting: "When I do good," the man
had said, "I feel good; when I do bad, I feel bad;
and that's my religion."

Although the Lincoln field has been worked
and winnowed year after year, from time to

time, happily enough, something new does turn up. It was not until some eighty years after his death that a printed statement was discovered in which he answered election campaign charges that he was "an open scoffer at Christianity" by saying, in part, "I have never denied the truth of the Scripture" and "I do not think I could myself, be brought to support a man for office whom I knew to be an open enemy of, and scoffer at, religion."

John Jay, grandson of the great Chief Justice and a notable Civil War figure himself, was reported by Frank B. Carpenter as saying he had seen Lincoln reading a "pocket edition of the New Testament." Cautious students have not accepted fully the report by Jay and others, due primarily to the lack of the Testament itself. Perhaps the discovery of this little book will increase research into the religious attitudes of Abraham Lincoln and throw new light on that long debated problem. In the meantime, some may ask themselves if the reported pocket Testament might not indeed have been this little devotional.

In "The Believer's Daily Treasure" Lincoln

could come upon many sentences and phrases famous, important and often quoted; and many of the passages in the book could have had special interest for him, and direct or indirect influence on his thought and speech. This daily devotional, unseen for many years, takes us no farther toward placing Lincoln within creed or denomination; but it is new testimony that he was a man of profound faith. "Take all this book upon reason that you can, and the balance on faith," Lincoln said of the Bible to his friend Joshua Speed in 1864, "and you will live and die a better man."

CARL SANDBURG

The devotional portion of this volume contains the entire text of "The Believer's Daily Treasure; or, Texts of Scripture Arranged for Every Day in the Year," published in 1852 by the Religious Tract Society of London, England. The material is reprinted as it appears in the copy of the book which Abraham Lincoln owned, and therefore contains the several inconsistencies and typographical errors found in the original edition.

Lincoln's signed copy of "The Believer's Daily Treasure" is now a part of the collection of Lincolniana owned by Mr. Carl Haverlin. No other copy of any edition of the book has been found at the time of this writing. Mr. Haverlin, president of Broadcast Music, Inc., is active in a number of organizations in the field of American history. He is president of the Civil War Centennial Association, founder and past president of the New York chapter of the Civil War Round Table, and a trustee of Lincoln Memorial University.

The photographs which follow show the book owned and inscribed by Abraham Lincoln.

46 MARCH.

20. INDWELLING OF THE SPIRIT.

Know ye not that ye are the temple of God, and that the Spirit of God dwelleth in you? 1 *Cor.* iii. 16.

Think what Spirit dwells within thee;
Think what Father's smiles are thine;
Think that Jesus died to win thee:
Child of heaven, canst thou repine?

21. INTERCESSION OF THE SPIRIT.

The Spirit also helpeth our infirmities: for we know not what we should pray for as we ought: but the Spirit itself maketh intercession for us with groanings which cannot be uttered. *Rom.* viii. 26.

Let pure devotion's fervours rise,
Let every holy feeling glow;
Oh, let the rapture of the skies
Kindle in our cold hearts below.
Come, vivifying Spirit, come,
And make our hearts thy constant home.

BELIEVER'S PRIVILEGES. 47

22. SANCTIFICATION BY THE SPIRIT.

Elect according to the foreknowledge of God the Father, through sanctification of the Spirit, unto obedience and sprinkling of the blood of Jesus. 1 *Pet.* i. 2.

Can aught beneath a power divine
The stubborn will subdue?
'Tis thine, eternal Spirit, thine,
To form our hearts anew.
'Tis thine the passions to recall,
And upwards bid them rise;
And make the scales of error fall
From reason's darkened eyes.

23. THE FRUITS OF THE SPIRIT.

The fruit of the Spirit is love, joy, peace, long-suffering, gentleness, goodness, faith, meekness, temperance: against such there is no law. *Gal.* v. 22, 23.

'Tis God himself the ground prepares,
His Spirit sows the land;
And every pleasant fruit it bears,
Is nurtur'd by his hand.

THE
BELIEVER'S
DAILY
TREASURE;

or,

Texts of Scripture,
arranged for every day in the year.

The law of thy mouth is better unto me
than thousands of gold and silver.
Psalm cxix. 72.

FOURTH EDITION

LONDON:

THE RELIGIOUS TRACT SOCIETY;

Depository, 56, Paternoster Row, and
65, St. Paul's Churchyard;

AND SOLD BY THE BOOKSELLERS.

1852.

C. Whittingham, Tooks Court, Chancery Lane.

CONTENTS

January

THE
TRUE BELIEVER

1

The Believer the Object of
Divine Love

In this was manifested the love of God toward us, because that God sent his only begotten Son into the world, that we might live through him. *1 John* iv. 9.

> Pause, my soul, adore and wonder,
> Ask, Oh, why such love to me?
> Grace hath put me in the number
> Of the Saviour's family:
> Hallelujah!
> Thanks, eternal thanks to thee.

2

Redeemed by the Blood of Christ

FORASMUCH as ye know that ye were not redeemed with corruptible things, as silver and gold—but with the precious blood of Christ, as of a lamb without blemish and without spot. *1 Pet.* i. 18, 19.

> Our sins and griefs on him were laid;
> He meekly bore the mighty load:
> Our ransom price he fully paid,
> By offering up himself to God.

3

Renewed by the Holy Ghost

NOT by works of righteousness which we have done, but according to his mercy he saved us, by the washing of regeneration, and renewing of the Holy Ghost.

Titus iii. 5.

> Vain is every outward rite,
> Unless thy grace be given:
> Nothing but thy life and light,
> Can form a soul for heaven.

4

Partaker of the Divine Nature

WHEREBY are given unto us exceeding great and precious promises: that by these ye might be partakers of the divine nature, having escaped the corruption that is in the world through lust. *2 Pet.* i. 4.

Blessed are the sons of God;
They are bought with Christ's own blood;
They produce the fruits of grace
In the works of righteousness:
Born of God, they hate all sin;
God's pure word remains within.

5

Justified Before God
Through Christ

BY him all that believe are justified from all things, from which ye could not be justified by the law of Moses. *Acts* xiii. 39.

Jesus, thy blood and righteousness
My beauty are, and glorious dress;
'Midst flaming worlds, in these array'd,
With joy shall I lift up my head.

7

6

United to Christ

I AM the vine, ye are the branches: he that
abideth in me, and I in him, the same
bringeth forth much fruit: for without me
ye can do nothing. *John* xv. 5.

> Lord of the vineyard, we adore
> That power and grace divine,
> Which plants our wild, our barren souls,
> In Christ the living Vine.
>
> For ever there may I abide,
> And from that vital root,
> Be influence spread through every branch,
> To form and feed the fruit.

7

Joint-Heir with Christ

IF children, then heirs; heirs of God, and
joint-heirs with Christ. *Rom.* viii. 17.

> Pronounce me, gracious God, thy son;
> Own me an heir divine;
> I'll pity princes on the throne,
> When I can call thee mine:
> Sceptres and crowns unenvied rise,
> And lose their lustre in mine eyes.

8

8

Complete in Christ

FOR in him dwelleth all the fulness of the Godhead bodily. And ye are complete in him. *Col.* ii. 9, 10.

> Thy saints on earth, and those above,
>   Here join in sweet accord:
> One body all in mutual love,
>   And thou their common Lord.
> Yes, thou that body wilt present
>   Before thy Father's face,
> Nor shall a wrinkle or a spot
>   Its beauteous form disgrace.

9

Christ the Believer's Advocate

IF any man sin, we have an advocate with the Father, Jesus Christ the righteous.
                                          1 John ii. 1.

> Look up, my soul, with cheerful eye,
>   See where the great Redeemer stands—
> Thy glorious Advocate on high,
>   With precious incense in his hands.
>
> He sweetens every humble groan,
>   He recommends each broken prayer;
> Recline thy hope on him alone,
>   Whose power and love forbid despair.

10

Christ the Hope of the Believer

PAUL, an apostle of Jesus Christ by the commandment of God our Saviour, and Lord Jesus Christ, which is our hope.

1 Tim. i. 1.

Jesus, my Lord, I look to thee;
  Where else can helpless sinners go?
Thy boundless love shall set me free
  From all my wretchedness and woe.

11

Christ the Life of the Believer

WHEN Christ, who is our life, shall appear, then shall ye also appear with him in glory.

Col. iii. 4.

If my immortal Saviour lives,
  Then my eternal life is sure;
His word a firm foundation gives,
  Here let me build, and rest secure.

Here, O my soul, thy trust repose;
  If Jesus is for ever mine,
Not death itself, that last of foes,
  Shall break a union so divine.

12

Christ the Peace of the Believer

Now in Christ Jesus ye who sometime were far off are made nigh by the blood of Christ. For he is our peace. *Eph.* ii. 13, 14.

> "He is our peace"—for by his blood
> Sinners are reconcil'd to God;
> Sweet harmony is now restor'd,
> And man beloved, and God ador'd.

13

Christ the Righteousness of the Believer

This is his name whereby he shall be called, The Lord our righteousness. *Jer.* xxiii. 6.

> Saviour divine, we know thy name,
>   And in that name we trust;
> Thou art the Lord our righteousness,
>   Thou art thine Israel's boast.
>
> That spotless robe which thou hast wrought,
>   Shall clothe us all around,
> Nor by the piercing eye of God
>   One blemish shall be found.

11

14

The Temple of the Spirit

KNOW ye not that your body is the temple of the Holy Ghost which is in you, which ye have of God. *1 Cor.* vi. 19.

> Creator Spirit! by whose aid
> The world's foundations first were laid,
> Come, visit every humble mind;
> Come, pour thy joys on human kind:
> From sin and sorrow set us free,
> And make us temples worthy thee.

15

Sanctified by the Spirit

GOD hath from the beginning chosen you to salvation through sanctification of the Spirit and belief of the truth.

2 Thess. ii. 13.

> Come, Holy Spirit, love divine,
>   Thy cleansing power impart;
> Each erring thought and wish refine
>   That wanders near my heart.

16

Upheld by the Spirit

THAT he would grant you, according to the riches of his glory, to be strengthened with might by his Spirit in the inner man.

Eph. iii. 16.

> Assisted by his grace,
> We still pursue our way;
> And hope at last to reach the prize,
> Secure in endless day.

17

The Spirit of Adoption Received

YE have not received the spirit of bondage again to fear; but ye have received the Spirit of adoption, whereby we cry, Abba, Father.

Rom. viii. 15.

> Assure my conscience of her part
> In the Redeemer's blood,
> And bear thy witness in my heart
> That I am born of God.

13

18

Comforted by the Spirit

WHEN the Comforter is come, whom I will send unto you from the Father, even the Spirit of truth, which proceedeth from the Father, he shall testify of me. *John* xv. 26.

> In the hour of my distress,
> When temptations me oppress,
> And when I my sins confess—
> Sweet Spirit, comfort me.

19

Sealed by the Spirit

GRIEVE not the holy Spirit of God, whereby ye are sealed unto the day of redemption.
Eph. iv. 30.

> Forbid it, Lord, that we
> Who from thy hands receive
> The Spirit's power to make us free,
> Should e'er that Spirit grieve.
>
> O keep our faith alive,
> Help us to watch and pray;
> Lest, by our carelessness, we drive
> The sacred Guest away.

20

Taught by the Spirit

WHEN he, the Spirit of truth, is come, he
will guide you into all truth: for he shall not
speak of himself; but whatsoever he shall
hear, that shall he speak: and he will show
you things to come. *John* xvi. 13.

> Thine inward teachings make me know
> The mysteries of redeeming love,
> The emptiness of things below,
> And excellence of things above.

21

Fellow-Citizen with the Saints

Now therefore ye are no more strangers and
foreigners, but fellow-citizens with the
saints, and of the household of God.
Eph. ii. 19.

> The kindred links of life are bright,
> Yet not so bright as those
> In which Christ's favoured friends unite,
> And each on each repose:
> Where all the hearts in union cling,
> With Him, the centre and the spring.

15

22

Lives a Life of Faith in Christ

I AM crucified with Christ: nevertheless I live; yet not I, but Christ liveth in me: and the life which I now live in the flesh I live by the faith of the Son of God. *Gal.* ii. 20.

> Close to the ignominious tree,
>   Jesus, my humbled soul would cleave;
> Despised and crucified with thee,
>   With Christ resolved to die and live:
> There would I bow my suppliant knee,
> And own no other Lord but thee.

23

Lives a Life of Consecration to God

I BESEECH you therefore, brethren, by the mercies of God, that ye present your bodies a living sacrifice, holy, acceptable unto God, which is your reasonable service.

Rom. xii. 1.

> Thine, wholly thine, I want to be;
>   The sacrifice receive:
> Made, and preserved, and saved by thee,
>   To thee myself I give.

24

Lives a Life of Hope

LOOKING for the mercy of our Lord Jesus Christ unto eternal life. *Jude* 21.

> Rejoice in glorious hope;
>   Jesus, the Judge, shall come,
> And take his servants up
>   To their eternal home:
> Lift up your heart, lift up your voice;
> Rejoice, he bids his saints rejoice.

25

Delivered from Condemnation

THERE is now no condemnation to them which are in Christ Jesus, who walk not after the flesh, but after the Spirit.

Rom. viii. 1.

> O Love, thou bottomless abyss!
>   My sins are swallow'd up in thee;
> Cover'd is my unrighteousness,
>   From condemnation now I'm free;
> While Jesus' blood through earth and skies,
> "Mercy, free boundless mercy!" cries.

26

Delivered from the Power of Satan

FORASMUCH then as the children are partakers of flesh and blood, he also himself likewise took part of the same; that through death he might destroy him that had the power of death, that is, the devil.

Heb. ii. 14.

Dry up your tears, ye saints, and tell
How high your great Deliverer reigns;
Sing, how he spoiled the host of hell,
And led the tyrant Death in chains.

27

Delivered from All Iniquity

LET Israel hope in the Lord: for with the Lord there is mercy, and with him is plenteous redemption. And he shall redeem Israel from all his iniquities. *Psalm* cxxx. 7, 8.

Fix'd on this ground will I remain,
Though my heart fail, and flesh decay;
This anchor shall my soul sustain,
When earth's foundations melt away:
Mercy's full power I then shall prove,
Lov'd with an everlasting love.

28

Delivered from All Enemies

HE delivereth me from mine enemies; yea, thou liftest me above those that rise up against me. *Psalm* xviii. 48.

> Foes are round us, but we stand
> On the borders of our land:
> Jesus, God's exalted Son,
> Bids us undismay'd go on:
> Onward then we gladly press
> Through this earthly wilderness.

29

Enjoys a Present Salvation

WHICH in time past were not a people, but are now the people of God: which had not obtained mercy, but now have obtained mercy. *1 Pet.* ii. 10.

> Fill'd with holy emulation
>   Let us vie with those above:
> Sweet the theme—a free salvation,
>   Fruit of everlasting love.

30

Preserved unto Eternal Salvation

WHO are kept by the power of God through faith unto salvation ready to be revealed in the last time. *1 Pet.* 1. 5.

> Saints by the power of God are kept
>   Till full salvation come;
> We walk by faith as strangers here
>   Till Christ shall call us home.

31

A Pilgrim to a Heavenly Country

Now they desire a better country, that is, an heavenly: wherefore God is not ashamed to be called their God: for he hath prepared for them a city. *Heb.* xi. 16.

> 'Tis true, we are but strangers
>   And sojourners below;
> And countless snares and dangers
>   Surround the path we go:
> Though painful and distressing,
>   Yet there's a rest above,
> And onward we are pressing
>   To reach that land of love.

February

EVIDENCES
OF THE BELIEVER

1
Supreme Love to God

MASTER, what shall I do to inherit eternal
life?—And he answering said, Thou shalt
love the Lord thy God with all thy heart,
and with all thy soul, and with all thy
strength, and with all thy mind.

Luke x. 25, 27.

Yes, I would love thee, blessed God!
　Paternal goodness marks thy name;
Thy praises, through thy high abode,
　The heavenly hosts with joy proclaim.

2

Gratitude to God

AND one of them, [the ten lepers,] when he saw that he was healed, turned back, and with a loud voice glorified God.

Luke xvii. 15.

What thanks I owe thee, and what love,
A boundless, endless store,
Shall echo through the realms above,
When time shall be no more.

3

Obedience to God

YE were the servants of sin, but ye have obeyed from the heart that form of doctrine which was delivered you. Being then made free from sin, ye became the servants of righteousness. *Rom.* vi. 17, 18.

Love is the fountain whence
All true obedience flows;
The Christian serves the God he loves,
And loves the God he knows.

4

Submission to God

WE have had fathers of our flesh which corrected us, and we gave them reverence: shall we not much rather be in subjection unto the Father of spirits, and live?

Heb. xii. 9.

Oh let my trembling soul be still,
    While darkness veils this mortal eye,
And wait thy wise, thy holy will
    Wrapp'd yet in tears and mystery:
I cannot, Lord, thy purpose see,
Yet all is well—since ruled by thee.

5

Faith in Christ

WHOSOEVER believeth that Jesus is the Christ is born of God. *1 John* v. 1.

Lord, I believe thy heavenly word;
Fain would I have my soul renew'd;
I mourn for sin, and trust the Lord
To have it pardon'd and subdued.

O may thy grace its power display,
Let guilt and death no longer reign;
Save me in thine appointed way,
Nor let my humble faith be vain.

6

Love to Christ

HE that loveth father or mother more than
me is not worthy of me: and he that loveth
son or daughter more than me is not worthy
of me. *Matt.* x. 37.

> Whom have I on earth below?
> Thee, and only thee, I know:
> Whom have I in heaven but thee?
> Thou art all in all to me.

7

Self-Denial for Christ

IF any man will come after me, let him deny
himself, and take up his cross daily, and
follow me. *Luke* ix. 23.

> Take up thy cross, let not its weight
>   Fill thy weak spirit with alarm,
> My strength shall bear thy spirit up,
>   And brace thy heart, and nerve thy arm.
>
> Take up thy cross, and follow me,
>   Nor think till death to lay it down;
> For only he who bears the cross
>   May hope to wear the glorious crown.

24

8

Confession of Christ

WHOSOEVER shall confess that Jesus is the Son of God, God dwelleth in him, and he in God. *1 John* iv. 15.

> I'll tell to all poor sinners round,
> How great a Saviour I have found;
> I'll point to his redeeming blood,
> And say, "Behold the way to God."

9

Devotedness to Christ

FOR whether we live, we live unto the Lord; and whether we die, we die unto the Lord: whether we live therefore, or die, we are the Lord's. *Rom.* xiv. 8.

> My soul, and all its powers,
>   Thine, wholly thine, shall be;
> All, all my happy hours
>   I consecrate to thee:
> Whate'er I have, whate'er I am,
> Shall magnify my Saviour's name.

10

Imitation of Christ

For I have given you an example, that ye should do as I have done to you.

John xiii. 15.

> Thy fair example may I trace,
> To teach me what I ought to be:
> Make me, by thy transforming grace,
> My Saviour, daily more like thee.

11

Christ Is Precious

Behold, I lay in Sion a chief corner stone, elect, precious: and he that believeth on him shall not be confounded. Unto you therefore which believe he is precious.

1 Pet. ii. 6, 7.

> Jesus, in thy transporting name
> What glories meet our eyes!
> Thou art the angels' sweetest theme,
> The wonder of the skies.
>
> Oh may our willing hearts confess
> Thy sweet, thy gentle sway;
> Glad captives of thy matchless grace,
> Thy righteous rule obey.

12

Possession of the Spirit of Christ

YE are not in the flesh, but in the Spirit, if so be that the Spirit of God dwell in you. Now if any man have not the Spirit of Christ, he is none of his. *Rom.* viii. 9.

> Author of our new creation,
>   Let us all thine influence prove;
> Make our souls thy habitation;
>   Shed abroad the Saviour's love.

13

Led by the Spirit

FOR as many as are led by the Spirit of God, they are the sons of God. *Rom.* viii. 14.

> Lead us to holiness—the road
> That we must take to dwell with God:
> Lead us to Christ—the living way,
> Nor let us from his pastures stray:
> Lead us to God—our final rest,
> In his enjoyment to be blest:
> Lead us to heaven—the seat of bliss,
> Where pleasure in perfection is.

14

Conviction of Sin

THERE is no soundness in my flesh because
of thine anger; neither is there any rest in
my bones because of my sin. For mine iniquities are gone over mine head: as an
heavy burden they are too heavy for me.

Psalm xxxviii. 3, 4.

> O Thou that hear'st the prayer of faith,
> Wilt thou not save my soul from death,
>   My soul that rests on thee?
> I have no refuge of my own,
> But fly to what my Lord hath done
>   And suffer'd once for me.

15

Repentance for Sin

GODLY sorrow worketh repentance to salvation not to be repented of: but the sorrow
of the world worketh death.

2 Cor. vii. 10.

> My lips with shame my sins confess
> Against thy law, against thy grace:
> Lo, should thy judgments grow severe,
> I am condemn'd, but thou art clear.

28

16

Hatred to Sin

WHOSOEVER is born of God doth not commit sin; for his seed remaineth in him: and he cannot sin, because he is born of God.
1 John iii. 9.

> Oh! give me, Lord, the tender heart
>   That trembles at the' approach of sin,
> A godly fear of sin impart,
>   Implant and root it deep within.

17

Mortification of Sin

THEY that are Christ's have crucified the flesh with the affections and lusts.
Gal. v. 24.

> Great God, assist me through the fight;
> Make me triumphant in thy might:
> Thou the desponding heart canst raise;
> The victory mine, and thine the praise.

18

Self-Righteousness Renounced

YEA doubtless, and I count all things but loss for the excellency of the knowledge of Christ Jesus my Lord: for whom I have suffered the loss of all things, and do count them but dung, that I may win Christ.

Phil. iii. 8.

On thee alone my hope relies;
    Beneath the cross I fall,
My Lord, my life, my sacrifice,
    My Saviour, and my all.

19

The World Overcome by Faith

WHATSOEVER is born of God overcometh the world: and this is the victory that overcometh the world, even our faith.

1 John v. 4.

'Tis faith that conquers earth and hell
    By a celestial power;
This is the grace that shall prevail
    In the decisive hour.

20

Non-Conformity to the World

LOVE not the world, neither the things that are in the world. If any man love the world, the love of the Father is not in him.

1 John ii. 15.

Why should our poor enjoyments here
Be thought so pleasant and so dear,
  And tempt our hearts astray?
Our brightest joys are fading fast,
The longest life will soon be past;
And if we go to heaven at last,
  We need not wish to stay.

21

Spiritual-Mindedness

THEY that are after the flesh do mind the things of the flesh; but they that are after the Spirit the things of the Spirit.

Rom. viii. 5.

Let worldly minds the world pursue,
  It has no charms for me;
Once I admired its trifles too,
  But grace has set me free.

31

22

Heavenly-Mindedness

OUR conversation is in heaven; from whence
also we look for the Saviour, the Lord Jesus
Christ. *Phil.* iii. 20.

> Beyond the bounds of time and space
> Look forward to that heavenly place,
>   The saints' secure abode;
> On faith's strong eagle pinion rise,
> And force your passage to the skies,
>   Strong in the strength of God.

23

Constrained by Love

THE love of Christ constraineth us; because
we thus judge, that if one died for all, then
were all dead: and that he died for all, that
they which live should not henceforth live
unto themselves, but unto him which died
for them, and rose again. *2 Cor.* v. 14, 15.

> Be all my heart, be all my days,
> Devoted to thy single praise;
> And let my glad obedience prove
> How much I owe, how much I love.

32

24

Love of the Truth

WE are of God: he that knoweth God heareth us; he that is not of God heareth not us. Hereby know we the spirit of truth, and the spirit of error. *1 John* iv. 6.

> Order my footsteps by thy word,
> And make my heart sincere;
> Let sin have no dominion, Lord,
> But keep my conscience clear.

25

Perseverance in the Truth

THEY went out from us, but they were not of us; for if they had been of us, they would no doubt have continued with us: but they went out, that they might be made manifest that they were not all of us. *1 John* ii. 19.

> When any turn from Zion's way,
> (Alas, what numbers do!)
> Methinks I hear my Saviour say,
> Wilt thou forsake me too?

26

Love to the Scriptures

I LOVE thy commandments above gold; yea, above fine gold. Thy testimonies are wonderful: therefore doth my soul keep them.
Ps. cxix. 127, 129.

Here mines of knowledge, love, and joy,
    Are open'd to our sight,
The purest gold without alloy,
    And gems divinely bright.

27

Love to Enemies

LOVE ye your enemies, and do good, and lend, hoping for nothing again; and your reward shall be great, and ye shall be the children of the Highest: for he is kind unto the unthankful and to the evil.

Luke vi. 3.

Lord, shall thy bright example shine
    In vain before my eyes?
Give me a soul akin to thine,
    To love my enemies.

28

Love to the Brethren

BELOVED, let us love one another: for love is of God; and every one that loveth is born of God, and knoweth God. *1 John* iv. 7.

> Bless'd be the tie that binds
> Our hearts in Christian love;
> The fellowship of kindred minds
> Is like to that above.

29 [*Leap Year*]

The Witness of Conscience

HEREBY we know that we are of the truth, and shall assure our hearts before him. Beloved, if our heart condemn us not, then have we confidence toward God.

1 John iii. 19. 21.

> How happy are the new-born race,
> Partakers of adopting grace!
>   How pure the bliss they share!
> Hid from the world and all its eyes,
> Within their hearts the blessing lies,
>   And conscience feels it there.

March

PRIVILEGES
OF THE BELIEVER

1
God the Believer's Sun and Shield

THE Lord God is a sun and shield: the Lord
will give grace and glory; no good thing will
he withhold from them that walk uprightly.
Ps. lxxxiv. 11.

> If thou art my shield and my sun,
>   The night is no darkness to me;
> And fast as my moments roll on,
>   They bring me but nearer to thee.

2

God the Portion of the Believer

GOD is the strength of my heart, and my portion for ever. *Ps.* lxxiii. 26.

His boundless grace shall all my need supply,
When streams of creature-comfort cease to flow:
And should he some inferior good deny,
'Tis but a greater blessing to bestow.

3

God the Refuge of the Believer

GOD is our refuge and strength, a very present help in trouble. Therefore will not we fear, though the earth be removed, and though the mountains be carried into the midst of the sea. *Psa.* xlvi. 1, 2.

God is our refuge in distress,
A present help when dangers press;
    In him undaunted I'll confide,
Though earth were from her centre toss'd,
And mountains in the ocean lost,
    Torn piece-meal by the roaring tide.

4

God the Guide of the Believer

THIS God is our God for ever and ever: he will be our guide even unto death.

Ps. xlviii. 14.

> Haste thee on from grace to glory,
> Arm'd by faith, and wing'd by prayer;
> Heaven's eternal day's before thee,
> God's own hand shall guide thee there.

5

God the Glory of the Believer

THOU, Lord, art a shield for me; my glory, and the lifter up of mine head. *Ps.* iii. 3.

> Lord, let thy grace surround me still,
> And like a bulwark prove,
> To guard my soul from every ill,
> Secured by sovereign love.

6

All Blessings Through Christ

ALL things are yours; whether Paul, or
Apollos, or Cephas, or the world, or life, or
death, or things present, or things to come;
all are yours; and ye are Christ's; and Christ
is God's. *1 Cor.* iii. 21-23.

> Let Christ assure me he is mine,
>   I nothing want beside;
> My soul shall at the fountain live,
>   When all the streams are dried.

7

All Blessings in Christ

BLESSED be the God and Father of our Lord
Jesus Christ, who hath blessed us with all
spiritual blessings in heavenly places in
Christ Jesus. *Eph.* i. 3.

> Oh the rich depths of love divine!
>   Of bliss a boundless store!
> Dear Saviour, let me call thee mine,
>   I cannot wish for more.

8

Pardon Through Christ

IN whom we have redemption through his blood, even the forgiveness of sin.

Col. i. 14.

> O Lamb of God, thy precious blood
>   Shall never lose its power,
> Till all the ransom'd church of God
>   Is saved, to sin no more.
>
> E'er since, by faith, I saw the stream
>   Thy flowing wounds supply,
> Redeeming love has been my theme,
>   And shall be till I die.

9

Justification Through Christ

BEING justified freely by his grace through the redemption that is in Christ Jesus.

Rom. iii. 24.

> No righteousness but his we own,
> No ransom but his blood alone:
> While on the Father's name we call,
> Our faith pleads Christ as all in all.

40

10

Reconciliation Through Christ

For if, when we were enemies, we were reconciled to God by the death of his Son, much more, being reconciled, we shall be saved by his life. *Rom.* v. 10.

Let us love, and sing, and wonder;
　Let us praise the Saviour's name:
He has hush'd the law's loud thunder,
　He has quench'd Mount Sinai's flame:
He has wash'd us with his blood,
He has brought us nigh to God.

11

Adoption Through Christ

As many as received him, to them gave he power to become the sons of God, even to them that believe on his name. *John* i. 12.

Let others boast their ancient line,
　In long succession great;
In the proud list, let heroes shine
　And monarchs swell their state:
Descended from the King of kings,
Each saint a nobler title sings.

12

Rest in Christ

COME unto me, all ye that labour and are heavy laden, and I will give you rest.

Matt. xi. 28.

Jesus, with thy word complying,
  Firm our faith and hope shall be;
On thy faithfulness relying,
  We will seek our rest in thee.

13

Safety in Christ

I GIVE unto them eternal life; and they shall never perish, neither shall any man pluck them out of my hand. *John* x. 28.

"Unnumber'd years of bliss
  I to my sheep will give;
And while my throne unshaken stands
  Shall all my chosen live."

Enough, my gracious Lord,
  Let faith triumphant cry;
My heart can on this promise live,
  Can with this promise die.

14

Strength Through Christ

I CAN do all things through Christ which strengtheneth me. *Phil.* iv. 13.

> I can do all things, and can bear
> All sufferings, if my Lord be near;
> Sweet pleasures mingle with the pains,
> While his left hand my head sustains.

15

Spiritual Freedom Through Christ

IF the Son shall make you free, ye shall be free indeed. *John* viii. 36.

> Sweet is the freedom Christ bestows,
> With which he makes his people free,
> A liberty no mortal knows
> Till they his great salvation see.

16

Consolation Through Christ

Now our Lord Jesus Christ himself, and
God, even our Father, which hath loved us,
and hath given us everlasting consolation
and good hope through grace. *2 Thess.* ii. 16.

> In every trouble, sharp and strong,
>   My soul to Jesus flies;
> My anchor-hold is firm on him,
>   When swelling billows rise.

17

Peace with God Through Christ

BEING justified by faith, we have peace with
God through our Lord Jesus Christ.
Rom. v. 1.

> No fiery vengeance now,
>   Nor burning wrath comes down;
> If justice call for sinners' blood,
>   The Saviour shows his own.

18

Access to God Through Christ

IN whom we have boldness and access with confidence by the faith of him. *Eph.* iii. 12.

> Come boldly to the throne of grace,
>   Where Jesus kindly pleads;
> Our's cannot be a desperate case
>   While Jesus intercedes.

19

Victory Through Christ

THANKS be to God, which giveth us the victory through our Lord Jesus Christ.
1 Cor. xv. 57.

> Thus strong in the Redeemer's strength,
>   Sin, death, and hell we trample down,
> Fight the good fight, and win at length,
>   Through mercy, an eternal crown.

20

Indwelling of the Spirit

KNOW ye not that ye are the temple of God, and that the Spirit of God dwelleth in you? *1 Cor*. iii. 16.

Think what Spirit dwells within thee;
Think what Father's smiles are thine;
Think that Jesus died to win thee:
Child of heaven, canst thou repine?

21

Intercession of the Spirit

THE Spirit also helpeth our infirmities: for we know not what we should pray for as we ought: but the Spirit itself maketh intercession for us with groanings which cannot be uttered. *Rom*. viii. 26.

Let pure devotion's fervours rise,
    Let every holy feeling glow;
Oh, let the rapture of the skies
    Kindle in our cold hearts below.
Come, vivifying Spirit, come,
And make our hearts thy constant home.

22

Sanctification by the Spirit

ELECT according to the foreknowledge of
God the Father, through sanctification of
the Spirit, unto obedience and sprinkling
of the blood of Jesus. *1 Pet.* i. 2.

> Can aught beneath a power divine
>   The stubborn will subdue?
> 'Tis thine, eternal Spirit, thine,
>   To form our hearts anew.
> 'Tis thine the passions to recall,
>   And upwards bid them rise;
> And make the scales of error fall
>   From reason's darkened eyes.

23

The Fruits of the Spirit

THE fruit of the Spirit is love, joy, peace,
long-suffering, gentleness, goodness, faith,
meekness, temperance: against such there is
no law. *Gal.* v. 22, 23.

> 'Tis God himself the ground prepares,
>   His Spirit sows the land;
> And every pleasant fruit it bears,
>   Is nurtur'd by his hand.

24

Inheritance Among the Sanctified

BRETHREN, I commend you to God, and to
the word of his grace, which is able to build
you up, and to give you an inheritance
among all them which are sanctified.

Acts xx. 32

From earth we shall quickly remove,
　　And mount to our native abode;
The house of our Father above,
　　The palace of angels and God.

25

Increase of Grace

THE righteous shall flourish like the palm
tree: he shall grow like a cedar in Lebanon.
They shall still bring forth fruit in old age;
they shall be fat and flourishing.

Ps. xcii. 12, 14

Lord, one thing we want,
More holiness grant;
For more of thy mind and thy image we pant:
While onward we move
To Canaan above,
Come, fill us with holiness, fill us with love.

48

26

Persevering Grace

THE righteous shall hold on his way, and he that hath clean hands shall be stronger and stronger. *Job* xvii. 9.

> The righteous, bless'd with light divine,
>   Shall prosper on their way;
> Brighter and brighter still shall shine,
>   To glory's perfect day.

27

Confidence in Prayer

THIS is the confidence that we have in him, that, if we ask any thing according to his will, he heareth us. *1 John* v. 14.

> He who for man their Surety stood,
> And poured on earth his precious blood,
> Pursues in heaven his mighty plan,
> The Saviour and the friend of man.

> With boldness, therefore, at the throne,
> Let us make all our sorrows known;
> And ask the aid of heavenly power,
> To help us in the evil hour.

49

28

Preservation in Trouble

IN the time of trouble he shall hide me in
his pavilion: in the secret of his tabernacle
shall he hide me; he shall set me upon a
rock. *Ps.* xxvii. 5.

> When I can trust my all with God,
>   In trial's fearful hour—
> Bow, all resign'd, beneath his rod,
>   And bless his sparing power;
> A joy springs up amid distress,
> A fountain in the wilderness.

29

All Things Work Together for Good

WE know that all things work together for
good to them that love God, to them who
are the called according to his purpose.

Rom. viii. 28.

> God will keep his own anointed;
>   Nought shall harm them, none condemn;
> All their trials are appointed;
>   All must work for good to them:
>   All shall help them
>   To their heavenly diadem.

30

Peace of Mind

THOU wilt keep him in perfect peace, whose mind is stayed on thee: because he trusteth in thee. *Isa.* xxvi. 3.

> Saviour, on earth I covet not
>   That every woe should cease;
> Only, if trouble be my lot,
>   In thee let me have peace.

31

Peace in Death

MARK the perfect man, and behold the upright: for the end of that man is peace.
Ps. xxxvii. 37.

> How bless'd the righteous when he dies,
>   When sinks a weary soul to rest!
> How mildly beam the closing eyes!
>   How gently heaves the' expiring breast!
>
> Life's labour done, as sinks the clay,
>   Light from its load the spirit flies;
> While heaven and earth combine to say,
>   "How bless'd the righteous when he dies!"

51

April

DUTIES OF THE BELIEVER—PERSONAL

1

Good Works to Be Done

THESE things I will that thou affirm constantly, that they which have believed in God might be careful to maintain good works. *Titus* iii. 8.

> Whate'er is noble, pure, refined,
> Just, generous, amiable, and kind,
> That may my constant thoughts pursue,
> That may I love and practise too.

2

Good Works to Be Done to the Glory of God

WHETHER therefore ye eat, or drink, or whatsoever ye do, do all to the glory of God.
1 Cor. x. 31.

> Through Jesus Christ the Just,
> My faint desires receive;
> And let me in thy goodness trust,
> And to thy glory live.

3

Good Works to Be Done

After the Example of Christ

HE that saith he abideth in him ought himself also so to walk, even as he walked.
1 John ii. 6.

To do his heavenly Father's will
  Was his employment and delight;
Humility and holy zeal
  Shone through his life divinely bright.

4

Good Works to Be Done

Through the Grace of Christ

Now the God of peace make you perfect in every good work to do his will, working in you that which is well pleasing in his sight, through Jesus Christ; to whom be glory for ever and ever. *Heb.* xiii. 20, 21.

Then shall we do, with pure delight,
Whate'er is pleasing in thy sight,
  As vessels of thy richest grace;
And, having thy whole counsel done,
To thee and thy co-equal Son
  Ascribe the everlasting praise.

5

Good Works to Be Done
in the Name of Christ

WHATSOEVER ye do in word or deed, do all
in the name of the Lord Jesus, giving thanks
to God and the Father by him. *Col.* iii. 17.

Whate'er I say or do,
Thy glory be my aim;
My offerings all be offered through
His ever blessed name.

6

Improvement of Time

KNOWING the time, that now it is high time
to awake out of sleep: for now is our salvation nearer than when we believed.
Rom. xiii. 11.

The time is short, but who can tell
How short his time below may be?
To-day on earth his soul may dwell,
To-morrow in eternity.

7

Improvement of Privileges

THAT on the good ground are they, which in an honest and good heart, having heard the word, keep it, and bring forth fruit with patience. *Luke* vii. 15.

> Father of mercies, we have need
>   Of thy preparing grace;
> Let the same hand that gives the seed
>   Provide a fruitful place.

8

Improvement of Opportunities

WHATSOEVER thy hand findeth to do, do it with thy might; for there is no work, nor device, nor knowledge, nor wisdom, in the grave, whither thou goest. *Eccles*. ix. 10.

> Whate'er our hands shall find to do,
>   To-day may we with zeal pursue;
> Seize fleeting moments as they fly,
>   And live as we would wish to die.

9

Spiritual Diligence

THIS one thing I do, forgetting those things which are behind, and reaching forth unto those things which are before, I press toward the mark for the prize of the high calling of God in Christ Jesus. *Phil.* iii. 13, 14.

A scrip on my back, and a staff in my hand,
I march on in haste through an enemy's land:
The road may be rough, but it cannot be long,
So I'll smooth it with hope, and I'll cheer it with song.

10

Entire Consecration

NEITHER yield ye your members as instruments of unrighteousness unto sin: but yield yourselves unto God, as those that are alive from the dead, and your members as instruments of righteousness unto God.

Rom. vi. 13.

Yield to the Lord, with simple heart,
All that thou hast, and all thou art:
Renounce all strength, but strength divine,
And peace shall be for ever thine.

56

11

Open Profession of Christ

WHOSOEVER shall confess me before men, him will I confess also before my Father which is in heaven. *Matt.* x. 32.

> Should I to gain the world's applause,
>   Or to escape its harmless frown,
> Refuse to countenance thy cause,
>   And make thy people's lot my own,
> What shame would fill me in that day,
> When thou thy glory shalt display!

12

Evil Appearances to Be Avoided

ABSTAIN from all appearance of evil.
1 Thess. v. 22.

> Our Saviour by a heavenly birth
> Calls us to holiness on earth,
> Bids us our former follies hate,
> And from the wicked separate.
>
> We must have holy hearts and hands,
> And feet that go where he commands;
> A holy will to keep his ways,
> And holy lips to speak his praise.

13

Diligence in Keeping the Heart

KEEP thy heart with all diligence; for out of it are the issues of life. *Prov.* iv. 23.

> Thy business be to keep thy heart,
>   Each passion to control;
> Nobly ambitious well to rule
>   The empire of thy soul.

14

Search the Scriptures

SEARCH the Scriptures; for in them ye think ye have eternal life: and they are they which testify of me. *John* v. 39.

> Lord, thy teaching grace impart,
>   That we may not read in vain;
> Write thy precepts on our heart,
>   Make thy truths and doctrine plain;
> Let the message of thy love
> Guide us to thy rest above.

15

Secret Prayer

THOU, when thou prayest, enter into thy closet, and when thou hast shut thy door, pray to thy Father which is in secret; and thy Father which seeth in secret shall reward thee openly. *Matt.* vi. 6.

> Far from the paths of men, to Thee
>   I solemnly retire;
> See Thou, who dost in secret see,
>   And grant my heart's desire.

16

Thanksgiving

IN every thing give thanks: for this is the will of God in Christ Jesus concerning you.
1 Thess. v. 18.

> Praise to God, immortal praise,
> For the love that crowns our days;
> Bounteous Source of every joy,
> Let thy praise our tongues employ.

17

Meditation

HIS delight is in the law of the Lord; and
in his law doth he meditate day and night.
Psalm i. 2.

I love in solitude to shed
  The penitential tear;
And all his promises to plead,
  When none but God is near.

I love to think on mercies past,
  And future good implore;
And all my cares and sorrows cast
  On him whom I adore.

18

Self-Examination

EXAMINE yourselves, whether ye be in the
faith; prove your own selves. *2 Cor.* xiii. 5.

At evening to myself I say,
My soul, where hast thou glean'd to-day,
  Thy labours how bestow'd?
What hast thou rightly said or done?
What grace attain'd, or knowledge won,
  In following after God?

60

19

In Prosperity to Be Humble

FOR I say, through the grace given unto me, to every man that is among you, not to think of himself more highly than he ought to think. *Rom.* xii. 3.

> Lord, if thou thy grace impart,
> Poor in spirit, meek in heart,
> I shall, as my Saviour, be
> Rooted in humility:
> Pleas'd with all the Lord provides,
> Wean'd from all the world besides.

20

In Adversity to Trust God

WHO is among you that feareth the Lord, that obeyeth the voice of his servant, that walketh in darkness, and hath no light? let him trust in the name of the Lord, and stay upon his God. *Isa.* 1. 10.

> If Providence our comforts shroud,
>   And dark distresses lower,
> Hope paints its rainbow on the cloud,
>   And grace shines through the shower.

21

Self-Government

HE that is slow to anger is better than the mighty; and he that ruleth his spirit than he that taketh a city. *Prov.* xvi. 32.

Happy the man, whose cautious steps
    Still keep the golden mean;
Whose life, by Scripture rules well form'd,
    Declares a conscience clean.

22

Self-Denial

ALL things are lawful for me, but all things are not expedient: all things are lawful for me, but all things edify not. *1 Cor.* x. 23.

Lord, ever let me freely yield
    What most I prize to thee,
Who never hast a good withheld,
    Or wilt withhold from me.

Thy favour all my journey through,
    Thou art engaged to grant;
What else I want, or think I do,
    'Tis better still to want.

23

Contentment

BE content with such things as ye have: for he hath said, I will never leave thee, nor forsake thee. *Heb.* xiii. 5.

Since he has said "I'll ne'er depart,"
I'll bind his promise to my heart,
   Rejoicing in his care:
This shall support while here I live,
And, when in glory I arrive,
   Will praise him for it there.

24

Patience

YE have need of patience, that, after ye have done the will of God, ye might receive the promise. *Heb.* x. 36.

I would submit to all thy will,
   For thou art good and wise;
Let every anxious thought be still,
   Nor one faint murmur rise.

Thy love can cheer the darksome gloom,
   And bid me wait serene,
Till hopes and joys immortal bloom
   And brighten all the scene.

25

Meekness

WALK worthy of the vocation wherewith ye are called, with all lowliness and meekness, with long suffering, forbearing one another in love. *Eph.* iv. 2.

> Meekness, humility, and love,
>   Did through thy conduct shine;
> Oh may my whole deportment prove
>   A copy, Lord, of thine.

26

Temperance

TAKE heed to yourselves, lest at any time your hearts be overcharged with surfeiting, and drunkenness, and cares of this life, and so that day come upon you unawares.
Luke xxi. 34.

> The world employs its various snares,
> Of hopes and pleasures, pains and cares,
>   And chain'd to earth I lie:
> When shall my fetter'd powers be free,
> And leave these seats of vanity,
>   And upward learn to fly?

27

Gravity and Sincerity

IN all things showing thyself a pattern of good works: in doctrine showing uncorruptness, gravity, sincerity. *Titus* ii. 7.

> Pure may I be, averse to sin,
>   Just, holy, merciful, and true;
> And let thine image form'd within,
>   Shine out in all I speak or do.

28

Watchfulness

BLESSED are those servants, whom the Lord when he cometh shall find watching: verily I say unto you, that he shall gird himself, and make them to sit down to meat, and will come forth and serve them.

Luke xii. 37.

> Arm me with jealous care,
>   As in thy sight to live:
> And oh, thy servant, Lord, prepare,
>   A strict account to give.
>
> Help me to watch and pray,
>   And on thyself rely;
> Assured if I my trust betray,
>   I shall for ever die.

29

Diligence in Worldly Calling

STUDY to be quiet, and to do your own business, and to work with your own hands, as we commanded you. *1 Thess.* iv. 11.

> Midst hourly cares, may love present
> Its incense to thy throne;
> And while the world our hands employs,
> Our hearts be thine alone.

30

Eminent Holiness
the Desire of the Believer

NOT as though I had already attained, either were already perfect: but I follow after, if that I may apprehend that for which also I am apprehended of Jesus Christ. *Phil.* iii. 12.

> Oh for a closer walk with God,
> A calm and heavenly frame,
> A light to shine upon the road
> That leads me to the Lamb!

May

DUTIES OF
THE BELIEVER—
IN THE CHURCH

1

To Show Forth the Praises of God

YE are a chosen generation, a royal priest-hood, an holy nation, a peculiar people; that ye should show forth the praises of him who hath called you out of darkness into his marvellous light. *1 Pet.* ii. 9.

> Not by your words alone,
> But by your actions show
> How much from him you have received,
> How much to him you owe.

2

To Depart from All Iniquity

LET every one that nameth the name of Christ depart from iniquity. *2 Tim.* ii. 19.

> Faith must obey her Father's will,
>   As well as trust his grace;
> A pardoning God is jealous still
>   For his own holiness.

3

Stedfastness in the Faith

STAND fast in the liberty wherewith Christ hath made us free, and be not entangled again with the yoke of bondage. *Gal.* v. 1.

> From Egypt lately freed
>   By the Redeemer's grace,
> A rough and thorny path we tread
>   In hopes to see his face.
>
> The flesh dislikes the way,
>   But faith approves it well;
> This only leads to endless day,
>   All others lead to hell.

4

Zeal in Defence of the Gospel

I EXHORT you that ye should earnestly contend for the faith which was once delivered unto the saints. *Jude* 3.

> In the conquests of thy might,
> May I loyally delight;
> In thy ever-spreading reign,
> Triumph as my greatest gain:
> Make me conscious by this sign,
> Gracious Saviour, I am thine.

5

Zeal for Good Works

LET us consider one another to provoke unto love and to good works. *Heb.* x. 24.

> Awake, my soul, awake, my love,
> And serve my Saviour here below,
> In works which all the saints above
> And holy angels cannot do.

6

Zeal for Divine Worship

NOT forsaking the assembling of ourselves together, as the manner of some is; but exhorting one another: and so much the more, as ye see the day approaching. *Heb*. x. 25.

> Oh let me always find a place,
> Within the temples of thy grace;
> Till God command my last remove,
> To dwell in temples made above!

7

Concern for the Peace of the Church

BE perfect, be of good comfort, be of one mind, live in peace; and the God of love and peace shall be with you. *2 Cor*. xiii. 11.

> Make us of one heart and mind,
> Courteous, pitiful, and kind;
> Lowly, meek in thought and word,
> Altogether like our Lord.

8

Concern for
the Prosperity of the Church

PEACE be within thy walls and prosperity within thy palaces. *Psa.* cxxii. 7.

> For our dear brethren's sake,
> Zion, we wish thee peace;
> Prosper, oh! prosper long,
> And may thy sons increase:
> We seek thy good, we love the road
> Which leads us to God's bless'd abode.

9

Mutual Love

WALK in love, as Christ also hath loved us, and hath given himself for us an offering and a sacrifice to God for a sweet-smelling savour. *Eph.* v. 2.

> Among the saints on earth
> Let mutual love be found;
> Heirs of the same inheritance,
> With mutual blessings crown'd.

10

Mutual Subjection

ALL of you be subject one to another, and be clothed with humility: for God resisteth the proud, and giveth grace to the humble.

1 Peter v. 5.

> Lord, for ever at thy side
> May my place and portion be;
> Strip me of the robe of pride;
> Clothe me with humility.

11

Mutual Honour

LET nothing be done through strife or vain-glory; but in lowliness of mind let each esteem other better than themselves.

Phil. ii. 3.

> Oh let each esteem his brother
> Better than himself to be;
> And let each prefer another,
> Full of love, from envy free:
> Happy are we,
> When in this we all agree.

12

Mutual Forbearance

FORBEARING one another, and forgiving one another, if any man have a quarrel against any: even as Christ forgave you, so also do ye. *Col.* iii. 13.

> May we each with each agree,
> Through thy uniting grace:
> Our gift shall thine accepted be,
> Our life be love and praise.

13

Mutual Candour

JUDGE not, that ye be not judged. Why beholdest thou the mote that is in thy brother's eye, but considerest not the beam that is in thine own eye? *Matt.* vii. 1, 3.

> Make us by thy transforming grace,
> Great Saviour, daily more like thee:
> Thy fair example may we trace,
> To teach us what we ought to be.

14

Mutual Forgiveness

BE ye kind one to another, tenderhearted, forgiving one another, even as God for Christ's sake hath forgiven you. *Eph.* iv. 32.

"Is Christ divided?" What can part
The members from the Head?
Oh how should those be one in heart
For whom our Saviour bled?

15

Mutual Admonition

I MYSELF am persuaded of you, my brethren, that ye also are full of goodness, filled with all knowledge, able also to admonish one another. *Rom.* xv. 14.

Bonds of everlasting love
Draw our souls in union,
To our Father's house above,
To the saints' communion.
Thither may our hopes ascend,
There may all our labours end.

16

Mutual Consolation and Edification

COMFORT yourselves together, and edify one another, even as also ye do. *1 Thess.* v. 11.

> While we journey, let us
>   Help each other on the road;
> Foes on every side beset us,
>   Snares through all the way are strew'd:
>   It behoves us,
>   Each to bear a brother's load.

17

Mutual Intercession

PRAY one for another.—The effectual fervent prayer of a righteous man availeth much. *James* v. 16.

> Before our Father's throne
>   We pour our ardent prayers;
> Our fears, our hopes, our aims are one—
>   Our comforts and our cares.

18

Unity of Sentiment

WHERETO we have already attained, let us
walk by the same rule, let us mind the same
thing. *Phil.* iii. 16.

> Bound to one Lord, by common vow
>   In one great enterprize;
> One faith, one hope, one centre now,
>   Our common home, the skies.

19

Unity of Judgment

I BESEECH you, brethren, by the name of
our Lord Jesus Christ, that ye all speak the
same thing, and that there be no divisions
among you; but that ye be perfectly joined
together in the same mind and in the same
judgment. *1 Cor.* i. 10.

> Lord, subdue our selfish will,
>   Each to each our tempers suit,
> By thy modulating skill,
>   Heart to heart, as lute to lute.

20

United Prayer

WHERE two or three are gathered together in my name, there am I in the midst of them. *Matt.* xviii. 20.

> Where two or three with sweet accord,
> Obedient to their sovereign Lord,
> Meet to recount his acts of grace,
> And offer solemn prayer and praise;
> There, saith the Saviour, will I be
> Amid the little company.

21

United Praise

TEACHING and admonishing one another in psalms and hymns and spiritual songs, singing with grace in your hearts to the Lord. *Col.* iii. 16.

> Teach us, though in a world of sin,
> Heaven's bless'd employment to begin,
> To sing our great Redeemer's praise;
> And love his name, and learn his ways.

22

Pious Conversation

LET no corrupt communication proceed out
of your mouth, but that which is good to
the use of edifying, that it may minister
grace unto the hearers. *Eph.* iv. 29.

> Wheresoever two or three
> Meet, a Christian company,
> Grant us, Lord, to meet with thee:
>   Gracious Saviour, hear!
> When with friends beloved we stray,
> Talking down the closing day,
> Saviour, meet us in the way:
>   Gracious Saviour, hear!

23

Compassion for the Weak

WE that are strong ought to bear the infirmities of the weak, and not to please
ourselves. *Rom.* xv. 1.

> When weaker Christians we despise,
>   We do the great Redeemer wrong;
> For God, the gracious and the wise,
>   Receives the feeble with the strong.

24

Compassion for the Afflicted

REMEMBER them that are in bonds, as
bound with them; and them which suffer
adversity, as being yourselves also in the
body. *Heb.* xiii. 3.

> With pity let my breast o'erflow,
> When I behold another's woe;
> And bear a sympathizing part,
> Whene'er I meet a wounded heart.

25

Compassion for the Poor

As we have therefore opportunity, let us do
good unto all men, especially unto them who
are of the household of faith. *Gal.* vi. 10.

> Awake, my charity, and feed
>   The hungry soul, and clothe the poor;
> In heaven are found no sons of need,
>   There all these duties are no more.

26

Compassion to
Those Who Have Erred

BRETHREN, if a man be overtaken in a fault,
ye which are spiritual, restore such an one
in the spirit of meekness; considering thyself, lest thou also be tempted. *Gal.* vi. 1.

> Lord, we would strive, and hope, and wait,
> The offending still to reinstate;
> And when a broken heart we view,
> Our Christian friendship quick renew.

27

Freedom from Slander

SPEAK not evil one of another, brethren. He
that speaketh evil of his brother, and judgeth his brother, speaketh evil of the law,
and judgeth the law: but if thou judge the
law, thou art not a doer of the law, but a
judge. *James* iv. 11.

> Love is a pure and heavenly flame,
> And much regards a brother's name;
> It hopeth all things, and believes,
> Nor easily a charge receives.

28

Esteem for the Ministry

WE beseech you to know them which labour among you, and are over you in the Lord, and admonish you; and to esteem them very highly in love for their work's sake.

1 Thess. v. 12, 13.

> How beauteous are their feet,
>   Who stand on Zion's hill;
> Who bring salvation on their tongues,
>   And words of peace reveal!

29

Prayer for the Ministry

PRAYING always with all prayer and supplication in the Spirit;—and for me, that utterance may be given unto me, that I may open my mouth boldly, to make known the mystery of the gospel. *Eph.* vi. 18, 19.

> With heavenly power, O Lord, defend
> Those whom we now to thee commend;
> Thy faithful messengers secure,
> And make them to the end endure.

30

Unbelief Should Be Guarded Against

TAKE heed, brethren, lest there be in any of you an evil heart of unbelief, in departing from the living God. *Heb.* iii. 12.

> How oft, deceived by self and pride,
> Has my weak heart been turn'd aside;
> And, Jonah-like, has fled from thee,
> Till thou hast look'd again on me!

31

Caution Against Apostasy

LOOKING diligently lest any man fail of the grace of God; lest any root of bitterness springing up trouble you, and thereby many be defiled. *Heb.* xii. 15.

> What bright exchange, what treasure shall be given,
> For the lost birthright of a hope in heaven?
> If lost the gem which empires could not buy,
> What yet remains?—a dark eternity.

June

DUTIES OF
THE BELIEVER—
IN THE WORLD

1
Believers Are the Salt of the Earth

YE are the salt of the earth: but if the salt
have lost his savour, wherewith shall it be
salted? it is thenceforth good for nothing,
but to be cast out, and to be trodden under
foot of men. *Matt.* v. 13.

> Strive thou with studious care to find
> Some good thy hands may do;
> Some way to serve and bless mankind,
> Console the heart, relieve the mind,
> And open comforts new.

2

Believers Are the Light of the World

YE are the light of the world. *Matt.* v. 14.

> Walk in the light—and thine shall be
> A path, though stormy, bright;
> For God in love shall dwell with thee—
> And God himself is light!

3

The Universal Rule of Equity

ALL things whatsoever ye would that men should do to you, do ye even so to them: for this is the law and the prophets.

Matt. vii. 12.

> Blessed Redeemer, how divine,
> How righteous is this rule of thine,
> To do to all men just the same
> As we expect or wish from them.
>
> How bless'd would every nation prove
> Thus ruled by equity and love!
> All would be friends without a foe,
> And form a paradise below.

4

To Glorify God by Holy Conduct

I BESEECH you as strangers and pilgrims, abstain from fleshly lusts, which war against the soul; having your conversation honest among the Gentiles. *1 Pet.* ii. 11.

> Help thy servant to maintain
> A profession free from stain;
> That my sole reproach may be,
> Following Christ, and fearing thee.

5

Abounding in the Work of the Lord

MY beloved brethren, be ye stedfast, unmoveable, always abounding in the work of the Lord, forasmuch as ye know that your labour is not in vain in the Lord.

1 Cor. xv. 58.

> Sow in the morn thy seed,
> At eve hold not thy hand,
> To doubt and fear give thou no heed,
> Broad-cast it round thy land.

6

Decision of Character

No man can serve two masters: for either he will hate the one, and love the other; or else he will hold to the one, and despise the other. Ye cannot serve God and mammon.
Matt. vi. 24.

Not a broken, brief obedience
Does the Lord of heaven demand;
He requires our whole allegiance,
Words and deeds, and heart and hand:
    God will hold divided sway
    With no deity of clay.

7

Holy Example

LET your light so shine before men, that they may see your good works, and glorify your Father which is in heaven. *Matt.* v. 16.

So let our lips and lives express
The holy gospel we profess;
So let our works and virtues shine
To prove the doctrine all divine.

8

Live in Peace with All Men

IF it be possible, as much as lieth in you, live peaceably with all men. *Rom.* xii. 18.

> His purpose is that we should bear
> His image now on earth,
> And by our peaceful lives declare
> Our new and heavenly birth.

9

Love to Our Neighbour

IF ye fulfil the royal law according to the scripture, Thou shalt love thy neighbour as thyself, ye do well. *James* ii. 8.

> Love lays its own advantage by
> To seek its neighbour's good;
> So God's own Son came down to die,
> And bought our lives with blood.
>
> Love is the grace that keeps its power
> In all the realms above;
> There faith and hope are known no more
> But saints for ever love.

10

Seek the

Edification of Our Neighbour

LET every one of us please his neighbour for his good to edification. *Rom.* xv. 2.

> May I from every act abstain,
> That hurts or gives another pain:
> Still may I feel my heart inclin'd
> To be the friend of all mankind.

11

Love to All Men

THE Lord make you to increase and abound in love one toward another, and toward all men, even as we do toward you.

1 Thess. iii. 12.

> May love, that shining grace,
> O'er all my powers preside;
> Direct my thoughts, suggest my words,
> And every action guide.

12

To Seek the Salvation of Others

HE which converteth the sinner from the
error of his way shall save a soul from death,
and shall hide a multitude of sins.

James v. 20.

> My God, I feel the mournful scene;
> My bowels yearn o'er dying men;
> And fain my pity would reclaim,
> And snatch the firebrands from the flame.

13

Give Due Honour to All

RENDER to all their dues: tribute to whom
tribute is due; custom to whom custom;
fear to whom fear; honour to whom honour.

Rom. xiii. 7.

> Our sovereign with thy favour bless;
> Stablish the throne in righteousness,
>   Let wisdom hold the helm:
> The counsels of our senate guide,
> Let justice in our courts preside,
>   Rule thou, and bless the realm.

14

Consistency

THAT ye may be blameless and harmless, the sons of God, without rebuke, in the midst of a crooked and perverse nation, among whom ye shine as lights in the world.
Phil. ii. 15.

That wisdom, Lord, on us bestow
  From every evil to depart,
To stop the mouth of every foe,
  While upright both in life and heart,
The proof of godly fear we give,
And show them how the Christians live.

15

Circumspection

SEE then that ye walk circumspectly, not as fools, but as wise. Redeeming the time, because the days are evil. *Eph.* v. 15, 16.

Let every flying hour confess
I gain the gospel fresh renown;
And when my life and labours cease,
May I possess the promised crown.

16

Discretion

A GOOD man sheweth favour, and lendeth:
he will guide his affairs with discretion.
Psalm cxii. 5.

Believers love what God commands,
  And in his ways delight;
Their gracious words, and holy hands
  Show that their faith is right.

Their converse is with God above,
  Their labours bless mankind;
Their works of mercy, peace, and love,
  Through Christ acceptance find.

17

Moderation

LET your moderation be known unto all
men. The Lord is at hand. *Phil.* iv. 5.

We'll look on all the toys below
With such disdain as angels do;
And wait the call that bids us rise
To mansions promised in the skies.

91

18

Forbearance

DEARLY beloved, avenge not yourselves, but rather give place unto wrath: for it is written, Vengeance is mine; I will repay, saith the Lord. *Rom.* xii. 19.

> May I feel beneath my wrongs
> Vengeance to the Lord belongs;
> Nor a worse requital dare,
> Than the meek revenge of prayer:
> Much forgiven, may I learn,
> Love for hatred to return.

19

Industry

LET a man labour, working with his hands the thing which is good, that he may have to give to him that needeth. *Eph.* iv. 28.

> To thee my very life I owe;
> From thee do all my comforts flow;
> And every blessing which I need
> Must from thy bounteous hand proceed.

20

Integrity

THAT ye may walk honestly toward them that are without, and that ye may have lack of nothing. *1 Thess.* iv. 12.

Come, let us search our ways, and try
　　Have they been just and right;
Is the great rule of equity
　　Our practice and delight?

In all we sell, in all we buy,
　　Is justice our design?
Do we remember God is nigh,
　　And fear the wrath Divine?

21

Fidelity

HE that is faithful in that which is least is faithful also in much: and he that is unjust in the least is unjust also in much.

Luke xvi. 10.

Thy gifts are only then enjoy'd
　　When used as talents lent;
Those talents only well employ'd
　　When in his service spent.

93

22

Truth and Sincerity

WHEREFORE, putting away lying, speak
every man truth with his neighbour: for we
are members one of another. *Eph.* iv. 25.

> Let those who bear the Christian name
>   Their holy vows fulfil;
> The saints, the followers of the Lamb,
>   Are men of honour still.

23

Gentleness and Meekness

SPEAK evil of no man, to be no brawlers,
but gentle, showing all meekness to all men.
Tit. iii. 2.

> Bless'd are the men of peaceful life,
> Who quench the coals of growing strife,
> They shall be called the heirs of bliss,
> The sons of God, the sons of peace.

24

Benevolence

PURE religion and undefiled before God and the Father is this, To visit the fatherless and widows in their affliction, and to keep himself unspotted from the world.

James i. 27.

> The poor are always with us here:
> 'Tis our great Father's plan,
> That mutual wants and mutual care
> Should bind us man to man.

25

Overcome Evil with Good

IF thine enemy hunger feed him: if he thirst, give him drink: for in so doing thou shalt heap coals of fire on his head. Be not overcome of evil, but overcome evil with good.

Rom. xii. 20, 21.

> Thus artists melt the sullen ore of lead,
> With heaping coals of fire upon its head;
> In the kind warmth the metal learns to glow,
> And loose from dross the silver runs below.

26

Perseverance in Doing Good

LET us not be weary in well doing: for in
due season we shall reap if we faint not.

Gal. vi. 9

> Meek pilgrim Zionward, if thou
> Hast put thy hand unto the plough,
> Oh look not back, nor droop dismay'd,
> At thought of victory delay'd:
> Doubt not that thou, in season due,
> Shall own his gracious promise true;
> And thou shalt share their glorious lot,
> Whom doing well hath wearied not.

27

Submission to Authority

PUT them in mind to be subject to principalities and powers, to obey magistrates, to
be ready to every good work. *Titus* iii. 1.

> Lord, thou hast bid thy people pray
> For all that bear the sovereign sway,
>   Who as thy servants reign;
> Rulers, and governors, and powers—
> Behold, in faith we pray for ours;
>   Nor let us plead in vain.

28

Universal Holiness
the Believer's Aim

WHATSOEVER things are true, whatsoever
things are honest, whatsoever things are
just, whatsoever things are pure, whatsoever things are lovely, whatsoever things
are of good report; if there be any virtue,
and if there be any praise, think on these
things. *Phil.* iv. 8.

> Father of eternal grace,
>   Glorify thyself in me;
> Meekly beaming in my face,
>   May the world thine image see.

29

Believer's Humble Confession

So likewise ye, when ye shall have done all
those things which are commanded you, say,
We are unprofitable servants: we have done
that which was our duty to do.
Luke xvii. 10.

> My present triumphs, and my past,
> Are thine, and must be to the last;
> And if the crown of life I wear,
> Thy hand alone must place it there.

97

30

The Great Motive to All Duty

YE are not your own; for ye are bought with
a price: therefore glorify God in your body,
and in your spirit, which are God's.

1 Cor. vi. 19, 20.

Oh! grant us, Lord, to feel and own
  The power of love divine;
The blood which doth for sin atone,
  The grace which makes us thine.

July

JOYS
OF THE BELIEVER

1
Joy in God

LET all those that put their trust in thee rejoice: let them ever shout for joy, because thou defendest them: let them also that love thy name be joyful in thee. *Psalm* v. 11.

When with his smiles my soul he deigns to bless,
  Nor cares nor crosses can my peace destroy,
Possessing all things if I him possess,
  Enjoying all things if I him enjoy.

2

Joy in Christ

WE are the circumcision, which worship
God in the spirit, and rejoice in Christ
Jesus, and have no confidence in the flesh.
Phil. iii. 3.

> The opening heavens around me shine
> With beams of sacred bliss,
> While Jesus shows his heart is mine,
> And whispers, I am his.

3

Joy in the Holy Ghost

THE kingdom of God is not meat and drink;
but righteousness, and peace, and joy in the
Holy Ghost. *Rom.* xiv. 17.

> Holy Ghost, dispel our sadness,
> Pierce the cloud of sinful night;
> Come, thou source of joy and gladness,
> Breathe thy life, and shed thy light.

4

The Gospel a Source of Joy

BLESSED is the people that know the joyful
sound: they shall walk, O Lord, in the light
of thy countenance. *Psalm* lxxxix. 15.

> Bless'd are the souls that hear and know
>   The gospel's joyful sound;
> Peace shall attend the path they go,
>   And light their steps surround.

5

The Atonement a Source of Joy

WE joy in God through our Lord Jesus
Christ, by whom we have now received the
atonement. *Rom.* v. 11.

> There is a fountain fill'd with blood,
>   Drawn from Immanuel's veins,
> And sinners plunged beneath that flood
>   Lose all their guilty strains.
>
> The dying thief rejoic'd to see
>   That fountain in his day;
> And here may I, though vile as he,
>   Wash all my sins away.

6

The Scriptures a Source of Joy

THY words were found, and I did eat them; and thy word was unto me the joy and rejoicing of mine heart: for I am called by thy name, O Lord God of hosts. *Jer.* xv. 16.

> Oh may these heavenly pages be
>   My ever dear delight;
> And still new beauties may I see,
>   And still increasing light.

7

The Sabbath a Source of Joy

THIS is the day which the Lord hath made; we will rejoice and be glad in it.

Psalm cxviii. 24.

Oft as this peaceful day shall come,
    Lord, raise my thoughts from earthly things,
And bear them to my heavenly home,
    On faith and hope's celestial wings:
Till the last gleam of life decay,
In one eternal sabbath day.

8

Faith a Source of Joy

WHOM having not seen, ye love; in whom, though now ye see him not, yet believing, ye rejoice with joy unspeakable and full of glory. *1 Pet.* i. 8.

> A bleeding Saviour, seen by faith,
>   A sense of pardoning love,
> A hope that triumphs over death,
>   Give joys like those above.

9

Pardon a Source of Joy

BLESSED is he whose transgression is forgiven, whose sin is covered. Blessed is the man unto whom the Lord imputeth not iniquity, and in whose spirit there is no guile. *Psalm* xxxii. 1, 2.

> The Saviour smiles! o'er my bless'd soul
> New tides of hope tumultuous roll;
> Earth has a joy unknown in heaven,
> The new-born peace of sin forgiven;
> Tears of such pure and deep delight,
> Ye angels! never dimm'd your sight.

10

Hope of Glory a Source of Joy

By whom [Jesus Christ] we have access by
faith into this grace wherein we stand, and
rejoice in hope of the glory of God.

Rom. v. 2.

By faith to Pisgah's top I fly,
    And there delighted stand,
To view beneath a cloudless sky,
    The spacious promised land.

The Lord of all the vast domain
    Has promised it to me;
The length and breadth of all the plain,
    As far as faith can see.

11

Godly Fear a Source of Joy

Blessed is every one that feareth the Lord;
that walketh in his ways. For thou shalt eat
the labour of thine hands: happy shalt thou
be, and it shall be well with thee.

Psalm cxxviii. 1, 2.

Happy, beyond description, he
    Who fears the Lord his God;
Who hears his threats with holy awe,
    And trembles at his rod.

12

Obedience a Source of Joy

I WILL delight myself in thy commandments
which I have loved. *Psalm* cxix. 47.

Then shall my heart have inward joy,
    And keep my face from shame,
When all thy statutes I obey,
    And honour all thy name.

13

Communion with God

a Source of Joy

THERE be many that say, Who will show
us any good? Lord, lift thou up the light of
thy countenance upon us. Thou hast put
gladness in my heart, more than in the time
that their corn and their wine increased.
                    Psalm iv. 6, 7.

Lord, what is life? if spent with thee,
    In humble praise and prayer,
How long or short my life may be
    I feel no anxious care:
Though life depart, my joys shall last,
When life and all its joys are past.

105

14

Communion of Saints
a Source of Joy

MY goodness extendeth not to thee; but to the saints that are in the earth, and to the excellent, in whom is all my delight.

Psalm xvi. 2, 3.

> If 'tis sweet to mingle where
> Christians meet for fervent prayer;
> If 'tis sweet with them to raise
> Songs of holy joy and praise;
> Passing sweet that state must be,
> Where they meet eternally.

15

Prayer a Source of Joy

EVEN them will I bring to my holy mountain, and make them joyful in my house of prayer. *Isaiah* lvi. 7.

> Prayer makes the darken'd cloud withdraw,
> Prayer climbs the ladder Jacob saw;
> Gives exercise to faith and love,
> Brings every blessing from above.

16

Salvation a Source of Joy

WE will rejoice in thy salvation, and in the name of our God we will set up our banners.
Psalm xx. 5.

> Salvation! oh the joyful sound!
>   'Tis pleasure to our ears;
> A sovereign balm for every wound,
>   A cordial for our fears.

17

Early Piety a Source of Joy

O SATISFY us early with thy mercy; that we may rejoice and be glad all our days.
Psalm xc. 14.

> Grace is a plant, where'er it grows,
>   Of pure and heavenly root;
> But fairest in the young it shows,
>   And yields the sweetest fruit.

18

A Good Conscience a Source of Joy

OUR rejoicing is this, the testimony of our conscience, that in simplicity and godly sincerity, not with fleshly wisdom, but by the grace of God, we have had our conversation in the world. *2 Cor.* i. 12.

> O happy soul, that lives on high,
>   While men lie grovelling here;
> Whose hopes are fix'd above the sky,
>   And faith forbids his fear.
>
> His conscience cleans'd from all his sins,
>   Love, peace, and joy combine
> To form a life whose holy springs
>   Are hidden and divine.

19

Benevolence a Source of Joy

REMEMBER the words of the Lord Jesus, how he said, It is more blessed to give than to receive. *Acts* xx. 35.

> Bless'd is the man whose heart expands
>   At melting pity's call,
> And the rich blessings of whose hands
>   Like heavenly manna fall.

20

Tribulation a Source of Joy

WE glory in tribulation: knowing that tribulation worketh patience; and patience, experience; and experience, hope.

Rom. v. 3, 4.

> Then let us wait the' appointed day,
>   Nor call this world our home;
> To pilgrims in a foreign land,
>   Afflictions needs must come.
>
> Who rules the world, o'errules their end,
>   They destined are for good;
> And bear the saints to realms of rest,
>   Though mighty as a flood.

21

Temporal Blessings Sources of Joy

YE shall eat in plenty, and be satisfied, and
praise the name of the Lord your God, that
hath dealt wondrously with you: and my
people shall never be ashamed. *Joel* ii. 26.

> Thy bounty gilds the path of life
>   With every cheering ray,
> And oft restrains the rising tear,
>   Or wipes that tear away.

22

The Divine Blessing
a Source of Joy

THE blessing of the Lord, it maketh rich, and he addeth no sorrow with it. *Prov.* x. 22.

> Better than life itself thy love,
> Dearer than all beside to me;
> For whom have I in heaven above,
> Or what on earth, compared to thee?

23

The Divine Protection
a Source of Joy

BECAUSE thou hast been my help, therefore in the shadow of thy wings will I rejoice.
Psalm lxiii. 7.

> Since thou hast been my help,
> To thee my spirit flies;
> And on thy watchful providence
> My cheerful hope relies.

24

Divine Acceptance a Source of Joy

Go thy way, eat thy bread with joy, and drink thy wine with a merry heart; for God now accepteth thy work. *Eccles.* ix. 7.

> Whilst I see thy love to me,
>   Every object teems with joy;
> Here, oh may I walk with thee,
>   Then into thy presence die!
> Let me but thyself possess,
> Total sum of happiness;
> Real bliss I then shall prove—
> Heaven below, and heaven above.

25

Joy Following Sorrow

WEEPING may endure for a night; but joy cometh in the morning. *Psalm* xxx. 5.

> When comforts are declining,
>   He grants the soul again,
> A season of clear shining,
>   To cheer it after rain.

26

Joy the Duty of the Believer

BE glad in the Lord, and rejoice, ye righteous: and shout for joy, all ye that are upright in heart. *Psalm* xxxii. 11.

> Let those refuse to sing
>   Who never knew the Lord;
> But children of the heavenly King
>   Should speak their joys abroad.

27

Joy to be Sought Through Christ

HITHERTO have ye asked nothing in my
name: ask, and ye shall receive, that your
joy may be full. *John* xvi. 24.

> Dark and cheerless is the morn,
>   Unaccompanied by thee;
> Joyless is the day's return,
>   Till thy mercy's beams we see:
> Day-spring from on high, be near;
> Day-star, in our hearts appear.

28

Believer's Joy Is Satisfying

BLESSED is the man whom thou choosest, and causest to approach unto thee, that he may dwell in thy courts: we shall be satisfied with the goodness of thy house, even of thy holy temple. *Psalm* lxv. 4.

> These are the joys which satisfy,
> And sanctify the mind;
> Which make the spirit mount on high,
> And leave the world behind.

29

Believer's Joy Is Abiding

THESE things have I spoken unto you, that my joy might remain in you, and that your joy might be full. *John* xv. 11.

> Art thou not mine, my living Lord?
> And can my hope, my comfort die,
> Fix'd on thine everlasting word—
> The word that built the earth and sky.

113

30

Believer Has Joy in Death

LORD, now lettest thou thy servant depart
in peace, according to thy word: for mine
eyes have seen thy salvation. *Luke* ii. 29, 30.

When we have number'd all our years,
    And stand, at length, on Jordan's brink;
Though the flesh fail with mortal fears,
    Oh! let not then the spirit sink:
But strong in faith, and hope, and love,
Plunge through the stream to rise above.

31

Heaven the Consummation of Joy

WELL done, thou good and faithful servant:
thou hast been faithful over a few things,
I will make thee ruler over many things:
enter thou into the joy of thy Lord.
                            Matt. xxv. 21.

Soldier of Christ, well done!
    Praise be thy new employ;
And while eternal ages run,
    Rest in thy Saviour's joy.

August

SORROWS
OF THE BELIEVER

1

Believer Forewarned of Sorrow

THESE things I have spoken unto you, that in me ye might have peace. In the world ye shall have tribulation: but be of good cheer; I have overcome the world. *John* xvi. 33.

The path of sorrow, and that path alone,
Leads to the land where sorrow is unknown.
No traveller e'er reached that bless'd abode,
Who found not thorns and briars in his road.

2

Sources of Sorrow—

Loss of Divine Favour

RESTORE unto me the joy of thy salvation; and uphold me with thy free Spirit.

Psalm li. 12.

> Ah! why, by passing clouds oppress'd,
> Should vexing thoughts distract thy breast?
> Turn, turn to Him, in every pain,
> Whom never suppliant sought in vain.

3

Sources of Sorrow—

Indwelling Sin

I SEE another law in my members, warring against the law of my mind, and bringing me into captivity to the law of sin which is in my members. *Rom.* vii. 23.

> Nature may raise her fleshly strife,
> Reluctant to the heavenly life:
> But grace omnipotent at length
> Shall arm the saint with saving strength,
> Through the sharp war with aids attend,
> And his last conflict sweetly end.

116

4

Sources of Sorrow—
A Deceitful Heart

THE heart is deceitful above all things, and
desperately wicked: who can know it?

Jer. xvii. 9.

With flowing tears, Lord, I confess,
My folly and unstedfastness;
When shall this heart more stable be,
Fix'd by thy grace alone on thee?

5

Sources of Sorrow—
Ingratitude of the Ungodly

THEY that render evil for good are mine
adversaries; because I follow the thing that
good is. Forsake me not, O Lord: O my
God, be not far from me.

Psalm xxxviii. 20, 21.

If wounded love my bosom swell,
Deceived by those I prized too well;
He shall his pitying aid bestow,
Who felt on earth severer woe:
At once betray'd, denied, or fled,
By those who shared his daily bread.

6

Sources of Sorrow—

Reproach of the World

LET us go forth therefore unto him without the camp, bearing his reproach. *Heb.* xiii. 13.

> If on my face, for thy dear name,
>   Shame and reproach shall be,
> I'll hail reproach, and welcome shame,
>   If thou remember me.

7

Sources of Sorrow—

Persecution

THOUGH I walk in the midst of trouble, thou wilt revive me: thou shalt stretch forth thine hand against the wrath of mine enemies, and thy right hand shall save me.

Ps. cxxxviii. 7.

> Man may trouble and distress me,
> 'Twill but drive me to thy breast;
> Life with trials hard may press me,
> Heaven will bring me sweeter rest.

8

Sources of Sorrow—

Earthly Losses and Bereavements

NAKED came I out of my mother's womb, and naked shall I return thither: the Lord gave and the Lord hath taken away; blessed be the name of the Lord. *Job* i. 21.

> Oh! blessed be the hand that gave;
>   Still blessed when it takes:
> Blessed be he who smites to save,
>   Who heals the heart he breaks:
> Perfect and true are all his ways
> Whom heaven adores, and earth obeys.

9

Sources of Sorrow—

The Sins of Others

RIVERS of water run down mine eyes, because they keep not thy law.
                        Psalm cxix. 136.

> I sorrow for the mental night
>   In which mankind around me lie:
> Almighty Father, by thy might,
>   Arouse them from their lethargy.

119

10

Sources of Sorrow—
The Number of the Wicked

BROAD is the way, that leadeth to destruction, and many there be which go in thereat: because strait is the gate, and narrow is the way, which leadeth unto life, and few there be that find it. *Matt.* vii. 13, 14.

> Strait is the way, the door is strait,
>   Which lead to joys on high:
> 'Tis but a few that find the gate,
>   While crowds mistake, and die.

11

Sorrow Chosen Rather than Sin

MOSES, when he was come to years, refused to be called the son of Pharaoh's daughter; choosing rather to suffer affliction with the people of God, than to enjoy the pleasures of sin for a season. *Heb.* xi. 24, 25.

> It is not for me to be seeking my bliss,
> And building my hopes in a region like this
> I look for a city which hands have not piled;
> I pant for a country by sin undefiled.

120

12

Believer's Confidence in Trouble

ALTHOUGH the fig tree shall not blossom, neither shall fruit be in the vines; the labour of the olive shall fail, and the fields shall yield no meat; the flock shall be cut off from the fold, and there shall be no herd in the stalls: yet I will rejoice in the Lord, I will joy in the God of my salvation.

Hab. iii. 17, 18.

> Although my wealth and comfort's lost,
>   My blooming hopes cut off I see,
> Yet will I in my Saviour trust,
>   Whose matchless grace can reach to me.

13

Believer's Comfort in Trouble

THIS is my comfort in my affliction: for thy word hath quickened me. *Psalm* cxix, 50.

> Thus trusting in thy word, I tread
>   The narrow path of duty on;
> What though some cherish'd joys are fled?
>   What though some flattering dreams are gone?
> Yet purer brighter joys remain:
> Why should my spirit then complain?

14

Christ an Example to the Afflicted

EVEN hereunto were ye called: because Christ also suffered for us, leaving us an example, that ye should follow his steps.
1 Pet. ii. 21.

> Our glorious Leader claims our praise
> For his own pattern given,
> While the long cloud of witnesses
> Show the same path to heaven.

15

The Patriarchs

Examples to the Afflicted

WHEREFORE seeing we also are compassed about with so great a cloud of witnesses, let us lay aside every weight, and the sin which doth so easily beset us, and let us run with patience the race that is set before us. *Heb*. xii. 1.

> Once they were mourning here below,
> And wet their couch with tears;
> They wrestled hard, as we do now,
> With sins, and doubts, and fears.

16

The Prophets

Examples to the Afflicted

TAKE, my brethren, the prophets, who have
spoken in the name of the Lord, for an example of suffering affliction, and of patience.
James v. 10.

> And shall not we aspire,
> Like them our course to run?
> The crown if we would wear,
> The cross must first be borne.
> Divinely taught, they show'd the way,
> First to believe, and then obey.

17

Benefits of Affliction—

Self-Abasement

SURELY after that I was instructed, I smote
upon my thigh: I was ashamed, yea, even
confounded, because I did bear the reproach
of my youth. *Jer.* xxxi. 19.

> Dumb at thy feet I lie,
> For thou hast brought me low;
> Remove thy judgments, lest I die;
> I faint beneath thy blow.

123

18

Benefits of Affliction—
Contrition for Sin

I will go and return to my place, till they acknowledge their offence, and seek my face: in their affliction they will seek me early. *Hos.* v. 15.

> What though afflictions pierced my heart!
> I bless the hand that caused the smart;
> It taught my tears awhile to flow,
> But saved me from eternal woe.

19

Benefits of Affliction—Patience

The trying of your faith worketh patience. But let patience have her perfect work, that ye may be perfect and entire, wanting nothing. *James* i. 3, 4.

> Through waves, and clouds, and storms,
>   He gently clears thy way:
> Wait thou his time—the darkest night
>   Shall end in brightest day.

20

Benefits of Affliction—Humility

IF I be wicked, woe unto me; and if I be righteous, yet will I not lift up mine head. I am full of confusion; therefore see thou mine affliction. *Job* x. 15.

> To the heart truly humbled by woe,
> The anointing of joy shall be given;
> To the tears that from penitence flow,
> The peace that's the' forerunner of heaven.

21

Benefits of Affliction—Submission

I WAS dumb, I opened not my mouth; because thou didst it. *Psalm* xxxix. 9.

> Take all, great God, I will not grieve,
> But still will wish that I had still to give:
> I hear thy voice, thou bidd'st me quit
> My paradise; I bless, and do submit;
> I will not murmur at thy word,
> Nor beg thy angel to sheath up his sword.

22

Benefits of Affliction—Hope

WHY art thou cast down, O my soul? and why art thou disquieted in me? hope thou in God: for I shall yet praise him for the help of his countenance. *Psalm* xlii. 5.

> The gloomiest day hath gleams of light,
>   The darkest wave hath bright foam near it;
> And twinkles through the cloudiest night
>   Some solitary star to cheer it.

23

Benefits of Affliction—Holiness

Now no chastening for the present seemeth to be joyous, but grievous: nevertheless, afterward it yieldeth the peaceable fruit of righteousness unto them which are exercised thereby. *Heb.* xii. 11.

> Our hearts are fasten'd to this world
>   By strong and endless ties;
> But every sorrow cuts a string,
>   And urges us to rise.

24

Benefits of Affliction—
Tries Our Sincerity

HE knoweth the way that I take: when he hath tried me, I shall come forth as gold.
Job xxiii. 10.

Though sorrows rise, and dangers roll
In waves of darkness o'er my soul;
Though friends are false, and love decays,
And few and evil are my days—
Yet even in nature's utmost ill,
I love thee, Lord! I love thee still.

25

Benefits of Affliction—Brings
Sin to Remembrance

IF they be bound in fetters, and be holden in cords of affliction; then he showeth them their work, and their transgressions that they have exceeded. *Job* xxxvi. 8, 9.

My former hopes are fled,
My terror now begins;
I feel, alas! that I am dead
In trespasses and sins.

26

Benefits of Affliction—

Leads to Prayer

O REMEMBER not against us former iniquities: let thy tender mercies speedily prevent
us: for we are brought very low.

Psalm lxxix. 8.

> Ah! whither could we flee for aid
> When tempted, desolate, dismay'd;
> Or how the hosts of hell defeat,
> Had suffering saints no mercy-seat?

27

Benefits of Affliction—

Brings Us Back to God

I WILL hedge up thy way with thorns, and
make a wall, that she shall not find her
paths.—Then shall she say, I will go and
return to my first husband; for then was it
better with me than now. *Hos.* ii. 6, 7.

> Long unafflicted, undismay'd,
> In pleasure's path secure I stray'd:
> Thou madest me feel thy chastening rod,
> And straight I turned unto my God.

28

Benefits of Affliction— Exercises Our Faith

YE are in heaviness through manifold temptations: that the trial of your faith, being much more precious than of gold that perisheth, though it be tried with fire, might be found unto praise and honour and glory at the appearing of Jesus Christ.

1 Pet. i. 6, 7.

> Dark are the ways of Providence,
>   While those who love thee groan;
> Thy reasons lie conceal'd from sense,
>   Mysterious and unknown.

29

Benefits of Affliction— Teaches Our Frailty

MINE age is departed, and is removed from me as a shepherd's tent: I have cut off like a weaver my life: he will cut me off with pining sickness. *Isa.* xxxviii. 12.

> Lord, let me know mine end,
>   My days, how brief their date,
> That I may timely comprehend
>   How frail my best estate.

129

30

Benefits of Affliction—Remind Us of Former Mercies

WE had the sentence of death in ourselves, that we should not trust in ourselves, but in God which raiseth the dead: who delivered us from so great a death, and doth deliver: in whom we trust that he will yet deliver us. *2 Cor.* i. 9. 10.

His love in times past forbids me to think
He'll leave me at last in trouble to sink:
Each sweet Ebenezer I have in review
Confirms his good pleasure to help me quite through.

31

Affliction Succeeded by Glory

OUR light affliction, which is but for a moment, worketh for us a far more exceeding and eternal weight of glory. *2 Cor.* iv. 17.

All trials and sorrows the Christian prepare
For the rest that remaineth above;
On earth tribulation awaits him, but there
The smile of unchangeable love.

September

TEMPTATIONS
OF THE BELIEVER

1

Temptations Permitted by God

THE Lord said unto Satan, Behold, all that he hath is in thy power; only upon himself put not forth thine hand. *Job* i. 12.

> Still thine integrity hold fast,
>   The tempter's counsel spurn,
> Hope against hope, and God at last,
>   Will for thy help return.

2

God Does Not Tempt to Sin

LET no man say when he is tempted, I am tempted of God: for God cannot be tempted with evil, neither tempteth he any man: but every man is tempted, when he is drawn away of his own lust, and enticed.
James i. 13, 14.

> My crimes, though great, do not surpass
> The power and glory of thy grace;
> Oh! wash my soul from every sin,
> And make my guilty conscience clean.

3

Temptations—From Satan

Lest Satan should get an advantage of us:
for we are not ignorant of his devices.

2 *Cor.* ii. 11.

Fear not Satan's strong temptations
 Though they tease thee day by day,
And thy evil inclinations
 Overwhelm thee with dismay!
 Thou shalt conquer,
Through the Lamb's redeeming blood.

4

Temptations—

From a Depraved Nature

I find then a law, that, when I would do
good, evil is present with me. *Rom.* vii. 21.

Oh! who can free my troubled mind
 From sin's oppressive load?
O wretched man! how shall I find
 Acceptance with my God.

My soul with transport turns to thee,
 To thee my Saviour turns;
Cleansed by thy blood, and saved by grace,
 My soul no longer mourns.

5

Temptations—
From the Love of Riches

THEY that will be rich fall into temptation
and a snare, and into many foolish and hurt-
ful lusts, which drown men in destruction
and perdition. *1 Tim.* vi. 9.

> Oh lay not up upon this earth
>   Your hopes, your joys, your treasure,
> Here sorrow clouds the pilgrim's path,
>   And blights each opening pleasure.
> All, all below must fade and die,
>   The dearest hopes we cherish,
> Scenes touch'd with brightest radiancy,
>   Are all decreed to perish.

6

Temptations—
From the Fear of Man

THE fear of man bringeth a snare: but
whoso putteth his trust in the Lord shall
be safe. *Prov.* xxix. 25.

> The taunts and frowns of men of earth,
>   What are they all to me!
> Oh they are things of little worth,
>   Weigh'd with one smile from Thee,
> Who bore a sorrow deeper far,
> Than all these stingless trifles are.

7

Temptation to Neglect Good Works

YE did run well; who did hinder you, that
ye should not obey the truth? *Gal.* v. 7.

> Better that we had never known
> The way to heaven through saving grace,
> Than basely in our lives disown,
> And slight and mock thee to thy face.

8

Temptation to Legal Dependance

ARE ye so foolish? having begun in the
Spirit, are ye now made perfect in the flesh?
Gal. iii. 3.

> Go, you that rest upon the law,
> And toil and seek salvation there;
> Look to the flame that Moses saw,
> And shrink, and tremble, and despair.
>
> But I'll retire beneath thy cross—
> Saviour, at thy dear feet I'll lie;
> And the keen sword that justice draws,
> Flaming and red, shall pass me by.

9

Temptation to
Formality in Religion

BE watchful, and strengthen the things which remain, that are ready to die: for I have not found thy works perfect before God. *Rev.* iii. 2.

> God is a Spirit just and wise;
>   He sees our inmost mind:
> In vain to heaven we raise our cries,
>   And leave our souls behind.

10

Temptation to
Slothfulness in Religion

NEVERTHELESS I have somewhat against thee, because thou hast left thy first love. Remember therefore from whence thou art fallen, and repent, and do the first works.
Rev. ii. 4, 5.

> I need the influence of thy grace
>   To speed me in the way,
> Lest I should loiter in my pace,
>   Or turn my feet astray.

135

11

Temptation to Self-Indulgence

I KEEP under my body, and bring it into subjection: lest that by any means, when I have preached to others, I myself should be a castaway. *1 Cor.* ix. 27.

> When thy statutes I forsake,
>   When my graces dimly shine,
> When my covenant I break,
>   Jesus, then remember thine:
>   Check my wanderings
>   By a look of love divine.

12

Temptation to Trifle with Sin

SHALL we continue in sin, that grace may abound? God forbid. How shall we, that are dead to sin, live any longer therein?
Rom. vi. 1.

> Shall we go on to sin,
>   Because thy grace abounds?
> Or crucify the Lord again,
>   And open all his wounds?
>   We will be slaves no more,
>   Since Christ has made us free;
> Has nail'd our tyrants to his cross,
>   And bought our liberty.

13

Temptation to Spiritual Pride

FOR who maketh thee to differ from another? and what hast thou that thou didst not receive? now if thou didst receive it, why dost thou glory, as if thou hadst not received it? *1 Cor.* iv. 7.

> Oft have I turn'd my eyes within,
> And brought to mind some latent sin
> But pride, the vice I most detest,
> Still lurks securely in my breast.

14

Temptation to Envy the Wicked

As for me, my feet were almost gone; my steps had well nigh slipped. For I was envious at the foolish, when I saw the prosperity of the wicked. *Psalm* lxxiii. 2, 3.

> Their feet are in a slippery place;
> Their riches swift as shadows fly;
> Their honours end in deep disgrace;
> In mirth they live, in anguish die.

15

Temptation to Mistrust Providence

IF God so clothe the grass of the field, which
to-day is, and to-morrow is cast into the
oven, shall he not much more clothe you,
O ye of little faith? *Matt.* vi. 30.

> I know not what may soon betide,
> Or how my wants shall be supplied;
> But Jesus knows, and will provide.
>
> When creature comforts fade and die,
> Worldlings may weep—but why should I?
> Jesus still lives, and still is nigh.

16

Temptation to Despair

I SINK in deep mire, where there is no standing: I am come into deep waters, where the
floods overflow me. I am weary of my crying: my throat is dried: mine eyes fail while
I wait for my God. *Psalm* lxix. 2, 3.

> Prostrate before thy mercy-seat,
>   I cannot if I would despair;
> None ever perish'd at thy feet,
>   And I would lie for ever there.

138

17

Temptation Humbles the Believer

LEST I should be exalted above measure through the abundance of the revelations, there was given to me a thorn in the flesh, the messenger of Satan to buffet me, lest I should be exalted above measure.

2 Cor. xii. 7.

What though a thorn my bosom bears,
And varied are the wants and cares,
   That mark my chequer'd way!
My God hath said, in whom I live,
"My grace is thine, and strength I give
   According to thy day."

18

Temptation to Be Resisted

FOR we wrestle not against flesh and blood, but against principalities, against powers, against the rulers of the darkness of this world, against spiritual wickedness in high places. *Eph.* vi. 12.

From strength to strength go on,
   Wrestle, and fight, and pray;
Tread all the powers of darkness down,
   And win the well-fought day.

19

Temptation to Be Avoided

ENTER not into the path of the wicked, and go not in the way of evil men. Avoid it, pass not by it, turn from it, and pass away. *Prov.* iv. 14, 15.

> A wicked world and wicked heart
>   With Satan are combined:
> Each acts a too successful part,
>   In harassing my mind.
>
> But fighting in my Saviour's strength,
>   Though mighty are my foes,
> I shall a conqueror be at length
>   O'er all that can oppose.

20

Temptation Avoided
by Watchfulness and Prayer

WATCH and pray, that ye enter not into temptation. *Matt.* xxvi. 41.

> Go to dark Gethsemane,
>   Ye that feel the tempter's power,
> Your Redeemer's conflict see,
>   Watch with him one bitter hour;
> Turn not from his griefs away,
> Learn of Jesus Christ to pray.

140

21

Temptation Overcome by Faith

ABOVE all, taking the shield of faith, wherewith ye shall be able to quench all the fiery
darts of the wicked. *Eph*. vi. 16.

> Let faith exert its conquering power,
> Say in thy tempted, trembling hour,
> "My God, my Father, save thy son!"
> 'Tis heard—and all thy fears are done.

22

Believer Armed Against Temptation

TAKE unto you the whole armour of God,
that ye may be able to withstand in the evil
day, and having done all, to stand.
Eph. vi. 13.

> The Christian warrior—see him stand
> In the whole armour of his God;
> The Spirit's sword is in his hand,
> His feet are with the gospel shod.

23

Preservation from Temptation

BECAUSE thou hast kept the word of my
patience, I also will keep thee from the hour
of temptation. *Rev.* iii. 10.

> Thus preserved from Satan's wiles,
>   Safe from dangers, free from fears,
> May I live upon thy smiles,
>   Till the promised hour appears:
> When the sons of God shall prove
> All their Father's boundless love.

24

Preservation in Temptation

BLESSED is the man that endureth temptation: for when he is tried, he shall receive
the crown of life, which the Lord hath promised to them that love him. *James* i. 12.

> When aught shall tempt my soul to stray
> From heavenly wisdom's narrow way,
> To shun the precept's holy light,
> Or quit my hold on Jesu's might,
> May He who felt temptation's power
> Still guard me in that dangerous hour.

142

25

Deliverance from Temptation

THE Lord knoweth how to deliver the godly out of temptations. *2 Pet.* ii. 9.

What though fierce and strong temptations
    Press around thee on the way,
And thy sinful inclinations
    Often cause thee great dismay!
        Look to Jesus,
    Thou through him shalt gain the day.

26

Christ the Strength of the Tempted

MY grace is sufficient for thee: for my strength is made perfect in weakness.
                    2 Cor. xii. 9.

Why should I fear the darkest hour,
Or tremble at the tempter's power!
Jesus vouchsafes to be my tower.

Though hot the fight, why quit the field?
Why must I either fear or yield,
Since Jesus is my mighty shield?

27

Christ's Sympathy
with the Tempted

In that he himself hath suffered being
tempted, he is able to succour them that
are tempted. *Heb.* ii. 18.

> Touch'd with a sympathy within,
>   He knows our feeble frame;
> He knows what sore temptations mean,
>   For he has felt the same.

28

Christ's Intercession
for the Tempted

The Lord said, Simon, Simon, behold, Satan
hath desired to have you, that he may sift
you as wheat: but I have prayed for thee,
that thy faith fail not. *Luke* xxii. 31, 32.

> Though faint my prayers, and cold my love
> My stedfast hope shall not remove,
> While Jesus intercedes above.
>
> Against me earth and hell combine;
> But on my side is power Divine;
> Jesus is all, and he is mine.

144

29

The Lord's Prayer for the Tempted

LEAD us not into temptation; but deliver us from evil. *Matt.* vi. 13.

> Protect us in the dangerous hour,
> And from the wily tempter's power,
>   Lord, set our spirits free;
> And if temptation should assail,
> May mighty grace o'er all prevail,
>   And lead our hearts to thee.

30

Freedom from Temptation
in Heaven

To him that overcometh, will I grant to sit with me in my throne, even as I also overcame, and am set down with my Father in his throne. *Rev.* iii. 21.

> Though temptations now attend thee,
>   And thou tread'st the thorny road,
> His right hand shall still defend thee,
>   Soon he'll bring thee home to God:
>   Full deliverance
>   Thou shalt have in heaven above.

145

October

RETROSPECTIONS
OF THE BELIEVER

1

Duty of Retrospection

THOU shalt remember all the way which
the Lord thy God led thee these forty years
in the wilderness, to humble thee, and to
prove thee, to know what was in thine heart,
whether thou wouldst keep his commandments. *Deut.* viii. 2.

> Thus far the Lord has led me on,
> And made his truth and mercy known;
> And while I tread this desert land,
> New mercies shall new songs demand.

2

Of the Divine Help

THEN Samuel took a stone, and set it between Mizpeh and Shen, and called the name of it Ebenezer, saying, Hitherto hath the Lord helped us. *1 Sam.* vii. 12.

> Here I raise my Ebenezer,
>   Hither, by thy help, I'm come:
> And I hope, by thy good pleasure,
>   Safely to arrive at home.

3

Of the Divine Guidance

WHO am I, O Lord God? and what is my house, that thou hast brought me hitherto? and this was yet a small thing in thy sight, O Lord God. *2 Sam.* vii. 18, 19.

> Render'd safe by his protection,
>   I shall pass the watery waste;
> Trusting to his wise direction,
>   I shall gain the port at last;
>   And with wonder,
>   Think on toils and dangers past.

147

4

Of the Divine Faithfulness

THOU hast dealt well with thy servant,
O Lord, according unto thy word.
Psalm cxix. 65.

Since first the maze of life I trod,
  Hast thou not hedged about my way,
My worldly vain designs withstood,
  And robb'd my passions of their prey?
Thrice happy loss, which makes me see
My happiness alone in thee!

5

Of the Divine Forbearance

IT is of the Lord's mercies that we are not
consumed, because his compassions fail not.
They are new every morning: great is thy
faithfulness. *Lam.* iii. 22, 23.

Lift up to God the voice of praise,
  Whose goodness, passing thought,
Loads every minute as it flies
  With benefits unsought.

6

Of the Divine Mercy

HE hath not dealt with us after our sins;
nor rewarded us according to our iniquities.
Psalm ciii. 10.

> He hath with a piteous eye
> Look'd upon our misery:
> Let us, then, with gladsome mind,
> Praise the Lord, for he is kind:
> For his mercies shall endure,
> Ever faithful, ever sure.

7

Of the Divine Counsel
and Instruction

I WILL bless the Lord, who hath given me
counsel: my reins also instruct me in the
night seasons. *Psalm* xvi. 7.

> Sure the Lord thus far has brought me,
>   By his watchful tender care;
> Sure, 'tis he himself has taught me
>   How to seek his face by prayer:
> After so much mercy past,
> Will he give me up at last?

149

8

Of Divine Promises Fulfilled

YE know in all your hearts and in all your souls, that not one thing hath failed of all the good things which the Lord your God spake concerning you; all are come to pass unto you, and not one thing hath failed thereof. *Josh.* xxiii. 14.

> In all my ways thy hand I own,
>   Thy ruling providence I see;
> Assist me still my course to run,
>   And still direct my paths to thee.

9

Of Unnumbered Blessings

MANY, O Lord my God, are thy wonderful works which thou hast done, and thy thoughts which are to us-ward: they cannot be reckoned up in order unto thee: if I would declare and speak of them, they are more than can be numbered. *Psalm* xl. 5.

> For mercies countless as the sand,
>   Which daily I receive
> From Jesus, my Redeemer's hand,
>   My soul, what canst thou give?

150

10

Of Early Pious Instruction

CONTINUE thou in the things which thou
hast learned and hast been assured of, knowing of whom thou hast learned them.
2 Tim. iii. 14.

> Lord, hast thou made me know thy ways?
>   Conduct me in thy fear;
> And grant me such supplies of grace
>   That I may persevere.

11

Of His Natural State

YOU that were sometime alienated and
enemies in your mind by wicked works, yet
now hath he reconciled. *Col.* i. 21.

> Plunged in a gulf of dark despair,
>   We wretched sinners lay,
> Without one cheerful beam of hope,
>   Or spark of glimmering day.

151

12

Of the Sins of His Life

How many are mine iniquities and sins?
make me to know my transgression and my
sin. *Job* xiii. 23.

> My past transgressions pain me;
>   Lord, cleanse my heart within;
> And evermore restrain me
>   From all presumptuous sin.
>
> So let my whole behaviour,
>   Thoughts, words, and actions be,
> O God, my strength and Saviour,
>   Acceptable to thee.

13

Of Past Unprofitableness

FOR when ye were the servants of sin, ye
were free from righteousness. What fruit
had ye then in those things whereof ye are
now ashamed? *Rom.* vi. 20, 21.

> Lord, I confess my numerous faults,
>   How great my guilt has been;
> Foolish and vain were all my thoughts,
>   And all my life was sin.

14

Of the Season of Conversion

GIVING thanks unto the Father, which hath made us meet to be partakers of the inheritance of the saints in light: who hath delivered us from the power of darkness, and hath translated us into the kingdom of his dear Son. *Col.* i. 12, 13.

Since the dear hour that brought me to thy foot,
And cut up all my follies by the root,
I never trusted in an arm but thine,
Nor hoped but in thy righteousness Divine:—
Cast at thy glorious feet, mine only plea
Is what it was, dependance upon Thee.

15

Of Spiritual Deliverance

GREAT is thy mercy toward me: and thou hast delivered my soul from the lowest hell.
Psalm lxxxvi. 13.

He pardon'd my transgressions,
Bade all my sorrows cease;
And, in his rich compassions,
Restored my soul to peace.

153

16

Of Spiritual Enjoyments

I SAT down under his shadow with great delight, and his fruit was sweet to my taste. He brought me to the banqueting house, and his banner over me was love.

Sol. Song ii. 3, 4.

> Kindly he brought me to the place
> Where stands the banquet of his grace;
> He saw me faint, and o'er my head
> The banner of his love he spread.

17

Of Support in Affliction

UNLESS thy law had been my delight, I should then have perished in mine affliction.

Psalm cxix. 92.

> God of my life, how good, how wise
> Thy judgments to my soul have been!
> They were but blessings in disguise,
> The painful remedies of sin.
> How different now thy ways appear,
> Most merciful, when most severe!

18

Of Answers to Prayer

I LOVE the Lord, because he hath heard my voice and my supplications. Because he hath inclined his ear unto me, therefore will I call upon him as long as I live. *Psalm* cxvi. 1, 2.

> Did ever trouble yet befall,
> And he refuse to hear thy call?
> And has he not his promise pass'd,
> That thou shalt overcome at last?

19

Of Deliverance from Adversity

I WILL be glad and rejoice in thy mercy: for thou hast considered my trouble; thou hast known my soul in adversities.

Psalm xxxi. 7.

> Oh, magnify the Lord with me;
>   Come, join his name to bless:
> To him did I in trouble flee;
>   He saved me from distress:
> Oh, let him then your refuge be,
>   Nor shall you fail success.

20

Of Deliverance from Danger

THOU drewest near in the day that I called upon thee: thou saidst, Fear not. O Lord, thou hast pleaded the causes of my soul; thou hast redeemed my life. *Lam*. iii. 57, 58.

> Be all my added life employ'd
> Thy image in my soul to see:
> Fill with thyself the mighty void;
> Enlarge my heart to compass thee.

21

Of Deliverance from Death

O LORD, thou hast brought up my soul from the grave: thou hast kept me alive, that I should not go down to the pit.

Psalm xxx. 3.

> Thy mercy chased the shades of death,
> And snatch'd me from the grave;
> Oh may thy praise employ that breath
> Which mercy deigns to save!

22

Of the Vanity of Human Life

AND Jacob said unto Pharaoh, The days of
the years of my pilgrimage are an hundred
and thirty years: few and evil have the days
of the years of my life been. *Gen.* xlvii. 9.

> This life's a dream, an empty show,
> But the bright world to which we go
> Hath joys substantial and sincere:
> When shall I wake, and find me there?

23

Of Departed Friends

I WOULD not have you to be ignorant, brethren, concerning them which are asleep, that
ye sorrow not, even as others which have no
hope. For if we believe that Jesus died and
rose again, even so them also which sleep in
Jesus will God bring with him.

1 Thess. iv. 13, 14.

Though loved and lost, not ours the pang of those
Whose earth-born grief no heavenly balsam knows:
We would not call their spirits from their home
Where sin assails them not, and sorrow cannot come.

24

Aged Believer's Retrospect

O GOD, thou hast taught me from my youth: and hitherto have I declared thy wondrous works. Now also when I am old and grey-headed, O God, forsake me not.

Psalm lxxi. 17, 18.

> Still hath my life new wonders seen
> Repeated every year:
> Behold, my days which yet remain
> I trust them to thy care.

25

Retrospection Should
Lead to Gratitude

WHAT shall I render unto the Lord for all his benefits toward me? I will take the cup of salvation, and call upon the name of the Lord. *Psalm* cxvi. 12, 13.

> When all thy mercies, O my God,
> My rising soul surveys,
> Transported with the view I'm lost
> In wonder, love, and praise.

26

Retrospection Should
Lead to Self-Examination

I HAVE considered the days of old, the years
of ancient times. I call to remembrance my
song in the night: I commune with mine
own heart: and my spirit made diligent
search. *Psalm* lxxvii. 5, 6.

> Help me, O Lord, to try my heart,
>   To search with strictest care,
> And all my thoughts, and words, and ways,
>   With Scripture to compare.

27

Retrospection Should
Lead to Self-Abasement

AND JACOB said, I am not worthy of the
least of all thy mercies, and of all the truth,
which thou hast shewed unto thy servant.
Gen. xxxii. 10.

> Unworthy, Lord, of all
>   Thy mercies though we be,
> Yet for the greatest we may call,
>   The greatest are most free.

159

28

Retrospection Should
Lead to Repentance

SURELY it is meet to be said unto God, I have borne chastisement, I will not offend any more: that which I see not teach thou me: if I have done iniquity, I will do no more. *Job* xxxiv. 31, 32.

> In thought, in will, in word and deed,
>   What evils have I done,
> Against the God of grace and love,
>   His Spirit and his Son?

29

Retrospection Should
Lead to Amendment of Life

I THOUGHT on my ways, and turned my feet unto thy testimonies. I made haste, and delayed not to keep thy commandments.
                              Psalm cxix. 59, 60.

> Thou art my portion, O my God;
>   Soon as I know thy way,
> My heart makes haste to obey thy word,
>   And suffers no delay.

30

Retrospection Should Lead to Confidence in God

RETURN unto thy rest, O my soul; for the Lord hath dealt bountifully with thee. For thou hast delivered my soul from death, mine eyes from tears, and my feet from falling. *Psalm* cxvi. 7, 8.

> For this, when future sorrows rise,
> To him will I direct my cries;
> For this, through all my future days,
> Adore his name, and sing his praise.

31

Retrospection Should Lead to Devotedness to God

ONLY fear the Lord, and serve him in truth with all your heart: for consider how great things he hath done for you. *1 Sam.* xii. 24.

> My God, my King, thy various praise
> Shall fill the remnant of my days;
> Thy grace employ my humble tongue
> Till death and glory raise the song.
>
> May every hour successive bear
> Some thankful tribute to thine ear;
> And by thy grace accepted be,
> As works of love perform'd for Thee.

November

ANTICIPATIONS
OF THE BELIEVER

1

Believer's Confidence in God

MY times are in thy hand: make thy face
to shine upon thy servant: save me for thy
mercies' sake. *Psalm* xxxi. 15, 16.

> "My times are in thy hand,"
> My God, I wish them there;
> My life, my friends, my soul, I leave
> Entirely to thy care.

2

Of Future Support

TRUST in the Lord, and do good; so shalt
thou dwell in the land, and verily thou shalt
be fed. *Psalm* xxxvii. 3, 4.

> The birds without barn or storehouse are fed;
> From them let us learn to trust for our bread:
> His saints what is fitting shall ne'er be denied,
> So long as 'tis written, The Lord will provide.

3

Of Deliverance from Trouble

THOU, which hast shewed me great and sore troubles, shalt quicken me again, and shalt bring me up again from the depths of the earth. *Psalm* lxxi. 20.

> From every piercing sorrow
>   That heaves our breast to-day,
> Or threatens us to-morrow,
>   Hope turns our eyes away;
> On wings of faith ascending,
>   We see the land of light,
> And feel our sorrows ending
>   In infinite delight.

4

Of Being Kept by Christ

I KNOW whom I have believed, and am persuaded that he is able to keep that which I have committed unto him against that day.
2 Tim. i. 12.

> Beneath his smiles my heart has liv'd,
>   And part of heaven possess'd;
> I thank him for the grace receiv'd,
>   And trust him for the rest.

5

Of the Completion
of the Work of Grace

BEING confident of this very thing, that he
which hath begun a good work in you will
perform it until the day of Jesus Christ.
Phil. i. 6.

> He will complete the work begun,
> He will his own defend;
> Will give me strength my course to run,
> And love me to the end.

6

Of the Triumphs of the Gospel

HIS name shall endure for ever: his name
shall be continued as long as the sun: and
men shall be blessed in him: all nations shall
call him blessed. *Psalm* lxxii. 17.

> Lord, let the thought of that bright day
> Kindle our hopes, and warm our love;
> Cheer us while here on earth we pray,
> And crown our songs in heaven above.

7

Of the End of His Warfare

THE time of my departure is at hand. I have fought a good fight, I have finished my course, I have kept the faith. *2 Tim.* iv. 6, 7.

> Oh most delightful hour by man
>   Experienced here below,
> The hour that terminates his span
>   Of conflict and of woe!

8

Of Victory Over Satan

THE God of peace shall bruise Satan under your feet shortly. *Rom.* xvi. 20.

> Now let my soul arise,
> And tread the tempter down;
> My Captain leads me forth
> To conquest and a crown:
> A feeble saint shall win the day,
> Though death and hell obstruct the way.

9

Of Victory Over Sin

O WRETCHED man that I am! who shall deliver me from the body of this death? I thank God, through Jesus Christ our Lord.
Rom. vii. 24, 25.

Now to the God of victory
  Immortal thanks be paid,
Who makes us conquerors while we die,
  Through Christ our living Head.

10

Of Victory Over the Grave

GOD will redeem my soul from the power of the grave: for he shall receive me.
Psalm xlix. 15.

There, till the archangel's trumpet sound,
  Ages of silence I shall lie;
Then from my earthly cell rebound,
  Glorious in immortality.

11

Of the Certainty of Death

WHEN a few years are come, then I shall go the way whence I shall not return.
Job xvi. 22.

> Welcome, sweet hour of full discharge,
> That sets my longing soul at large;
> Unbinds my chains, breaks up my cell,
> And gives me with my God to dwell.

12

Of Support in the Hour of Death

YEA, though I walk through the valley of the shadow of death, I will fear no evil: for thou art with me; thy rod and thy staff they comfort me. *Psalm* xxiii. 4.

> When the vale of death appears,
>   (Faint and cold this mortal clay,)
> Kind Forerunner, soothe my fears,
>   Light me through the darksome way:
>   Break the shadows,
>   Usher in eternal day.

167

13

Of the End of the World

THE day of the Lord will come as a thief in the night; in the which the heavens shall pass away with a great noise, and the elements shall melt with fervent heat, the earth also and the works that are therein shall be burned up. *2 Pet.* iii. 10.

> Lo! it comes—that day of wonder!
> Louder chorals shake the skies:
> Hades' gates are burst asunder;
> See the new-clothed myriads rise!

14

Of a Joyful Resurrection

I KNOW that my Redeemer liveth, and that he shall stand at the latter day upon the earth: and though after my skin worms destroy this body, yet in my flesh shall I see God. *Job* xix. 25, 26.

> Though worms may waste this with'ring clay,
> When flesh and spirit sever;
> My soul shall see eternal day,
> And dwell with God for ever.

15

Of the Coming
of Christ to Judgment

BEHOLD, he cometh with clouds; and every eye shall see him, and they also which pierced him: and all kindreds of the earth shall wail because of him. *Rev.* i. 7.

> Great God! what do I see and hear!
>   The end of things created:
> The Judge of mankind doth appear
>   In clouds of glory seated;
> The trumpet sounds, the graves restore
> The dead which they contain'd before:
>   Prepare, my soul, to meet him.

16

Of Meeting the Judge

WE must all appear before the judgment seat of Christ; that every one may receive the things done in his body, according to that he hath done, whether it be good or bad. *2 Cor.* v. 10.

> Oh! on that day, that wrathful day,
> When man to judgment wakes from clay,
> Lord, be the trembling sinner's stay,
> Though heaven and earth shall pass away.

17

Of Entire Acquittal

WHO shall lay any thing to the charge of God's elect? It is God that justifieth. Who is he that condemneth? It is Christ that died; yea rather, that is risen again, who is even at the right hand of God, who also maketh intercession for us. *Rom.* viii. 33, 34.

> Fear not the drum's earth-rending sound,
> Dread not the day of doom;
> For He that is to be thy Judge,
> Thy Saviour is become.

18

Of Participation in the Judgment

Do ye not know that the saints shall judge the world? *1 Cor.* vi. 2.

> See the Judge, our nature wearing,
> Cloth'd in majesty divine;
> Ye who long for his appearing
> Then shall say, "This God is mine:"
> Gracious Saviour,
> Own us in that day of thine!

19

Of Being Presented Faultless

UNTO him that is able to keep you from falling, and to present you faultless before the presence of his glory with exceeding joy.
Jude 24.

What transport then shall fill my heart,
    When thou my worthless name wilt own;
When I shall see thee as thou art,
    And know as I myself am known!

20

Of an Incorruptible Body

So when this corruptible shall have put on incorruption, and this mortal shall have put on immortality, then shall be brought to pass the saying that is written, Death is swallowed up in victory. *1 Cor.* xv. 54.

Where then thy triumph, Grave? and where thy sting,
O sullen Death? what terror dost thou bring?
We burst thine iron band, and soar on high—
Glory to Christ the Lord, who brings us victory!

171

21

Of a Glorious Body

WHO shall change our vile body, that it may be fashioned like unto his glorious body, according to the working whereby he is able even to subdue all things unto himself.

Phil. iii. 21.

My flesh shall slumber, in the ground
Till the last trumpet's joyful sound;
Then burst the chains, with sweet surprise,
And in my Saviour's image rise.

22

Of Being with Christ

To me to live is Christ, and to die is gain. For I am in a strait betwixt two, having a desire to depart, and to be with Christ, which is far better. *Phil.* i. 21, 23.

'Tis best, 'tis infinitely best,
To go where tempests never come;
Where saints and angels, ever blest,
Dwell, and enjoy their heavenly home.

23

Of Being Ever with Christ

THEN we which are alive and remain shall be caught up together with them in the clouds, to meet the Lord in the air: and so shall we ever be with the Lord.

1 Thess. iv. 17.

Oh, who can tell what joy shall beam
On all the ransom'd race,
When they shall join the hallow'd strains
And see the Saviour's face!

24

Of Reigning with Christ

IT is a faithful saying: For if we be dead with him, we shall also live with him: if we suffer, we shall also reign with him.

2 Tim. ii. 11, 12.

Ever upward may we move,
Wafted on the wings of love:
Looking when our Lord shall come,
Longing, gasping after home!
There may we with thee remain,
Partners of thine endless reign.

25

Of Being Like Christ

BELOVED, now are we the sons of God, and it doth not yet appear what we shall be: but we know that, when he shall appear, we shall be like him; for we shall see him as he is. *1 John* iii. 2.

> Him eye to eye we there shall see,
>   Our face like his shall shine:
> Oh, what a glorious company,
>   When saints and angels join!

26

Of an Heavenly Habitation

WE know that if our earthly house of this tabernacle were dissolved, we have a building of God, an house not made with hands, eternal in the heavens. *2 Cor.* v. 1.

> There is a home for weary souls,
>   By sin and sorrow driven;
> When toss'd on life's tempestuous shoals,
> Where storms arise, and ocean rolls,
>   'Tis found above—in heaven.

27

Of Perfection of Knowledge in Heaven

Now we see through a glass, darkly; but then face to face: now I know in part; but then shall I know even as also I am known. *1 Cor*. xiii. 12.

> As through a glass I dimly see
> The wonders of thy love;
> How little do I know of thee,
> Or of the joys above!
>
> 'Tis but in part I know thy will—
> I bless thee for the sight—
> When will thy love the rest reveal
> In glory's clearer light?

28

Of a Crown of Righteousness

HENCEFORTH there is laid up for me a crown of righteousness, which the Lord, the righteous Judge, shall give me at that day.
2 Tim. iv. 8.

> God has laid up in heaven for me
> A crown which cannot fade;
> The righteous Judge, in that great day,
> Shall place it on my head.

29

Of Reunion with Glorified Spirits

WHAT is our hope, or joy, or crown of rejoicing? Are not even ye in the presence of our Lord Jesus Christ at his coming?
1 Thes. ii. 19.

We soon shall join the throng,
  Their pleasures we shall share,
And sing the everlasting song
  With all the ransom'd there:
    Hallelujah!
  We are on our way to God.

30

Believer's Anticipations
a Call to Holiness

WHEREFORE, beloved, seeing that ye look for such things, be diligent that ye may be found of him in peace, without spot, and blameless. *2 Pet.* iii. 14.

Yet with these prospects full in sight
I'll wait thy signal for my flight;
For while thy service I pursue,
I find a heaven in all I do.

December

FINAL BLESSEDNESS
OF THE BELIEVER

1
Eternal Life the Gift of God

Now being made free from sin, and become servants to God, ye have your fruit unto holiness, and the end everlasting life. For the wages of sin is death; but the gift of God is eternal life through Jesus Christ our Lord. *Rom.* vi. 22, 23.

> From thee, my God, my joys shall rise,
>   And run eternal rounds,
> Beyond the limits of the skies,
>   And all created bounds.

2

Eternal Life the Purchase of Christ

NEITHER by the blood of goats and calves, but by his own blood he entered in once into the holy place, having obtained eternal redemption for us. *Heb*. ix. 12.

> Pardon and peace to dying men,
> And endless life are given:
> By the rich blood that Jesus shed
> Our souls are brought to heaven.

3

Eternal Life Secured by the Spirit

THE Holy Spirit of promise is the earnest of our inheritance until the redemption of the purchased possession, unto the praise of his glory. *Eph*. i. 13, 14.

> Dost thou not dwell in all the saints,
> And seal the heirs of heaven?
> When wilt thou banish my complaints,
> And show my sins forgiven.

4

Heaven the Desire of the Saints

WHILST we are at home in the body, we are absent from the Lord, we are confident, and willing rather to be absent from the body, and to be present with the Lord.

2 Cor. v. 6, 8.

In that bright city I would dwell,
  With that bless'd church the Saviour praise,
And, safe, redeem'd from death and hell,
  Sit at his feet through endless days.

5

Heaven a Rest

THERE remaineth a rest to the people of God. *Heb.* iv. 9.

Oh where shall rest be found,
  Rest for the weary soul?
'Twere vain the ocean-depths to sound,
  Or pierce to either pole.

Beyond this vale of tears,
  There is a life above,
Unmeasured by the flight of years—
  And all that life is love.

179

6

Heaven Compared
to a Marriage Supper

WRITE, Blessed are they which are called
unto the marriage supper of the Lamb.
Rev. xix. 9.

"Worthy the Lamb!" aloud they cry,
"That brought us here to God:"
In ceaseless hymns of praise they shout
The merits of his blood.

7

Heaven an Inheritance

HE is the mediator of the new testament,
that by means of death, for the redemption
of the transgressions that were under the
first testament, they which are called might
receive the promise of eternal inheritance.
Heb. ix. 15.

There is my house and portion fair,
My treasure and my heart are there,
And my abiding home;
For me my elder brethren stay,
And angels beckon me away,
And Jesus bids me come.

8

Heaven a Kingdom

I APPOINT unto you a kingdom, as my Father hath appointed unto me; that ye may eat and drink at my table in my kingdom. *Luke* xxii. 29, 30.

> O God! O Good beyond compare!
> If all thy meaner works are fair,
> How glorious must that kingdom be,
> Where thy redeem'd shall dwell with thee!

9

Heaven Is Prepared Mansions

IN my Father's house are many mansions: if it were not so, I would have told you. I go to prepare a place for you. *John* xiv. 2.

> High in yonder realms of light,
> Far above these lower skies,
> Fair and exquisitely bright,
> Heaven's unfading mansions rise.
>
> Glad within these bless'd abodes,
> Dwell the' enraptur'd saints above,
> Where no anxious care corrodes,
> Happy in Immanuel's love.

10

Heaven Compared to Paradise

JESUS said unto him, Verily I say unto thee, To-day shalt thou be with me in paradise.
Luke xxiii. 43.

> There is a land of pure delight,
>   Where saints immortal reign;
> Infinite day excludes the night,
>   And pleasures banish pain.
>
> There everlasting spring abides,
>   And never-withering flowers:
> Death, like a narrow sea, divides
>   This heavenly land from ours.

11

Heaven a State of Holiness

THERE shall in no wise enter into it any thing that defileth, neither whatsoever worketh abomination, or maketh a lie: but they which are written in the Lamb's book of life. *Rev.* xxi. 27.

> The soul, from sin for ever free,
>   Shall mourn its power no more,
> But clothed in spotless purity,
>   Redeeming love adore.

12

Heaven a State of Happiness

THOU wilt show me the path of life: in thy presence is fulness of joy; at thy right hand there are pleasures for evermore.

Psalm xvi. 11.

> Love, in an ever-deepening tide,
>   O'er all the plains above
> Spreads, like a sea immensely wide—
>   For God himself is Love.

13

Heaven a State of Service

THEY serve him day and night in his temple: and he that sitteth on the throne shall dwell among them. *Rev.* vii. 15.

> And swift to do his high behest
>   Each spirit wings its flight;
> And virtue glows on every breast,
>   A gem of purest light.

14

No Sorrow in Heaven

GOD shall wipe away all tears from their eyes; and there shall be no more death, neither sorrow, nor crying, neither shall there be any more pain: for the former things are passed away. *Rev.* xxi. 4.

> Joy and gladness banish sighs,
>   Perfect love dispels their fears,
> And for ever from their eyes,
>   God shall wipe away all tears.

15

No Curse in Heaven

THERE shall be no more curse: but the throne of God and the Lamb shall be in it.
Rev. xxii. 3.

> When we shall Christ in glory meet,
> Our utmost joys shall be complete:
> When landed on that heavenly shore,
> Death and the curse shall be no more.

16

No Night in Heaven

THERE shall be no night there; and they need no candle, neither light of the sun; for the Lord God giveth them light: and they shall reign for ever and ever. *Rev.* xxii. 5.

> Nor needed is the shining moon,
>   Nor e'en the sun's bright ray;
> For glory, from the sacred throne,
>   Spreads everlasting day.

17

No Death in Heaven

THEY which shall be accounted worthy to obtain that world, and the resurrection from the dead, neither marry nor are given in marriage: neither can they die any more: for they are equal unto the angels.
Luke xx. 35, 36.

> There pain and sickness never come,
>   And grief no more complains;
> Health triumphs in immortal bloom,
>   And endless pleasure reigns.

18

Praises of Heaven

THEY sung a new song, saying, Thou wast slain, and hast redeemed us to God by thy blood out of every kindred, and tongue, and people, and nation. *Rev.* v. 9.

> Hark! hark! the voice of ceaseless praise
> Around Jehovah's throne,
> Songs of celestial joy they raise,
> To mortal lips unknown.

19

Society of Heaven

THESE are they which came out of great tribulation, and have washed their robes, and made them white in the blood of the Lamb: therefore are they before the throne of God. *Rev.* vii. 14, 15.

> Clad in raiment pure and white,
> Victor-palms in every hand,
> Through their great Redeemer's might,
> More than conquerors they stand.

20

Saints Shall Be with God

HE will dwell with them, and they shall be his people, and God himself shall be with them, and be their God. *Rev.* xxi. 3.

Oh glorious hour! oh bless'd abode!
I shall be near and like my God;
And flesh and sin no more control
The sacred pleasures of the soul.

21

Saints Shall Be with Christ

FATHER, I will that they also, whom thou hast given me, be with me where I am; that they may behold my glory. *John* xvii. 24.

Oh then shall the veil be remov'd,
    And round me thy brightness be pour'd:
I shall meet Him whom absent I lov'd,
    I shall see Him whom unseen I ador'd!

22

Saints Shall Inherit All Things

HE that overcometh shall inherit all things; and I will be his God, and he shall be my son. *Rev.* xxi. 7.

> The saints in his presence receive
> Their great and eternal reward;
> With Jesus in heaven they live;
> They reign in the smile of their Lord.

23

Saints Shall Be Perfect

YE are come unto the general assembly and church of the first-born, which are written in heaven, and to God the Judge of all, and to the spirits of just men made perfect.
Heb. xii. 22, 23.

> A life in heaven! oh what is this?
> The sum of all that faith believed;
> Fullness of joy, and perfect bliss,
> Unseen—unfathom'd—unconceiv'd.

24

Saints Shall Be
Glorious in Appearance

THEN shall the righteous shine forth as the sun in the kingdom of their Father.
Matt. xiii. 43.

The Lamb is their light and their sun,
   And, lo, by reflection they shine;
With Jesus ineffably one,
   And bright in effulgence divine.

25

Saints Shall Be
Honoured as Victors

I BEHELD, and, lo, a great multitude, which no man could number, of all nations, and kindreds, and people, and tongues, stood before the throne, and before the Lamb, clothed with white robes, and palms in their hands. *Rev*. vii. 9.

Now the conquerors bring their palms
   To the Lamb amidst the throne,
And proclaim in joyful psalms,
   Victory through his cross alone.

189

26

Saints Shall Be

Kings and Priests Unto God

THOU hast made us unto our God kings and priests: and we shall reign on the earth.

Rev. v. 10.

Thou hast redeem'd our souls with blood,
  Hast set the prisoners free,
Hast made us kings and priests to God,
  And we shall reign with thee.

27

Joys of Heaven Are Sure

OH how great is thy goodness, which thou hast laid up for them that fear thee; which thou hast wrought for them that trust in thee before the sons of men! *Psalm* xxxi. 19.

This is the hope that shall sustain me
  Till life's pilgrimage be past;
Fears may vex, and troubles pain me,
  I shall reach my home at last.

28

Joys of Heaven Are Abundant

THE Lamb which is in the midst of the throne shall feed them, and shall lead them unto living fountains of water. *Rev.* vii. 17.

> The Lamb that fills the middle throne
> Shall shed around his milder beams,
> There shall they feast on his rich love,
> And drink full joys from heavenly streams.

29

Joys of Heaven Are Satisfying

I WILL behold thy face in righteousness: I shall be satisfied, when I awake, with thy likeness. *Psalm* xvii. 15.

> Oh! when awaken'd by thy care,
> Thy face I view, thy image bear,
> How shall my breast with transport glow!
> What full delight my heart o'erflow!

30

Joys of Heaven Are Eternal

HIM that overcometh will I make a pillar in the temple of my God, and he shall go no more out. *Rev.* iii. 12.

> The everlasting doors
>   Shall soon the saints receive,
> Above, with angel powers,
>   In glorious joy to live:
> Far from a world of grief and sin,
> With God eternally shut in.

31

Believers to Wait for Heaven

BLESSED is he that waiteth, and cometh to the thousand three hundred and five and thirty days. But go thou thy way till the end be: for thou shalt rest, and stand in thy lot at the end of the days. *Dan.* xii, 12, 13.

> Jerusalem, my happy home,
>   My soul still pants for thee;
> When shall my labours have an end
>   In joy, and peace, and thee.

The passionate, comic, candid memoirs
of America's greatest woman of letters

Lillian Hellman's plays—including **The Little Foxes**, **Watch
on the Rhine**, **The Children's Hour**, **The Autumn Garden**,
Toys In the Attic—speak eloquently for themselves and
for Miss Hellman's place in the world of letters. In **AN
UNFINISHED WOMAN**, she offers a detailed, unsparing
self-scrutiny and frank account of her experiences in
New York, New Orleans, Hollywood, in Spain during the
Civil War, in Moscow and Leningrad during the Second
World War, and after.

As this book makes clear, since childhood she has hated
hypocrisy and has refused to settle for soft answers,
least of all from herself. The qualities she values most
are courage, loyalty and integrity, and she has found
them in her closest relationships. Her extraordinary
thirty-year love affair with Dashiell Hammett, her warm
and completely unsentimental portrait of her close friend
Dorothy Parker, a revealing chapter on two black women
who profoundly influenced her life, and her involvement
with the great events of her time have formed the basis
of a book that calls upon all Miss Hellman's formidable
powers of intellect, imagination and style.

This is the book that received the National Book Award
in March 1970 as the best book of the year in the cate-
gory of Arts and Letters.

AN UNFINISHED WOMAN
by Lillian Hellman
a memoir

An
Unfinished
Woman
A MEMOIR
Lillian Hellman

AN UNFINISHED WOMAN
A MEMOIR

*A Bantam Book | published by arrangement with
Little, Brown & Company*

PRINTING HISTORY
Little, Brown edition published June 1969
Literary Guild alternate selection published June 1969
Reader's Subscription alternate selection published July 1969

Bantam edition | July 1970

2nd printing .... August 1970	6th printing .... March 1975
3rd printing .... August 1970	7th printing .... August 1976
4th printing .. November 1973	8th printing ...... January 1977
5th printing ...... October 1974	9th printing .... March 1978
	10th printing...... January 1979

Portions of this book originally appeared in the NEW YORK
REVIEW OF BOOKS, ATLANTIC, *and* PARTISAN REVIEW.
The introduction to The Big Knockover *by Dashiell Hammett,
Copyright © 1965, 1966 by Lillian Hellman,
is reprinted by permission of Random House, Inc.*

ISBN 0–553–12710–1

Published simultaneously in the United States and Canada

To Hannah, Dick and Mike

An
Unfinished
Woman

up and down the long stretches ... miles from being
finished at the present time ... a big
in the ... that ...
devel ... T ...
... my road ... me ... until I was home early ... out
..., and work late into the night. I enjoyed the basic

1

I was born in New Orleans
to Julia Newhouse from Demopolis, Alabama, who had
fallen in love and stayed in love with Max Hellman, whose
parents had come to New Orleans in the German
1845-1848 immigration to give birth to him and his two
sisters. My mother's family, long before I was born, had
moved from Demopolis to Cincinnati and then to New
Orleans, both desirable cities, I guess, for three marriage-
able girls.

But I first remember them in a large New York apartment: my two young and very pretty aunts; their taciturn,
tight-faced brother; and the silent, powerful, severe woman, Sophie Newhouse, who was their mother, my grandmother. Her children, her servants, all of her relatives
except for her brother Jake were frightened of her, and so
was I. Even as a small child I disliked myself for the fear
and showed off against it.

The Newhouse apartment held the upper-middle-class
trappings, in touch of things and in spirit of people, that

never manage to be truly stylish. Heavy weather hung over the lovely oval rooms. True, there were parties for my aunts, but the parties, to a peeping child in the servants' hall, seemed so muted that I was long convinced that on fancy occasions grown people moved their lips without making sounds. In the days after the party one would hear exciting stories about the new suitors, but the suitors were never quite good enough and the parties were, obviously, not good enough for those who might have been. Then there were the Sunday dinners with great-uncles and aunts sometimes in attendance, full of open ill will about who had the most money, or who spent it too lavishly, who would inherit what, which had bought what rug that would last forever, who what jewel she would best have been without. It was a corporation meeting, with my grandmother unexpectedly in the position of vice-chairman. The chairman was her brother Jake, the only human being to whom I ever saw her defer. Early, I told myself that was because he was richer than she was, and did something called managing her money. But that was too simple: he was a man of great force, given, as she was given, to breaking the spirit of people for the pleasure of the exercise. But he was also witty and rather worldly, seeing his own financial machinations as natural not only to his but to the country's benefit, and seeing that as comic. (I had only one real contact with my Uncle Jake: when I graduated from school at fifteen, he gave me a ring that I took to a 59th Street hock shop, got twenty-five dollars, and bought books. I went immediately to tell him what I'd done, deciding, I think, that day that the break had to come. He stared at me for a long time, and then he laughed and said the words I later used in *The Little Foxes*: "So you've got spirit after all. Most of the rest of them are made of sugar water.")

But that New York apartment where we visited several times a week, the summer cottage where we went for a visit each year as the poor daughter and granddaughter,

2

made me into an angry child and forever caused in me a wild extravagance mixed with respect for money and those who have it. The respectful periods were full of self-hatred and during them I always made my worst mistakes. But after *The Little Foxes* was written and put away, this conflict was to grow less important, as indeed, the picture of my mother's family was to grow dim and almost fade away.

It was not unnatural that my first love went to my father's family. He and his two sisters were free, generous, funny. But as I made my mother's family all one color, I made my father's family too remarkable, and then turned both extreme judgments against my mother.

In fact, she was a sweet eccentric, the only middle-class woman I have ever known who had not rejected the middle class—that would have been an act of will—but had skipped it altogether. She liked a simple life and simple people, and would have been happier, I think, if she had stayed in the backlands of Alabama riding wild on the horses she so often talked about, not so lifelong lonely for the black men and women who had taught her the only religion she ever knew. I didn't know what she was saying when she moved her lips in a Baptist church or a Catholic cathedral or, less often, in a synagogue, but it was obvious that God could be found anywhere, because several times a week we would stop in a church, any church, and she seemed to be at home in all of them.

But simple natures can also be complex, and that is difficult for a child, who wants all grown people to be sharply one thing or another. I was puzzled and irritated by the passivity of my mother as it mixed with an unmovable stubbornness. (My father had not been considered a proper husband for a rich and pretty girl, but my mother's deep fear of her mother did not override her deep love for my father, although the same fear kept my two aunts from ever marrying and my uncle from marrying until after his mother's death.)

3

Mama seemed to do only what my father wanted, and yet we lived the way my mother wanted us to live. She deeply wanted to keep my father and to please him, but no amount of protest from him could alter the strange quirks that Freud already knew about. Windows, doors and stoves haunted her and she would often stand before them for as long as half an hour, or leaving the house, would insist upon returning to it while we waited for her in any weather. And sad, middle-aged ladies would be brought home from a casual meeting on a park bench to fill the living room with woe: plain tales of sickness, or poverty, or loneliness in the afternoon often led to their staying on for dinner with my bored father.

I remember a time when our apartment was being painted and the week it was supposed to take stretched into three because one of the two painters, a small, sickly man with an Italian accent, soon found that my mother was a sympathetic listener. He would, in duty, climb the ladder at nine in the morning, but by eleven he was sitting on the sofa with the tale of the bride who died in child-birth, the child still in Italy, his mother who ailed and half starved in Tuscany, the nights in New York where he knew nobody to eat with or talk to. After lunch, cooked by our bad-tempered Irish lady, and served to him by my mother to hide the bad temper, he would climb the ladder again and paint for a few hours while my mother urged him to stop work and go for a nice day in the sunshine. Once, toward the end of the long job—the other painter never returned after the first few days—I came home carrying books from the library, annoyed to find the painter in my favorite chair. As I stood in the doorway, frowning at my mother, the painter said, "Your girl. How old?"

"Fifteen," said my mother.

"In Italy, not young, fifteen. She is healthy?"

"Very healthy," said my mother. "Her generation has larger feet than we did."

An Unfinished Woman

"I think about it," said the painter. "I let you know."

I knew my mother didn't understand what he meant because she smiled and nodded in the way she always did when her mind had wandered. but I was angry and told my father about it at dinner. He laughed and I left the table, but later he told my mother that the painter was not to come to the house again. A few years later when I brought home for dinner an aimless, handsome young man who got roaring drunk and insisted upon climbing down the building from our eighth-floor apartment, my father, watching him from the window, said, "Perhaps we should try to find that Italian house painter." My mother was dead for five years before I knew that I had loved her very much.

My mother's childbearing had been dangerously botched by a fashionable doctor in New Orleans, and forever after she stood in fear of going through it again, and so I was an only child. (Twenty-one years later, when I was married and pregnant, she was as frightened for me, and unashamedly happy when I lost the child.) I was thirty-four years old, after two successful plays, and fourteen or fifteen years of heavy drinking in a nature that wasn't comfortable with anarchy, when a doctor told me about the lifelong troubles of an only child. Most certainly I needed a doctor to reveal for me the violence and disorder of my life, but I had always known about the powers of an only child. I was not meaner or more ungenerous or more unkind than other children, but I was off balance in a world where I knew my grand importance to two other people who certainly loved me for myself, but who also liked to use me against each other. I don't think they knew they did that, because most of it was affectionate teasing between them, but somehow I knew early that my father's jokes about how much my mother's family liked money, how her mother had crippled her own children, my grandmother's desire to think of him—and me—as strange vagabonds of no property value, was more than

5

teasing. He wished to win me to his side, and he did. He was a handsome man, witty, high-tempered, proud, and—although I guessed very young I was not to be certain until much later—with a number of other women in his life. Thus his attacks on Mama's family were not always for the reasons claimed.

When I was about six years old my father lost my mother's large dowry. We moved to New York and were shabby poor until my father finally settled for a life as a successful traveling salesman. It was in those years that we went back to New Orleans to stay with my father's sisters for six months each year. I was thus moved from school in New York to school in New Orleans without care for the season or the quality of the school. This constant need for adjustment in two very different worlds made formal education into a kind of frantic tennis game, sometimes played with children whose strokes had force and brilliance, sometimes with those who could barely hold the racket. Possibly it is the reason I never did well in school or in college, and why I wanted to be left alone to read by myself. I had found, very early, that any other test found me bounding with ease and grace over one fence to fall on my face as I ran towards the next.

2

THERE was a heavy fig tree on
the lawn where the house turned the corner into the side
street, and to the front and sides of the fig tree were three
live oaks that hid the fig from my aunts' boardinghouse. I
suppose I was eight or nine before I discovered the pleasures of the fig tree, and although I have lived in many
houses since then, including a few I made for myself, I
still think of it as my first and most beloved home.

I learned early, in our strange life of living half in New
York and half in New Orleans, that I made my New
Orleans teachers uncomfortable because I was too far
ahead of my schoolmates, and my New York teachers
irritable because I was too far behind. But in New Orleans, I found a solution: I skipped school at least once a
week and often twice, knowing that nobody cared or
would report my absence. On those days I would set out
for school done up in polished strapped shoes and a prim
hat against what was known as "the climate," carrying my
books and a little basket filled with delicious stuff my

7

Aunt Jenny and Carrie, the cook, had made for my school lunch. I would round the corner of the side street, move on toward St. Charles Avenue, and sit on a bench as if I were waiting for a streetcar until the boarders and the neighbors had gone to work or settled down for the post-breakfast rest that all Southern ladies thought necessary. Then I would run back to the fig tree, dodging in and out of bushes to make sure the house had no dangers for me. The fig tree was heavy, solid, comfortable, and I had, through time, convinced myself that it wanted me, missed me when I was absent, and approved all the rigging I had done for the happy days I spent in its arms: I had made a sling to hold the school books, a pulley rope for my lunch basket, a hole for the bottle of afternoon cream-soda pop, a fishing pole and a smelly little bag of elderly bait, a pillow embroidered with a picture of Henry Clay on a horse that I had stolen from Mrs. Stillman, one of my aunts' boarders, and a proper nail to hold my dress and shoes to keep them neat for the return to the house.

It was in that tree that I learned to read, filled with the passions that can only come to the bookish, grasping, very young, bewildered by almost all of what I read, sweating in the attempt to understand a world of adults I fled from in real life but desperately wanted to join in books. (I did not connect the grown men and women in literature with the grown men and women I saw around me. They were, to me, another species.)

It was in the fig tree that I learned that anything alive in water was of enormous excitement to me. True, the water was gutter water and the fishing could hardly be called that: sometimes the things that swam in New Orleans gutters were not pretty, but I didn't know what was pretty and I liked them all. After lunch—the men boarders returned for a large lunch and a siesta—the street would be safe again, with only the noise from Carrie and her helpers in the kitchen, and they could be counted on never to move past the back porch, or the chicken coop.

Then I would come down from my tree to sit on the side street gutter with my pole and bait. Often I would catch a crab that had wandered in from the Gulf, more often I would catch my favorite, the crayfish, and sometimes I would, in that safe hour, have at least six of them for my basket. Then, about 2:30, when house and street would stir again, I would go back to my tree for another few hours of reading or dozing or having what I called the ill hour. It is too long ago for me to know why I thought the hour "ill," but certainly I did not mean sick. I think I meant an intimation of sadness, a first recognition that there was so much to understand that one might never find one's way and the first signs, perhaps, that for a nature like mine, the way would not be easy. I cannot be sure that I felt all that then, although I can be sure that it was in the fig tree, a few years later, that I was first puzzled by the conflict which would haunt me, harm me, and benefit me the rest of my life: simply, the stubborn, relentless, driving desire to be alone as it came into conflict with the desire not to be alone when I wanted not to be. I already guessed that other people wouldn't allow that, although, as an only child, I pretended for the rest of my life that they would and must allow it to me.

I liked my time in New Orleans much better than I liked our six months apartment life in New York. The life in my aunts' boardinghouse seemed remarkably rich. And what a strange lot my own family was. My aunts Jenny and Hannah were both tall, large women, funny and generous, who coming from a German, cultivated, genteel tradition had found they had to earn a living and earned it without complaint, although Jenny, the prettier and more complex, had frequent outbursts of interesting temper. It was strange, I thought then, that my mother, who so often irritated me, was treated by my aunts as if she were a precious Chinese clay piece from a world they didn't know. And in a sense, that was true: her family was rich, she was small, delicately made and charming—she was a

9

sturdy, brave woman, really, but it took years to teach me that—and because my aunts loved my father very much, they were good to my mother, and protected her from the less wellborn boarders. I don't think they understood—I did, by some kind of child's malice—that my mother enjoyed the boarders and listened to them with the sympathy Jenny couldn't afford. I suppose none of the boarders were of great interest, but I was crazy about what I thought went on behind their doors.

I was conscious that Mr. Stillman, a large, loose, good-looking man, flirted with my mother and sang off key. I knew that a boarder called Collie, a too thin, unhappy looking, no-age man, worked in his uncle's bank and was drunk every night. He was the favorite of the lady boarders, who didn't think he'd live very long. (They were wrong: over twenty years later, on a visit to my retired aunts, I met him in Galatoire's restaurant looking just the same.) And there were two faded, sexy, giggly sisters called Fizzy and Sarah, who pretended to love children and all trees. I once overheard a fight between my mother and father in which she accused him of liking Sarah. I thought that was undignified of my mother and was pleased when my father laughed it off as untrue. He was telling the truth about Sarah: he liked Fizzy, and the day I saw them meet and get into a taxi in front of a restaurant on Jackson Avenue was to stay with me for many years. I was in a black rage, filled with fears I couldn't explain, with pity and contempt for my mother, with an intense desire to follow my father and Fizzy to see whatever it was they might be doing, and to kill them for it. An hour later, I threw myself from the top of the fig tree and broke my nose, although I did not know I had broken a bone and was concerned only with the hideous pain.

I went immediately to Sophronia, who had been my nurse when I was a small child before we moved, or half moved, to New York. She worked now for people who lived in a large house a streetcar ride from ours, and she took care of two little red-headed boys whom I hated with pleasure in my wicked jealousy. Sophronia was the first and most certain love of my life. (Years later, when I was a dangerously rebellious young girl, my father would say that if he had been able to afford Sophronia through the years, I would have been under the only control I ever recognized.) She was a tall, handsome, light tan woman— I still have many pictures of the brooding face—who was for me, as for so many other white Southern children, the one and certain anchor so needed for the young years, so forgotten after that. (It wasn't that way for us: we wrote and met as often as possible until she died when I was in my twenties, and the first salary check I ever earned she returned to me in the form of a gold chain.) The mother of the two red-haired boys didn't like my visits to Sophronia and so I always arrived by the back door.

But Sophronia was not at home on the day of my fall. I sat on her kitchen steps crying and holding my face until the cook sent the upstairs maid to Audubon Park on a search for Sophronia. She came, running, I think for the first time in the majestic movements of her life, waving away the two redheads. She took me to her room and washed my face and prodded my nose and put her hand over my mouth when I screamed. She said we must go immediately to Dr. Fenner, but when I told her that I had thrown myself from the tree, she stopped talking about the doctor, bandaged my face, gave me a pill, put me on her bed and lay down beside me. I told her about my father and Fizzy and fell asleep. When I woke up she said that she'd walk me home. On the way she told me that I must say nothing about Fizzy to anybody ever, and that if my nose still hurt in a few days I was only to say that I had fallen on the street and refuse to answer any questions about how I fell. A block away from my aunts' house we sat down on the steps of the Baptist church. She looked sad and I knew that I had displeased her. I touched her face, which had always been between us a way of saying that I was sorry.

She said, "Don't go through life making trouble for people."

I said, "If I tell you I won't tell about Fizzy, then I won't tell."

She said, "Run home now. Goodbye."

And it was to be goodbye for another year, because I had forgotten that we were to leave for New York two days later, and when I telephoned to tell that to Sophronia the woman she worked for said I wasn't to telephone again. In any case, I soon forgot about Fizzy, and when the bandage came off my nose—it looked different but not different enough—our New York doctor said that it would heal by itself, or whatever was the nonsense they believed in those days about broken bones.

We went back to New Orleans the next year and the years after that until I was sixteen, and they were always the best times of my life. It was Aunt Hannah who took me each Saturday to the movies and then to the French Quarter, where we bought smelly old leather books and she told me how it all had been when she was a girl: about my grandmother—I remembered her—who had been a very tall woman with a lined, severe face and a gentle nature; about my grandfather, dead before I was born, who, in his portrait over the fireplace, looked too serious and distinguished. They had, in a middle-class world, evidently been a strange couple, going their own way with little interest in money or position, loved and respected by their children. "Your grandfather used to say" was a common way to begin a sentence, and although whatever he said had been law, he had allowed my father and aunts their many eccentricities in a time and place that didn't like eccentrics, and to such a degree that not one of his children ever knew they weren't like other people. Hannah, for example, once grew angry—the only time I ever saw her show any temper—when my mother insisted I finish my dinner: she rose and hit the table, and told my mother and the startled boarders that when she was twelve years old she had decided she didn't ever want to eat with people again and so she had taken to sitting on the steps of the front porch and my grandmother, with no comment, had for two years brought her dinner on a tray, and so what was wrong with one dinner I didn't feel like sitting through?

I think both Hannah and Jenny were virgins, but if they were, there were no signs of spinsterhood. They were nice about married people, they were generous to children, and sex was something to have fun about. Jenny had been the consultant to many neighborhood young ladies before their marriage night, or the night of their first lover. One of these girls, a rich ninny, Jenny found irritating and unpleasant. When I was sixteen I came across the two of them in earnest conference on the lawn, and later Jenny told me that the girl had come to consult her about how to avoid pregnancy.

"What did you tell her?"

"I told her to have a glass of ice water right before the sacred act and three sips during it."

When we had finished laughing, I said, "But she'll get pregnant."

"He's marrying her for money, he'll leave her when he gets it. This way at least maybe she'll have a few babies for herself."

And four years later, when I wrote my aunts that I was going to be married, I had back a telegram: FORGET ABOUT THE GLASS OF ICE WATER TIMES HAVE CHANGED.

I think I learned to laugh in that house and to knit and embroider and sew a straight seam and to cook. Each Sunday it was my job to clean the crayfish for the wonderful bisque, and it was Jenny and Carrie, the cook, who taught me to make turtle soup, and how to kill a chicken without ladylike complaints about the horror of dealing death, and how to pluck and cook the wild ducks that were hawked on our street every Sunday morning. I was taught, also, that if you gave, you did it without piety and didn't boast about it. It had been one of my grandfather's laws, in the days when my father and aunts were children, that no poor person who asked for anything was ever to be refused, and his children fulfilled the injunction. New Orleans was a city of many poor people, particularly black people, and the boardinghouse kitchen after the house dinner was, on most nights, a mighty pleasant place: there would often be as many as eight or ten people, black and white, almost always very old or very young, who sat at the table on the kitchen porch while Carrie ordered the kitchen maids and me to bring the steaming platters and the coffeepots.

It was on such a night that I first saw Leah, a light tan girl of about fifteen with red hair and freckles, a flat, ugly face, and a big stomach. I suppose I was about fourteen years old that night, but I remember her very well because she stared at me through her hungry eating. She came again about a week later, and this time Carrie herself took the girl aside and whispered to her, but I don't think the girl answered her because Carrie shrugged and moved away. The next morning, Hannah, who always rose at six to help Jenny before she went to her own office job, screamed outside my bedroom window. Leaning out, I saw Hannah pointing underneath the house and saying softly, "Come out of there."

Slowly the tan-red girl crawled out. Hannah said, "You must not stay under there. It's very wet. Come inside, child, and dry yourself out." From that day on Leah lived somewhere in the house, and a few months later had her baby in the City Hospital. The baby was put out for adoption on Sophronia's advice with a little purse of money from my mother. I never knew what Leah did in the house, because when she helped with the dishes Carrie lost her temper, and when she tried making beds Jenny asked her not to, and once when she was raking leaves for the gardener he yelled, "You ain't in your proper head," so in the end, she took to following me around.

I was, they told me, turning into a handful. Mrs. Stillman said I was wild, Mr. Stillman said that I would, of course, bring pain to my mother and father, and Fizzy said I was just plain disgusting mean. It had been a bad month for me. I had, one night, fallen asleep in the fig tree and, coming down in the morning, refused to tell my mother where I had been. James Denery the Third had hit me very hard in a tug-of-war and I had waited until the next day to hit him over the head with a porcelain coffee pot and then his mother complained to my mother. I had also refused to go back to dancing class.

And I was now spending most of my time with a group from an orphanage down the block. I guess the orphan group was no more attractive than any other, but to be an orphan seemed to me desirable and a self-made piece of independence. In any case, the orphans were more interesting to me than my schoolmates, and if they played rougher they complained less. Frances, a dark beauty of my age, queened it over the others because her father had been killed by the Mafia. Miriam, small and wiry, regularly stole my allowance from the red purse my aunt had given me, and the one time I protested she beat me up. Louis Calda was religious and spoke to me about it. Pancho was dark, sad, and, to me, a poet, because once he said, *"Yo te amo."* I could not sleep a full night after this declaration, and it set up in me forever after both sympathy and irritability with the first sexual stirrings of little girls, so masked, so complex, so foolish as compared with the sex of little boys. It was Louis Calda who took Pancho and me to a Catholic Mass that could have made me a fourteen-year-old convert. But Louis explained that he did not think me worthy, and Pancho, to stop my tears, cut off a piece of his hair with a knife, gave it to me as a gift from royalty, and then shoved me into the gutter. I don't know why I thought this an act of affection, but I did, and went home to open the back of a new wristwatch my father had given me for my birthday and to put the lock of hair in the back. A day later when the watch stopped, my father insisted I give it to him immediately, declaring that the jeweler was unreliable.

It was that night that I disappeared, and that night that Fizzy said I was disgusting mean, and Mr. Stillman said I would forever pain my mother and father, and my father turned on both of them and said he would handle his family affairs himself without comments from strangers. But he said it too late. He had come home very angry with me: the jeweler, after my father's complaints about his unreliability, had found the lock of hair in the back of the watch. What started out to be a mild reproof on my father's part soon turned angry when I wouldn't explain about the hair. (My father was often angry when I was most like him.) He was so angry that he forgot that he was attacking me in front of the Stillmans, my old rival Fizzy, and the delighted Mrs. Dreyfus, a new, rich boarder who only that afternoon had complained about my bad manners. My mother left the room when my father grew angry with me. Hannah, passing through, put up her hand as if to stop my father and then, frightened of the look he gave her, went out to the porch. I sat on the couch, astonished at the pain in my head. I tried to get up from the couch, but one ankle turned and I sat down again, knowing for the first time the rampage that could be caused in me by anger. The room began to have other forms, the people were no longer men and women, my head was not my own. I told myself that my head had gone somewhere and I have little memory of anything after my Aunt Jenny came into the room and said to my father, "Don't you remember?" I have never known what she meant, but I knew that soon after I was moving up the staircase, that I slipped and fell a few steps, that when I woke up hours later in my bed, I found a piece of angel cake—an old love, an old custom—left by my mother on my pillow.

The headache was worse and I vomited out of the window. Then I dressed, took my red purse, and walked a long way down St. Charles Avenue. A St. Charles Avenue mansion had on its back lawn a famous doll's-house, an elaborate copy of the mansion itself, built years before for the small daughter of the house. As I passed this show-piece, I saw a policeman and moved swiftly back to the doll palace and crawled inside. If I had known about the fantasies of the frightened, that ridiculous small house would not have been so terrible for me. I was surrounded by ornate, carved reproductions of the mansion furniture, scaled for children, bisque figurines in miniature, a working toilet seat of gold leaf in suitable size, small draperies of damask with a sign that said "From the damask of Marie Antoinette," a miniature samovar with small bronze cups, and a tiny Madame Récamier couch on which I spent the night, my legs on the floor. I must have slept, because I woke from a nightmare and knocked over a bisque figurine. The noise frightened me, and since it was now almost light, in one of those lovely mist mornings of late spring when every flower in New Orleans seems to melt and mix with the air, I crawled out. Most of that day I spent walking, although I had a long session in the ladies' room of the railroad station. I had four dollars and two bits, but that wasn't much when you meant it to last forever and when you knew it would not be easy for a fourteen-year-old girl to find work in a city where too many people knew her. Three times I stood in line at the railroad ticket windows to ask where I could go for four dollars, but each time the question seemed too dangerous and I knew no other way of asking it.

Toward evening, I moved to the French Quarter, feeling sad and envious as people went home to dinner. I bought a few Tootsie Rolls and a half loaf of bread and went to the St. Louis Cathedral in Jackson Square. (It was that night that I composed the prayer that was to become, in the next five years, an obsession, mumbled over and

over through the days and nights: "God forgive me, Papa
forgive me, Mama forgive me, Sophronia, Jenny, Hannah,
and all others, through this time and that time, in life and
in death." When I was nineteen, my father, who had made
several attempts through the years to find out what my lip
movements meant as I repeated the prayer, said, "How
much would you take to stop that? Name it and you've
got it." I suppose I was sick of the nonsense by that time
because I said, "A leather coat and a feather fan," and the
next day he bought them for me.) After my loaf of bread,
I went looking for a bottle of soda pop and discovered, for
the first time, the whorehouse section around Bourbon
Street. The women were ranged in the doorways of the
cribs, making the first early evening offers to sailors, who
were the only men in the streets. I wanted to stick around
and see how things like that worked, but the second or
third time I circled the block, one of the girls called out to
me. I couldn't understand the words, but the voice was
angry enough to make me run toward the French Market.

The Market was empty except for two old men. One of
them called to me as I went past, and I turned to see that
he had opened his pants and was shaking what my circle
called "his thing." I flew across the street into the coffee
stand, forgetting that the owner had known me since I was
a small child when my Aunt Jenny would rest from her
marketing tour with a cup of fine, strong coffee.

He said, in the patois, *"Que faites, ma 'fant? Je suis
fermé."*

I said, *"Rien. My tante attend*—Could I have a dough-
nut?"

He brought me two doughnuts, saying one was *lagni-
appe,* but I took my doughnuts outside when he said,
"Mais où est vo' tante à c' heure?"

I fell asleep with my doughnuts behind a shrub in
Jackson Square. The night was damp and hot and through
the sleep there were many voices and, much later, there
was music from somewhere near the river. When all

18

sounds had ended, I woke, turned my head, and knew I was being watched. Two rats were sitting a few feet from me. I urinated on my dress, crawled backwards to stand up, screamed as I ran up the steps of St. Louis Cathedral and pounded on the doors. I don't know when I stopped screaming or how I got to the railroad station, but I stood against the wall trying to tear off my dress and only knew I was doing it when two women stopped to stare at me. I began to have cramps in my stomach of a kind I had never known before. I went into the ladies' room and sat bent in a chair, whimpering with pain. After a while the cramps stopped, but I had an intimation, when I looked into the mirror, of something happening to me: my face was blotched, and there seemed to be circles and twirls I had never seen before, the straight blonde hair was damp with sweat, and a paste of green from the shrub had made lines on my jaw. I had gotten older.

Sometime during that early morning I half washed my dress, threw away my pants, put cold water on my hair. Later in the morning a cleaning woman appeared, and after a while began to ask questions that frightened me. When she put down her mop and went out of the room, I ran out of the station. I walked, I guess, for many hours, but when I saw a man on Canal Street who worked in Hannah's office, I realized that the sections of New Orleans that were known to me were dangerous for me.

Years before, when I was a small child, Sophronia and I would go to pick up, or try on, pretty embroidered dresses that were made for me by a colored dressmaker called Bibettera. A block up from Bibettera's there had been a large ruin of a house with a sign, ROOMS—CLEAN —CHEAP, and cheerful people seemed always to be moving in and out of the house. The door of the house was painted a bright pink. I liked that and would discuss with Sophronia why we didn't live in a house with a pink door.

Bibettera was long since dead, so I knew I was safe in this Negro neighborhood. I went up and down the block several times, praying that things would work and I could take my cramps to bed. I knocked on the pink door. It was answered immediately by a small young man.

I said, "Hello." He said nothing.

I said, "I would like to rent a room, please."

He closed the door but I waited, thinking he had gone to get the lady of the house. After a long time, a middle-aged woman put her head out of a second-floor window and said, "What you at?"

I said, "I would like to rent a room, please. My mama is a widow and has gone to work across the river. She gave me money and said to come here until she called for me."

"Who your mama?"

"Er. My mama."

"What you at? Speak out."

"I told you. I have money . . ." But as I tried to open my purse, the voice grew angry.

"This is a nigger house. Get you off. *Vite.*"

I said, in a whisper, "I know. I'm part nigger."

The small young man opened the front door. He was laughing. "You part mischief. Get the hell out of here."

I said, "Please"—and then, "I'm related to Sophronia Mason. She told me to come. Ask her."

Sophronia and her family were respected figures in New Orleans Negro circles, and because I had some vague memory of her stately bow to somebody as she passed this house, I believed they knew her. If they told her about me I would be in trouble, but phones were not usual then in poor neighborhoods, and I had no other place to go.

The woman opened the door. Slowly I went into the hall.

I said, "I won't stay long. I have four dollars and Sophronia will give more if . . ."

The woman pointed up the stairs. She opened the door of a small room. "Washbasin place down the hall. Toilet place behind the kitchen. Two-fifty and no fuss, no bother."

I said, "Yes ma'am, yes ma'am," but as she started to close the door, the young man appeared.

"Where your bag?"

"Bag?"

"Nobody put up here without no bag."

"Oh. You mean the bag with my clothes? It's at the station. I'll go and get it later . . ." I stopped because I knew I was about to say I'm sick, I'm in pain, I'm frightened.

He said, "I say you lie. I say you trouble. I say you get out."

I said, "And I say you shut up."

Years later, I was to understand why the command worked, and to be sorry that it did, but that day I was very happy when he turned and closed the door. I was asleep within minutes.

Toward evening, I went down the stairs, saw nobody, walked a few blocks and bought myself an oyster loaf. But the first bite made me feel sick, so I took my loaf back to the house. This time, as I climbed the steps, there were three women in the parlor, and they stopped talking when they saw me. I went back to sleep immediately, dizzy and nauseated.

I woke to a high, hot sun and my father standing at the foot of the bed staring at the oyster loaf.

He said, "Get up now and get dressed."

I was crying as I said, "Thank you, Papa, but I can't."

From the hall, Sophronia said, "Get along up now. *Vite.* The morning is late."

My father left the room. I dressed and came into the hall carrying my oyster loaf. Sophronia was standing at the head of the stairs. She pointed out, meaning my father was on the street.

I said, "He humiliated me. He did. I won't . . ."

She said, "Get you going or I will never see you whenever again."

I ran past her to the street. I stood with my father until Sophronia joined us, and then we walked slowly, without speaking, to the streetcar line. Sophronia bowed to us, but she refused my father's hand when he attempted to help her into the car. I ran to the car meaning to ask her to take me with her, but the car moved and she raised her hand as if to stop me. My father and I walked again for a long time.

He pointed to a trash can sitting in front of a house. "Please put that oyster loaf in the can."

At Vanalli's restaurant, he took my arm. "Hungry?"

I said, "No, thank you, Papa."

But we went through the door. It was, in those days, a New Orleans custom to have an early black coffee, go to the office, and after a few hours have a large breakfast at a restaurant. Vanalli's was crowded, the headwaiter was so sorry, but after my father took him aside, a very small table was put up for us—too small for my large father, who was accommodating himself to it in a manner most unlike him.

He said, "Jack, my rumpled daughter would like cold crayfish, a nice piece of pompano, a separate bowl of Béarnaise sauce, don't ask me why, French fried potatoes . . ."

I said, "Thank you, Papa, but I am not hungry. I don't want to be here."

My father waved the waiter away and we sat in silence until the crayfish came. My hand reached out instinctively and then drew back.

My father said, "Your mother and I have had an awful time."

I said, "I'm sorry about that. But I don't want to go home, Papa."

He said, angrily, "Yes, you do. But you want me to

apologize first. I do apologize but you should not have made me say it."

After a while I mumbled, "God forgive me, Papa forgive me, Mama forgive me, Sophronia, Jenny, Hannah . . ."

"Eat your crayfish."

I ate everything he had ordered and then a small steak. I suppose I had been mumbling throughout my breakfast.

My father said, "You're talking to yourself. I can't hear you. What are you saying?"

"God forgive me, Papa forgive me, Mama forgive me, Sophronia, Jenny . . ."

My father said, "Where do we start your training as the first Jewish nun on Prytania Street?"

When I finished laughing, I liked him again. I said, "Papa, I'll tell you a secret. I've had very bad cramps and I am beginning to bleed. I'm changing life."

He stared at me for a while. Then he said, "Well, it's not the way it's usually described, but it's accurate, I guess. Let's go home now to your mother."

We were never, as long as my mother and father lived, to mention that time again. But it was of great importance to them and I've thought about it all my life. From that day on I knew my power over my parents. That was not to be too important: I was ashamed of it and did not abuse it too much. But I found out something more useful and more dangerous: if you are willing to take the punishment, you are halfway through the battle. That the issue may be trivial, the battle ugly, is another point.

3

My mother had gone to Sophie Newcomb College in New Orleans, and although the experience had left little on the memory except a fire in her dormitory, she felt it was the right place for me. (My aunts Jenny and Hannah could keep an eye on me.) But I had had enough of Southern education and wanted to go to Smith. A few months before the autumn entrance term, when I thought the matter had been settled, my mother and father held out for Goucher on the strange ground that it was closer to New York. But a month before I was to leave for Goucher, my mother became ill and it was obvious that I was meant to stay at home. I do not remember any sharp words about these changes and that in itself is odd, because sharp words came often in those years, but I do remember a feeling of what difference did it make. I knew, without rancor, that my parents were worried about a wild and headstrong girl; and then, too, a defeat for an only child can always be turned into a later victory.

New York University had started its Washington Square branch only a few years before, with an excellent small faculty and high requirements for the students it could put into one unattractive building. I was, of course, not where I wanted to be and I envied those of my friends who were. And yet I knew that in another place I might have been lost, because the old story was still true: I was sometimes more advanced but often less educated than other students and I had little desire to be shown up. And by seventeen, I was openly rebellious against almost everything. I knew that the seeds of the rebellion were scattered and aimless in a nature that was wild to be finished with something-or-other and to find something-else-or-other, and I had sense enough to know that I was overproud, oversensitive, overdaring because I was shy and frightened. Ah, what a case can be made for vanity in the shy. (And what a losing game is self-description in the long ago.)

It was thus in the cards that college would mean very little to me, although one professor opened up a slit into another kind of literature: I began an exciting period of Kant and Hegel, a little, very little, of Karl Marx and Engels. In a time when students didn't leave classes or even skip them very often, I would slip away from a class conducted by a famous editor, annoyed at the glimpses of his well-bred life, and would slam my seat as I left in the middle of a lecture by the famous Alexander Woollcott whenever he paraded the gibe-wit and shabby literary taste of his world. (My bad manners interested Woollcott. He went out of his way, on several occasions, to find me after class and to offer a ride uptown. But the kindness or interest made me resentful and guilty, and I remember a tart exchange about a novel written by a friend of his. Years later, because Woollcott admired Hammett, who did not admire him, I was to meet him again. And after that, when I wrote plays, he was pleasant to me—if saying

26

that I looked like a prow head on a whaling ship is pleasant.)

A good deal of the college day I spent in a Greenwich Village restaurant called Lee Chumley's curled up on a dark bench with a book, or arguing with a brilliant girl called Marie-Louise and her extraordinary, foppish brother, up very often from Princeton, carrying a Paris copy of *Ulysses* when he wasn't carrying Verlaine. (Hal was a handsome, strange young man and we all hoped to be noticed by him. A few years later he married one of our group and a few years after that he killed himself and a male companion in a Zurich hotel room.)

In my junior year, I knew I was wasting time. My mother took me on a long tour to the Midwest and the South, almost as a reward for leaving college. We returned to New York for my nineteenth birthday and the day after I began what was then called an "affair." It was an accident: the young man pressed me into it partly because it satisfied the tinkering malice that has gone through the rest of his life, mostly because it pained his best friend. The few months it lasted did not mean much to me, but I have often asked myself whether I underestimated the damage that so loveless an arrangement made on my future. But my generation did not often deal with the idea of love—we were ashamed of the word, and scornful of the misuse that had been made of it—and I suppose that the cool currency of the time carried me past the pain of finding nastiness in what I had hoped would be a moving adventure.

In the autumn, feeling pleasantly aimless, but knowing that I deeply wanted to work at something, I went to a party and met Julian Messner, the vice-president of Horace Liveright. I had never met a publisher before, never before had a conversation with a serious man much older than myself, and I mistook what was an automatic flirtatious interest for a belief that Julian thought I was intelligent. In any case, by the time the party was over, I had a job.

A job with any publishing house was a plum, but a job with Horace Liveright was a bag of plums. Never before, and possibly never since, has an American publishing house had so great a record. Liveright, Julian, T. R. Smith, Manuel Komroff, and a few even younger men had made a new and brilliant world for books. In the years before I went to work, and in the few years after I left, they discovered, or persuaded over, Faulkner, Freud, Hemingway, O'Neill, Hart Crane, Sherwood Anderson, Dreiser, E. E. Cummings, and many other less talented but remarkable people, all of them attracted by the vivid, impetuous, high-living men who were the editors. It didn't hurt that Horace was handsome and daring, Julian serious and kind, Tom Smith almost erudite with his famous collection of erotica and odd pieces of knowledge that meant nothing but seemed to; that the advances they gave were large and the parties they gave even larger, full of lush girls and good liquor; that the sympathy and attention given to writers, young or old, was more generous than had been known before, possibly more real than has been known since. They were not truly serious men, I guess, nor men of the caliber of Max Perkins, but they had respect for serious writing. Their personal capers, which started out as outrageous and dashing in the fusty world of older publishing houses, became comic and, in time, dangerous and destructive. In the case of Horace himself, the end was sad, broken, undignified. But I was there at a good time and had a good time while I was there.

4

By the time I grew up the fight for the emancipation of women, their rights under the law, in the office, in bed, was stale stuff. My generation didn't think much about the place or the problems of women, were not conscious that the designs we saw around us had so recently been formed that we were still part of the formation. (Five or ten years' difference in age was a greater separation between people in the 1920's, perhaps because the older generation had gone through the war.) The shock of Fitzgerald's flappers was not for us: by the time we were nineteen or twenty we had either slept with a man or pretended that we had. And we were suspicious of the words of love. It was rather taken for granted that you liked one man better than the other and hoped he would marry you, but if that didn't happen you did the best you could and didn't talk about it much. We were, I suppose, pretend cool, and paid for it later on, but our revolt against sentimentality had come, at least, out of distaste for pretense. Of the five girls I knew best, three

29

married for money and said so, and we were not to know then that two of them, in their forties, would crack up under deprivation or boredom.

I was not, therefore, attracted by the lady intellectuals I met at Liveright's. They puzzled me. They talked so much about so little, they were weepy about life and men, and I was too young to be grateful for how much I owed them in the battle of something-or-other in the war for equality. They came through the office door as novelists or poets or artists and, there, I caught only glimpses and heard only gossip. But at parties I saw them in action and felt envy for their worldliness, their talent, their clothes, their age—and bewilderment at their foreign, half-glimpsed problems.

Liveright gave a great many parties. Any writer on a New York visit, any new book, any birthday was an excuse for what he called an A party or a B party. (Liveright was possibly the first publisher to understand that writers care less for dollars than for attention.) The A parties were respectable and high-class chatty. The B parties were drunk, cutup sex stuff and often lasted into another day and night with replacements. I was invited to both the A and B parties, maybe because I was young and thought to be unjudging, maybe for reasons not so good.

The respectable parties were filled with wives, single or divorced ladies, and a few wellborn Lesbians. They chatted about books and Freud. Not many of them had read Freud carefully and so he was considered by some as a metaphysician and by others as a welcome emancipator. And his conclusions about children were considerably misunderstood: I remember one of Maxwell Bodenheim's wives deploring, in Freud's name, the stodgy mind of her very young son who would not admit that when his mama flapped her arms she really rose in the air and soared above the city. She had been cursed, she felt, with a seven-year-old banker type. When she turned to me for agreement, I truly ran across the room feeling younger than her son and more ignorant. But I felt that way most of the time: Edmund Wilson, who met me somewhere in those years, says that I was a shy girl who spoke very little. I like him to say that, but the shyness was a cover for the fear of being shown up.

The B parties were filled with pretty ladies, semi-ins, almost-actresses or newspaper girls, and they slept quite openly with the gentlemen guests, or executives of Live-right's, or the bankers Horace so often had at his parties because he so often needed their money. Some of the ladies had permanent alliances—permanent meant about six months, and semi-permanent meant a few weeks. The B party girls puzzled me as much as the A party ladies and seemed to me no livelier. (If I had known the word square, I would have used it.) I felt that the words of emotion they spoke were not the truth, but then I was not yet old enough to be kind about lost ladies. Whatever step my generation had taken, forward or backward, it was large enough to separate us from people not too much older than ourselves.

Sometimes the parties were given at Horace's apartment, more often they were given at the office. And the office was a wacky joint in a brownstone house on 48th Street. Certain jobs were more clearly defined than others, but even the stenographers and shipping clerks often wandered about reading manuscripts, offering opinions about how to advertise or sell a book, and there was seldom a day without excitement. Some days a "great" new book was found; some days no corner could be found for work because too many writers were in town or had just dropped by; sometimes one of the editors had been in mysterious trouble the night before and everybody went around to his house or hospital to call upon him; on no day could you ever be sure what you would see through a half-open office door, or how long lunch hour would be for Horace and the editors, or who was taking a long nap afterwards. All the men in the office made routine passes at the girls who worked there—one would have had to be hunchbacked to be an exception—and one of the more pleasant memories of my life is the fast sprinting I would do up and down the long staircases to keep from being idly pinched or thrown by a clutching hand on a leg.

But the nicest times came when an efficiency cleanup was ordered. Then for a short time we would look and act like every other office and return from lunch prompt and sober, and work late into the night. I enjoyed the calm and was sorry that such periods never lasted more than a few days.

It was in one of those efficiency periods that I knew there was talk of firing me—I had misplaced an important manuscript, I didn't know how to file, my typing was erratic, my manuscript reports were severe. I would have been fired if I hadn't, that very week, discovered that I was pregnant by the man who, a half year later, I would marry.

A young man called Donald Friede had just been made a partner because Horace needed the money Donald brought into the firm. (He always needed money and often found it by selling part of the business to rich young men.) Donald seemed friendly, more my age, and I was so desperate to find an abortionist that, foolishly, I asked if he knew such a doctor. He found one immediately, swore himself to secrecy, and I made an appointment with the doctor for the following week. The morning following Donald's vow of secrecy, every member of the firm called me into his office to offer money, to ask the name of my child's father, to guess that it was one of them, to make plans and plots for help I didn't want. I was suddenly a kind of showcase. I was angry about that and so, throughout the good-natured questionings, I sat sullen, staring into space, refusing answers, trying not to think about the vicarious, excited snoopiness I knew was mixed with the kindness.

The operation, done without an anesthetic in a Coney

Island half-house, with the doctor's mother as assistant, was completed on a Monday evening. I went home, weak and more frightened than I had ever been about anything, and so ignorant that I was awake all night worried that my parents could tell what had happened by just looking at me. On Tuesday morning feeling sick, but sure that my mother would call a doctor if I said that, I went back to work. Horace called me in to ask how I was and to give me a glass of midmorning champagne; Friede stopped by my desk to ask if I had now decided to reveal the name of the father; Julian Messner asked me out to lunch and bought me a drink that was called a pink-un, and stared at me throughout lunch as if I were a recent arrival from a distant land. We didn't talk much at lunch, but as we walked back to the office he said, gently, "I don't understand what you're about."

I said, "That's all right, Julian," and knew he didn't like the answer.

As we climbed the steps of the brownstone, T. R. Smith yelled, "Julian, tell that ninny to go home to bed. She shouldn't have come to work today. Tell her to get out of here."

I was sure this was his way of firing me, so on my way past his office, I stopped in. I said, "I know I've lost the manuscript, Tom, but I've been nervous and tomorrow I'll find it--"

He said, "What are you made of, Lilly?"

I said, "Pickling spice and nothing nice."

He said, "That kind of talk. I don't understand you kids. Go home."

I said I couldn't, that if I went home too early my mother would be nervous and make a fuss, so I'd go to the movies.

He said, "You look awful. Lie down on the couch. I'll send you in some supper. When you feel better, go home, or go wherever you go."

He went back to the manuscript he was reading, the

33

phone calls he was making, and I went to sleep on the couch.

When I woke up he said, "What's your generation about?"

"I don't know what it's about and I don't know why all of you keep asking questions like that. Everybody here seems angry with me for a reason I don't understand, and I'm angry with Donald for breaking his word."

Smith said, "It isn't that we're angry with you. We're worried about ourselves. We're used to bums and we're used to nice or near nice girls who make speeches and cause a fuss. We're not used to a respectable girl who doesn't make trouble for the man, says she is probably going to marry him anyway, but won't when she's pregnant, doesn't even tell him what day the abortion is—"

"I didn't tell him because it would have made me more nervous."

"How many men have you slept with?"

"Three hundred and thirty-three, Tom, not counting my brothers and uncles who don't much like to be counted."

I came toward his desk, took a deep breath, and no longer cared about being fired. "And it's none of your business. I haven't much liked being everybody's pregnant pet the last few days and all the questions. It's as if all of you were waiting for me to cry or to throw myself from a window or to tell you the man had deserted me and wouldn't I come home with one of you nicer boys—"

He said, "Not me. I don't want you home with me. You're not up my alley. But you're right. Exactly right."

"Funny," I said, "because none of you gives a damn about me."

"Not one damn. They even forgot you were here until this happened. But you acted too calm, wouldn't talk, came to work and so on, so now we realize that you're younger, different than the women we know. There *is* a new generation and nobody here likes to think that. But

34

we'd better catch up on it if we want to publish it. I don't think we're going to like it, but maybe you'd better start telling us about it."

A waiter came into Smith's office, bringing a tray from the speakeasy next door. Smith moved a table in front of me, gave me a drink, and stared at me as I ate all of the good food. I grinned at him and he said, "So?"

I said, "I don't know how to answer you. I don't know about my generation. It's just us. We think we sound better than your ladies, but we don't know even that much because we haven't had time to make theories or maybe even need any."

"What do you think of what you call our ladies?"

I said, "All the talk about love, all the stuff."

"Did you ever read *Flaming Youth?*"

"Certainly not."

"Well, smarty, a lot of people did. We want Sam Adams to do a new book, maybe a sequel. But I think things have changed even in these few years, and I don't think we know, or he knows, what we're talking about. You can help."

I said I wasn't flaming youth, didn't even know what it meant.

"Yes, you do. You're it. Or it to us."

He came and sat by me and patted my hand. "It was I who wanted to fire you. You're not very efficient. But I'll make you a bargain. Get a couple of your bright friends, bring them over to Horace's this Saturday night, let Sam Adams ask all of you a few questions, and you can keep the job. For a while, anyway."

Saturday night my two friends, Marie-Louise and Alice, and I were escorted to Horace's apartment entrance by Alice's two brothers. As flaming youth we'd each had a root beer and a sandwich in a delicatessen. The boys left us at the door with a few bad jokes and the three of us went up to Horace's duplex apartment.

I should have guessed there would be a party, there was

a party almost every Saturday night, but I couldn't have guessed how noisy it would be. We stood in the door, knowing nobody, feeling awkward and foolish, until Tom Smith saw us and, crossing the room, motioned us up the stairs. I remember Liveright calling out from his place on the sofa, telling us to come and join him, but Tom hurried us to a kind of small library—guest room, and then, having made a leering examination of my friends, went out, closing the door. None of us talked: we felt like new patients in a hospital ward. In a few minutes Tom came back carrying glasses and a bottle. He was followed by Mr. Adams, who sat down on the couch bed and motioned us to chairs around him.

I would like to say these many years later that I remember his questions. But I don't, and for a good reason: he had already decided on whatever he meant to write and the questions were fitted to his decisions. So most of the time we didn't know what he was talking about.

After a few drinks, Mr. Adams's boredom with us was no longer concealed. (I think he had agreed to meet us only because Smith had insisted upon it. And the hour was late and he wasn't young.) The three of us felt silly and resentful, so when he got down to stuff like "How old were you when you had your first sexual encounter?" Marie-Louise said she didn't know what encounter meant, kind of, and when Mr. Adams explained that it meant being in bed with a man, she said that in Bombay, where she had been born, things like that didn't take place in a bed. She had been born in Albany, New York, was a virgin until she married two years later, but it was a good thing to say because it put a little fire under Alice and me, who had been acting sulky. I said I had my first encounter in a chicken coop in New Orleans when I was four years old, but Mr. Adams was more interested in Alice, who was a beautiful girl and who could cry any time she felt like it. She was crying now over her first encounter, an imaginary geographer-explorer who had disappeared on what she sometimes called the Niger and sometimes called the Amazon. Marie-Louise, tired of Alice's overlong fantasy, took to singing. She had a pretty voice and she was improvising about her love in Bombay. Mr. Adams liked the singing and asked her if she wanted him to speak to Liveright, who would speak to Otto Kahn, the culture-kick banker, about money for singing lessons. Alice had now left the geographer behind and was trying to tell Mr. Adams that she had had so many encounters that only her priest could remember the details, but she'd make him write them all down for Mr. Adams because her father was a papal count. (Her father was a rich Jew from Detroit and she was already started on the road to Marxism that would lead her, as a student doctor, to be killed in the Vienna riots of 1934.)

The three of us had had too many drinks, were talking at the same time, were laughing too much at nothing. Mr. Adams rose, thanked us, suggested that we all go downstairs and join Horace's party.

But the door wouldn't open. I don't know why it wouldn't open, and although he later denied it, I've always believed that Tom Smith had locked us in and forgotten about us. In any case, there we were. We tried hitting the door, we shouted, we stamped on the floor, but no sounds could overreach the noise of the party below. Mr. Adams finally threw himself against the door with such angry force that he reeled and fell back over a chair, and pushed Alice when she tried to help him up. She stayed on the floor and claimed that it was the first time in all of her many encounters that a man had been mean to her. When she started to cry, Marie-Louise said to cut it, but by now the tears were real and they were soon being nasty to each other.

The only other door in the room led to a bathroom, and when Mr. Adams went in there we had no reason to be curious. (In any case we were too busy: Marie-Louise and

37

Alice were shouting at each other and I was explaining the damage alcohol did to the brain.) When the three of us quieted down, and Alice and Marie-Louise had apologized to one another, we whispered and giggled about the new encounters we were making up for Mr. Adams's return. It took us quite a while to realize that he had been missing for 'longer than a toilet usually requires. We knocked on the bathroom door, got no reply, consulted, and finally opened the door. There was no sign of him, but the bathroom window was open and sounds were coming from below. We climbed the bathtub ledge to see that Mr. Adams was on a fire escape three flights below us, one story above ground level. He was shouting into a window that faced him, but nobody answered. He took to pounding on the window and then to pushing it. He was sweating and he looked sick. Slowly he walked to the opening of the fire escape, crouched, and began to shake the ladder. But the ladder had rusted through the years and would not budge. Mr. Adams stood erect as if to jump. But he didn't make the jump and he was right: it was a long jump, he was not young, and frustration and anger had turned him clumsy. He slipped and fell the length of the fire escape landing.

Marie-Louise said, "Ssh. He wouldn't want us to see him."

Alice said, "He's going to hurt himself." She pushed us both aside, climbed out the window, going young and rapid down the ladders. Adams didn't see her until she had almost reached him and then, in some kind of panic, or shame, he grabbed her leg and motioned her to go back. Alice kicked his hand and made the long jump to the ground with an athlete's soft, forward motion. Adams shouted something to her we couldn't hear, but we could see that her face changed to anger.

She stepped back to look up at us and called out, "Don't ever have encounters with old gentlemen on fire escapes." Then she disappeared around a corner of the building and in a few minutes Mr. Adams rose from his fire escape and began a slow climb back to our bathroom window.

I said to Marie-Louise, "Take your clothes off, get in the shower, and when he gets here, pop out and offer yourself. I think that's what flaming youth does every Saturday night."

She said, "Don't be mean," and backed me out of the bathroom.

The three of us didn't speak during the half hour it took the janitor and his assistant to take the door off the hinges. We faced a large group of people from the party who treated us as if we were a vaudeville turn put on for their amusement. By the time we got past them and downstairs, Mr. Adams had disappeared and Alice was sitting next to Tom Smith.

I said, "Tom, flaming youth thinks you locked us in and it was a dirty trick."

Tom put his arm around Alice. "This little girl has sense. Some little girls don't have too much. I think we'll fire you tomorrow."

I wasn't fired, but I left a few months later to get married. Mr. Adams never wrote a sequel to *Flaming Youth*, although he did write a book called *The Flagrant Years* about the "beauty market." I don't think that could have been us.

After I was married I would often drop around to the office to see my old friend Louis Kronenberger, who had gone to work there, and sometimes Julian Messner would take me out to lunch. I wanted very much to ask him to give me back my old job, but I guess I knew I wouldn't get it. In any case, I had a feeling that the place was in a decline. Rumors went about that Horace was wasting money producing plays and was drinking too much; and because the depression had now set in, the rich, available young men partners were no longer to be found. Gradually the firm began to disappear, its assets and contracts taken over by a man who had been the head of the shipping room. It was, of course, a sad story, but there were so many sad stories in the early 1930's that I don't remember any special pain when I met Horace again in Hollywood. He had become a producer at Paramount Pictures: some of the old glamour was there, where his name was still famous and his recent history not yet fully understood. But every time I saw him—not many times, perhaps five or six—I knew, for a simple reason, that the pride was breaking: he would, immediately, cross the room to sit beside me because I alone in the room was the respectful young girl who had known him in the great days, and the more he drank the more we talked of those days, not so many years before. (He had, as a mistress, a very nice actress, and was by this time divorced from his wife. The nice actress was good to him and faithful, and we all took for granted that he would marry her.)

Then for a long time I didn't see him, and I no longer can remember whether he was fired from Paramount or resigned. I saw him again after I was divorced and Hammett and I had moved to New York. About a year after that, I had a call from him asking me to his wedding reception the following week. I didn't want to go, although I don't know what instinct dictated that, but Hammett, who didn't know him very well and didn't like him very much, unexpectedly insisted that we go.

The reception was given at the apartment of one of his respectable lady cousins. The room was filled with people I had never seen before, although an occasional familiar face would float in and float out. The party seemed in the managerial hands of two brothers who, when they weren't kissing the gentlemen guests, were kissing each other.

I said to one of them, "Where's Horace?"

"Passed out," he shrieked with laughter, "and so has the bride. They had a simply, simply splendid fight."

"She never used to drink," I said.

"Always. Always. How do you know? You never met her."

When we got that straight, it turned out that Horace had not married the nice actress, but another actress, recently met, a dark beauty who appeared in a few minutes, lurching, demanding that somebody find the bridegroom because she wanted an immediate divorce.

I said to Hammett, "Let's get out."

Hammett said, "No. Wait for him, the poor bastard."

And so we sat through the long afternoon and night, neither of us having much to drink, although those were the heavy drinking days. Hammett, sober, was always a silent man, and after a while I couldn't bring myself to even the smallest conversation with the strange men and women in the room. We must have been an odd pair, sitting silent on a big couch as the place emptied, filled again, grew quiet, then noisy with new visitors, the bride screaming "darlings" at some, curses at others, explaining over and over again that the bridegroom had given her a black eye. (Her eyes were beautiful and clear.) Toward midnight, I think I must have dozed, because I remember being surprised to see Hammett on his feet as Horace came through the door. The fine clothes were rumpled, the strong, handsome face was set as if it had been arranged before a mirror. He came directly towards me and I rose to meet him.

Horace said, "You don't have to rise to greet me. Nobody does anymore."

Hammett said, "Don't tell her things like that. I'm having enough trouble keeping her respectful."

It was a good thing to say because it made Horace smile. He said, "I need a drink. Lilly, were you the only one to come today?"

I said that all his old friends and writers had been there—it was not true—but it was late now, and they had gone when they couldn't find him.

He said, "I've been resting. Where's the bride?" When

he went to look for her, and Hammett came back with the drink Horace had forgotten about, we decided to go home. On the way down the stairs, voices were suddenly raised, and I recognized Horace angry, and the bride even angrier.

I was never to see him again. But in 1933 one of his former secretaries called to tell me that he was very ill and broke and living alone. She gave me the address, I took five hundred dollars from the bureau where Hammett always left money for me, and took a taxi to the address. But I had the wrong address and had to telephone home to ask Hammett to find the piece of paper on which I had written it.

I said, "I'm taking him five hundred dollars. Is that enough?"

Hammett said, "Enough to make you feel noble. Get yourself in a taxi and come back here. He won't want money from you, have a little sense. Find somebody else to take it to him."

I said, "That's foolish. Why wouldn't he want it from me?"

Hammett said, "O.K., do what you want."

But I went home and called Dick Simon, of Simon and Schuster, who had once worked for Liveright. Simon's secretary said he was out of town, would be back in a week. But three days later Horace died.

5

          I HAD left my job at Liveright's to marry Arthur Kober, who was a charming young man working as a theatre press agent and just beginning to write about his friends in the emerging Jewish-American lower middle class world.

We didn't have much money, but we had enough for a pleasant life of reading, afternoon bridge for me, and nice, aimless evenings. I found that I liked to do the good New Orleans cooking of my childhood and wanted to learn more about the excellent backwoods cooking of my mother's Alabama. I went back to writing short stories in fits of long hours of secret work. But I knew the stories were not very good and so I always put them aside.

Those first few years of marriage included a long trip to Paris, where Arthur worked on a magazine. I wandered around Europe in a jumble of passivity and wild impatience. I believed I was not doing or living the way I had planned. I had planned nothing, of course. I was bewildered: if I really felt there were a million years ahead of me, why then did I feel so impatient, so restless?

I think we were younger in our twenties than people are now because the times allowed us to be and because we were not very concerned with position or the future or money. (That came to most of us a few years later.) And I was even younger than my friends. I was rash, overdaring, certain only that any adventure was worth having, and increasingly muddled by the Puritan conscience that made me pay for the adventures. I needed a teacher, a cool teacher, who would not be impressed or disturbed by a strange and difficult girl. I was to meet him, but not for another four or five years.

The time came when my idle life didn't suit Arthur and didn't suit me. I wasn't any good at finding jobs or keeping them, and so Arthur found them for me in the theatre. I worked as a press agent for an arty little group who didn't pay me after the second week. I worked as a play reader for Anne Nichols, the author of *Abie's Irish Rose,* who wanted to become a producer. I had a good time for four months in Rochester, New York, working for a stock company and gambling every night for money to spend in Europe that summer. Once, for a few weeks, I went back to the short stories, but I convinced myself that I was not meant to be a writer. I was rather relieved by that discovery—it gave me more time to listen to a gangster who ran Rochester's underworld, more time to win money at bridge from Rochester society, more time to read and drink.

I have no clear memories of those days, those years, not of myself where and when, not of other people. I know only that I was ignorant pretending to be wise, lazy pretending to work hard, so oversensitive to a breath of reservation that I called it unfriendliness and swept by it with harsh intolerance. It was the fashion then to like the witty insult behind the back, the goose-grease compliment before the face. (That fashion has now returned and we

like only those we consider "pleasant.") But I did not
want that form of human exchange. I respected only those
I thought told the "truth," without fear for themselves,
independent of popular opinion. And thus, like so many
lady extremists, I began a history of remarkable men,
often difficult, sometimes even dangerous.

I did win enough money in those scrubby Rochester
days to go to Europe that summer of 1929. I went to
Germany, liked Bonn, and decided to study there for a
year. I lived in a university boardinghouse waiting for the
day of enrollment and went on nice picnics with large
healthy blondes. I thought I was listening to a kind of
socialism, I liked it, and agreed with it. But one day on an
autobus, riding out to the picnic grounds, two of them
gave me a cheesy-looking pamphlet about their organization—I cannot remember its name but it was, of course, a
youth group publication of Hitler's National Socialism—
and asked if I wouldn't like to become a member, no dues
for foreigners if they had no Jewish connections. I said I
had no other connections that I knew of, although a
second cousin in Mobile had married the owner of a
whorehouse, non-Jewish. But nobody paid attention to
what I said, because Hellman in Germany is often not a
Jewish name. I left Bonn the next day and came back to
New York.

It has been forgotten that for many people the depression years were the good years. True, my father, like so
many of his generation, took a beating from which he did
not recover, but Arthur was offered a job as a scenario
writer for Paramount Pictures at more money than we had
ever seen. We had been living in a beat-up old house on
Long Island and I was reluctant to leave it. So Arthur
went ahead of me to Hollywood and I fooled and fiddled
with excuses until the day when I did go, knowing even
then, I think, that I would not stay.

6

We rented a dark house in Hollywoodland, the hilly section above the already junky Hollywood Boulevard. I do not know why we chose such an ugly house nor why we employed an ex-actress to cook bad dinners. The ex-actress was a sad, lonely woman who gave me my first concern about middle age because she so often cried and spoke about growing bald. Arthur and I felt sorry for her, but my father didn't ever feel sorry for bad cooks, and so, when he and my mother came West for a visit, at the second night's dinner he said to me, "How can you eat salad before the soup and what kind of people eat grapefruit at dinner? What has happened to you?"

He was right. Something had happened to me. Torpor had touched down. I spent most of the day reading in a leather chair and at night I was learning to drink hard. I was out of place and the drinking made uninteresting people matter less and, late at night, matter not at all. I was twenty-five years old that June and I had stepped too early into solitude.

After my father spoke to me, I was worried enough to try again for a job. My husband pulled strings and I was given fifty dollars a week at Metro-Goldwyn-Mayer to read manuscripts and write reports about them. In order to get the job, you had to read two languages—or pretend that you did—and you had to write the kind of idiot-simple report that Louis Mayer's professional lady storyteller could make even more simple when she told it to Mr. Mayer.

Twelve men and two women sat in a large room in a rickety building on stilts, and every small tremor—and California had a number of tremors that year—sent the building atilt. When you finished a manuscript (you were expected to read at least two a day) you went into another large room and waited your turn for one of the half-broken typewriters. It was said that if your reports showed signs of promise you would be promoted to what was called a junior writer position, but after that I don't know what became of you because I was never promoted. The job didn't matter to me after the first few weeks' pleasure of having any job at all, but it did matter to the learned Austrian who sat next to me, and to the former English lady writer who sat by herself in a corner, and most of all it mattered to what had been a most respected editor of a New York publishing house who had left his wife to live with a young girl and ended up here. I used to stare at him a good deal hoping we could become friends, but while he was polite to me, as he was to all others, I was the one person in the room who knew about him and thus most to be avoided. (I knew the girl he had run away with and the fact that she was an ugly girl somehow made the whole story more interesting.) In the third or fourth month of our bowing acquaintance, his girl picked him up one evening and invited me to dinner the following week. I looked forward to the evening, but a few days before the dinner he did not appear in the office, and the head lady of the typewriters told me that his daughter had killed herself and he had returned to New York. I tried to find his girl, but the landlady at the sad little half-house said she had moved without leaving an address. I was never to see or hear from them again, although many years later he did a distinguished piece of scholarly research.

The days and the months went clipclop along, much as they had done in the leather chair in our ugly house, except that now I was reading junk when, alone, I had been with good books. I would leave home at eight-thirty, drive to Culver City carrying a small basket with my lunch and a bottle of wine. I would, by one o'clock, have a vague headache that would disappear as I ate my picnic on the back lot of the studio and got fuzzy on the wine and the surrounding dream of old movie sets piled next to one another, early Rome at right angles to the painted roses of a girlie musical, at the left of a London street, side by side with a giant, empty whaling ship.

It was not a good place to eat lunch, but it was better than going to the studio commissary where I had to pass a large table for famous directors and writers, some of whom knew my husband and thus had to make the kind of half rise-bow, acknowledged in all worlds where classes are sharply marked to mean you are above the ordinary but not enough above it to include you in the circle. Nor was I interested in looking at the almost stars, and occasional real stars, who sat at special tables spooning the chicken soup that was Mr. Mayer's special pride. (I did not know then that the glamour of theatre people was never to mean anything to me, which was forever to make me difficult for those who have the right to think it should.) I remember once seeing Garbo there and thinking she was the most beautiful woman in the world, and I often remember John Gilbert, whose career was about to come to an end because his voice shocked the talking picture audiences, and Norma Shearer, the face unclouded by thought. (Years later, after *The Children's Hour*, Mrs. Patrick Campbell, broke and anxious for a job,

borrowed four hundred dollars from me "to go to dinner
with Shearer and her husband Irving Thalberg, because
he's the head of the studio, duckie, and crazy about her the
way Jews are about women who aren't." I didn't understand why that should cost four hundred dollars until a
few days after the dinner when Mrs. Campbell showed me
a dress she had bought for the occasion. Four hundred
dollars was a fortune for a dress in those days, but I
thought it a splendid gesture for a proud old lady and
asked her if Thalberg had given her the job she wanted.
"No, duckie, and I don't think I'll get it. So I'll give you a
few of Bernard Shaw's letters as repayment." I said I
didn't want Mr. Shaw's letters, but by this time she was
giggling and playing with a little dog called Moonbeam.
Through the giggles she said, "You see, dearie duckie, I
was doing rather splendidly at first. And then, well, it's
true, isn't it, and *that's* the important thing, I said to Mr.
Thalberg, 'Your wife has the most beautiful little eyes I've
ever seen.' ")

After my picnic lunch, warm with wine, I would go
back to work and try for a nap if the head lady of the
typewriters was out of the building. But two and sometimes three and four reports of plays or novels is a lot of
work for one day, and by four o'clock there wasn't a face
in the room that didn't show the strain. But I would stay
late, always with the excuse that I wasn't finished or the
typewriter had broken or that I was waiting for somebody
to call me.

In truth, I was avoiding the ride home. I do not know
why that drive in the dark of six o'clock was so terrible to
me. Maybe because the flat, soggy land of the main road
was the kind of country I had never seen before, maybe
the awful speed and jerkiness of California drivers, maybe
the ugly house I was going home to, maybe because I
knew this shabby job had solved nothing. Maybe all of
that and maybe little of it, I don't know anymore, but the
drive had become so bad for me that I would tremble as I

got into the car and would often have to stop the car and press my hands together to stop the movements they were making. Sometimes when I stopped I fell asleep for a while; once I leaned from the window and screamed; once I left the car, went to a small hotel and phoned to say I couldn't get home and didn't want anybody to come for me; twice I had minor accidents and once I killed a rabbit and sat by it for a few hours. I did not yet know about "inhuman cities" or roads built with no relief for the eye, or the effects of a hated house upon the spirit. I didn't even understand about my marriage, or my life, and had no knowledge of the new twists I was braiding into the kinks I was already bound round with.

Certainly I did not know that fear, to many, was no disgrace. Like most of the middle class I had been brought up to swim, drive cars, climb around. Irrational fear was no part of your own world and you had contempt for the few times you had seen it in other people. Now here it was, out in the open, and I realized it had been with me before, and would now be with me forever unless I did something, a favorite phrase of my time. I did nothing more than go home because I had no place else to go.

That is the way I saw it then, because that is the way I wrote about it then, but now I know it is not a whole nor a true picture. We often had nice weekends in Tia Juana, where my father found an oyster shucker he had known in New Orleans. The oyster shucker owned a small restaurant and was so happy to see my father that he would go quail shooting at dawn and broil them for us at breakfast, drinking pernod as he told us of the old days when he would open oysters for my father and the other young bloods and their "girlies." Once, when he told about a ball in New Orleans that had lasted three days and punched my father in the ribs with teasing about "seven girlies" in those three days, my mother's pleasant face changed so sharply that I thought she was sick. She went to the

51

An Unfinished Woman

ladies' room and I followed her there. She was sitting in a
chair, staring at the floor. I don't think we spoke, but I
remember thinking that I had never in my life been
jealous about a man and had contempt for what I was
watching. A few years later, when I had gone to live with
Dashiell Hammett, I remember being ashamed of that
contempt and always wishing to apologize to my mother
for it.

And we had pleasant evenings with our best friends,
Laura and Sidney Perelman and Laura's brother, Nathanael West. The five of us, and a few others, stayed
close together not only because we liked each other but
because we were in what was called "the same salary
bracket." Then, and probably now, if you were a writer
who earned five hundred dollars a week you didn't see
much of those who earned fifteen hundred a week. That
was O.K. with me because other, richer and more important groups puzzled me and made me disorderly: the remarkable gadgets in their houses, the then new swimming
pools, the earnest talk made me irritable and nasty. It took
me years to understand that it had been a comic time,
with its overperfect English antiques that were replacing
the overcarved Spanish furniture and hanging shawls; the
flutey, refined language—one producer spoke often of his
daughter's "perberty," and Hammett phoned me one night
from Jean Harlow's house to tell me that she had rung the
bell for the butler and said, "Open the window, James,
and leave in a tiny air"—and the attempt, running side by
side with the new life, to stand by the old roots: Jewish
mama stories and Jewish mamas proudly imported from
the East; French cooks and stuffed derma; and one studio
executive who lived in a Colonial house with early American furniture and a mezuzah above the door encased in
pickled pine. And there was the wife of a composer who
had two ermine coats exactly alike in case one should
burn, and the ex-star, our neighbor, who often came
calling to show me the knife cuts on her body put there

the night before by a very religious movie director, and over our own fireplace in the ugly house there was a portrait of a lion whose eyes lit up if you pressed a button, and we knew a pug dog who would not eat his meat unless his Polish mistress flavored it with what she called a *soupçon d'ail.*

More interesting to me was the foggy edge-world of people who had come to Hollywood for reasons they had long ago forgotten. They lived in the Murphy-bed, modern apartments that were already the slums off Hollywood Boulevard, or in the rickety houses that stuck out like broken tree-geraniums from the Hollywood mud hills. There were still traces of the days when most of them had wanted to act or write or paint, but those days passed into years of drinking and doping or grubbing. I saw this world only after I knew Hammett but, because of my nature and theirs, I saw it only through a crack in the door. It seemed to me a world of independent spirits and I envied the long, free nights and the sleeping days, but they thought my envy was something else, and were suspicious of me. I remember an older woman asking, "Where did you get that suit?" And before I could answer she said, "It takes too damned long to tell that your clothes are good." They saw me, I think, as a tight, tense sightseer, and believed that my unspoken romantic view of them was an outlander's patronage. Hammett saw this world for what it was, and turned to it only during drinking bouts, turning sharply away when they were over. Pep West saw it through his own wonderfully original mind and wrote, in *The Day of the Locust,* the only good book about Hollywood ever written. (Fitzgerald's *The Last Tycoon* was a sentimental view of Irving Thalberg: Scott had written magnificently of the rich and powerful in the East and in Europe, but he got sticky moon-candy about a man who was only a bright young movie producer.)

The people of that world are now, in my memory, rolled into one mass in one room, and I cannot be sure that I do not mix up the men with the women, their dogs with their children or mothers. But I do remember an artist who went barefoot along the streets and picked up a job when he had to as a first-rate captain or engineer on one of the yachts of the rich. His leaning house in the hills was full of china and glass and sheets bearing the names of the many large boats from which they had been taken, and he did funny imitations of movie moguls on the water.

And I remember a small, faded woman called Sis who lived with and exchanged men with her mother. Sis was always too doped to talk much, and as she sat in a chair holding a small dog on her lap, silent, waited upon by her vigorous green-blonde mother, she seemed to me an interesting girl, but the one time I tried talking to her she suddenly slapped my face. She died a few month later when, according to her mother, she was so drunk that she fell to the floor and hit her head on a radiator. Hammett said he didn't believe that because he had never known anybody who doped heavily to drink heavily, and evidently somebody agreed with him because there were a few days of excitement when the mother was arrested and charged with throwing Sis against the radiator during a fight. Nothing ever came of that except a party the mother gave when the police could prove nothing, or didn't want to. And there was a man, an ex-actor, who played the flute and lived with a fat woman everybody said was a man, and there was the American Indian who sold postcards on Hollywood Boulevard and went to every fancy movie opening in top hat and tails. One night Hammett and I were having dinner in the Brown Derby and the Indian came in, pushing his way past the headwaiter, to sit down next to Hammett. He said, "My grandfather was chief of the Sioux, my great-grandfather was killed by ..."

"How much do you want?" Hammett asked.

"Nothing as a gift from you. You told me once you arrested an Indian for murder . . ."

Hammett put his wallet on the table and said, "Take it any way you want, but don't tell me what you think."

The Indian opened the wallet and took out five twenty-dollar bills. "Be sure I do not take it as a gift. I take it as a loan. You are better than most, but you . . ."

Hammett said wearily, "Arrested an Indian for murder. That's right."

The Indian said, "And thus it is impossible for me . . ."

"Sure, sure," Hammett said. "Mail it to me someday." The Indian bowed, kissed my hand, and was gone.

I said, "He's proud, isn't he?"

Hammett said, "No. He's a Negro pretending to be an Indian. He's a no-good stinker."

I said, "Then why did you give him the money?"

"Because no-good stinkers get hungry too."

But all that came after I left the job at Metro. I was there for about a year, and then one night, driving home, I knew I could not make that drive again. It had, of course, became a symbol of much else that had gone wrong. A short time later Arthur and I separated without ill feeling and I went back to New York.

I forgot about those rides in the car, don't think I ever thought about them again until seven or eight years later. By that time I had written two plays and two movies, was earning a lot of money, and was able to write a clause in a contract with Samuel Goldwyn that allowed me a choice of scripts and did not require me, except for short periods, to go to Hollywood.

And so I was living on an island off the shore of Connecticut when the Spanish Civil War began in 1936. Never before and never since in my lifetime were liberals, radicals, intellectuals and the educated middle class to come together in single, forceful alliance. (The present feeling against the war in Vietnam is stronger, of course, and more widespread. But it took us four or five years to realize that *we,* our own people, my hairdresser's husband, and the son of my friend's friend, and a former student of my own at Harvard, and a garage mechanic who should never have been trusted with a penknife, had all been drafted to murder for reasons neither they nor we understood.) Therefore when Archibald MacLeish, in 1937, suggested that he, Hemingway, Joris Ivens and I make a documentary movie about Spain, I jumped at the chance to do something. Sitting in New York it was easy enough to write a check, but too hard to write a shooting script, or even an outline, about a war I did not know in a place I had never seen. I decided to join Ivens in Spain, but I came down with pneumonia in Paris, came home, and didn't get to Spain for another eight or nine months. But Hemingway was already in Spain and he was much better qualified than I to make the picture.

In 1938, after I had been to Spain and was back in Hollywood for a short stay, Ernest and Joris brought the final cut of *The Spanish Earth* to California. It was a good picture, with remarkable work by Ivens and a narration by Ernest that I still like—I saw the picture again about a year ago—because he felt deeply enough not to care that he often sounded like a parody of himself. Frederic and Florence March offered us their house for a private showing of the picture. We invited a few well-heeled people and raised thirteen thousand dollars, a great deal of money in those days, to buy ambulances for Spain. (We all felt so good that night that nobody much cared that Errol Flynn, invited because he claimed he had been to Spain during the war—Ernest said that Flynn had crossed the border and crossed right back again—went to the toilet during the money raising and was not seen again.)

When we left the Marches, Dorothy Parker asked a few of us to her house for a nightcap. (She had known Ernest for many years, and while they didn't like each other, the night was pleasant enough to make both of them affectionate.) I had met Scott Fitzgerald years before in Paris, but I had not seen him again until that night and I was shocked by the change in his face and manner. He hadn't seemed to recognize me and so I was surprised and pleased when he asked if I would ride with him to Dottie's. My admiration for Fitzgerald's work was very great, and I looked forward to talking to him alone. But we didn't talk: he was occupied with driving at ten or twelve miles an hour down Sunset Boulevard, a dangerous speed in most places, certainly in Beverly Hills. Fitzgerald crouched over the wheel when cars honked at us, we jerked to the right and then to the left, and passing drivers leaned out to shout at us. I could not bring myself to speak, or even to look at Fitzgerald, but when I saw that his hands were trembling on the wheel, all my rides from Metro came rushing back, and I put my hand over his hand. He brought the car to the side of the road and I told him about my old job at Metro, the awful rides home, my fears of California drivers, until he patted my arm several times and then I knew he hadn't been listening and had different troubles.

He said, "You see, I'm on the wagon. I'll take you to Dottie's but I don't want to go in."

When we finally got to Dottie's, he came around to open the door for me. He said softly, "It's a long story. Ernest and me."

In those days I knew no stories about Hemingway and Fitzgerald, just that they had been friends and weren't anymore, but I remembered that Dottie had once told me that she and Scott had slept together years before I knew her, in a casual one or two night affair.

I said, "But Dottie wants to see you. Everybody in that room wants to meet you."

He shook his head and smiled. "No, I'm riding low now."

"Not for writers, nor will you ever. *The Great Gatsby* is the best . . ."

He smiled and touched my shoulder. "I'm afraid of Ernest, I guess, scared of being sober when . . ."

I said, "Don't be. He could never like a good writer, certainly not a better one. Come. You'll have a nice time."

I put out my hand and, after a second, he smiled and took it. We went into the hall and turned left to the living room. Nobody saw us come in because the four or five people in the room were all turned toward Ernest, who stood with his back to the door, facing the fireplace. I don't know why he did it, or what had gone on before, but as we started into the room, Hemingway threw his highball glass against the stone fireplace. Fitzgerald and I stopped dead at the sound of the smashing glass: he stepped back into the hall and turned to leave, but I held his arm and he followed me through a swinging door as if he didn't know or care where he was going. Dottie and Hammett were in the kitchen talking about Errol Flynn as they watched Alan Campbell, Dottie's husband, grow irritable about ice trays.

I said, "Ernest just threw a glass."

Dottie said, "Certainly," as she kissed Fitzgerald.

I moved toward Dash and said in a whisper, "Please help Mr. Fitzgerald. He's frightened of Ernest and the glass throwing didn't help."

Hammett, when he was drinking heavily, and he was that night, seldom paid any attention to what anybody said but continued with whatever was in his head at the minute.

So now he said, "Ernest has never been able to write a woman. He only puts them in books to admire him."

By the time I asked what the hell that had to do with what I was saying, he was out of the kitchen, and when I went back into the hall he was saying the same thing to somebody else. The rest of the evening was quiet, but I don't remember how long Fitzgerald stayed and I was never to see him again.

But somewhere through the liquor fog of that night,

and many others like it, what had been said to him, or what he had seen or sensed himself, stayed in Dash's mind. (Often he would forget a night or a week, could not remember where or with whom he had been, only to discover that many of the details of such periods were recorded almost accurate.)

A year or so later, we were in the Stork Club and the table grew, as it so often did, until it included Ernest and Gustav Regler, a German writer I had known in Spain. (Ernest and Dash had seemed to like each other—they had dined alone a few times when Ernest was in New York—and once I had said, "Ernest is generous about your books, that's nice." Hammett laughed. "Must mean I'm a bad writer.")

The Spanish War was just ended and many Republicans and their supporters had been caught in France, or in northern Spain, and had to be bailed or bought out. We had all given money to make that possible, but Ernest was in a bad humor that Stork Club night and gave small jab lectures about safe people in New York. People began to leave our table until nobody was left but Ernest, Regler, Dash and me, and by that time Dash had had as much to drink as Ernest, and had grown too quiet. Now he put his head in his hands as Ernest spoke again of the friends who must be saved.

Ernest said, "What's the matter with you, Hammett?"

"I don't always like lectures."

I remember an angry silence, and then suddenly Ernest seemed in a good humor and Dash in a bad humor as they talked of saving intellectuals or saving ordinary people, and when Regler or I tried to speak neither of them cared. When I came back from a trip to the ladies' room, Ernest had a tablespoon between the muscles of his upper and lower arm and was pressing it hard. Hammett was staring down at the tablecloth. Just as I settled myself the spoon crumpled and Ernest threw it down with a happy grin.

He turned to Hammett, "All right, kid, let's see you do that."

Kid looked up, stared at Ernest, returned his head to his hands, and I knew there was going to be trouble. I tinkled and giggled and chatted and chittered, but nobody paid any attention. I didn't hear anything for a few minutes until Ernest said, "So you're against saving the intellectuals?"

Hammett spoke through his hands. "I didn't say that. I said there were other people in the world." He turned to me, "Come on. Let's go."

He half rose. Ernest's hand shot out and held him down. Ernest was grinning. "No. Let's see you do the spoon trick first."

Dash stared at Ernest's hand, settled in his chair again, put his head back in his hands. Regler began to talk about something, but I don't remember what he said. Ernest was holding out another tablespoon as he whispered to Dash.

Dash said, "Why don't you go back to bullying Fitzgerald? Too bad he doesn't know how good he is. The best."

The hand on Dash's arm came away and the fingers spread open as the grin disappeared. Ernest said, very sharply, "Let's see you bend the spoon."

Dash got up. He was drunk now and the rise was unsteady. He said, very softly, "I don't think I could bend the spoon. But when I did things like that I did them for Pinkerton money. Why don't you go roll a hoop in the park?"

He left the table and by the time I got up to follow he was nowhere to be found on the street.

7

Two years earlier, in the late summer of 1937, I had been invited to a theatre festival in Moscow. I showed the cable to Dash and suggested he might like to make his first trip to Europe. I pointed to four handsome volumes he had just bought on the art of the Hermitage. "You could see the pictures for yourself."

"The books will do me fine. Why are you going?"

I said I had never been to Russia, that I wanted to see the Russian theatre.

Dash said, "No, you don't."

"Why do you think I don't?"

He shrugged. "I'll write it down for you some day soon."

A few days later I left for Paris en route to Moscow.

I wanted to get out of Hollywood partly because George Gershwin had died a few weeks before, and although I could not yet believe in the terrible death, I was sleepless with the memory of a night when what we all thought was a mildly sick, overanxious man came downstairs for dinner in a dressing gown and, as usual, went immediately to the piano. I was talking to somebody, only half listening to the piano, when I turned my head: his fingers had moved to the wrong notes for a passage of *An American in Paris*. Startled, I went over to the piano, but by the time I reached it, George had stopped playing and was staring at his hands as if he had never seen them before. Then he looked up and saw me, but I don't think he recognized me and the shock of thinking that kept me from speaking. In a minute, George's brother Ira came into the room and we all went in to dinner. George was a bewildered man that night, but the diagnosis had not as yet been made and there was no further sign of the brain tumor that would kill him a week later.

About the third week I was in Paris, in reply to two letters asking him to tell me why he was so certain I didn't want to see the Russian theatre, Hammett wrote: "I think, I don't know, of course, but I think that you would not betray anybody for any reason about anything—and I am not a man who thinks in such terms—unless somebody offered you a free subway ride to Jersey City and then we'd all be in danger. That's one reason you made this trip, and always will. So have a good wasted time but stop telling yourself you want to see the theatre. You don't. You'll see three plays and I'll bet you'll leave all of them by intermission. Then somebody'll give you a party and if the guests include an electrician or a property man, you'll find him and not want to talk to anybody else. I am told that foreigners like to gather cultivated questions for their cultivated guests, so when they get around to asking you your work methods and such, your face will grow very stern because you won't, thank God, know what they're talking about. Or you will be asked about your theatre experiences, and you'll say you never have had any, and you'll believe what you're saying. The truth is you don't like the theatre except the times when you're in a room by yourself putting the play on paper."

Like, not like, were not the words, but there was

enough truth in what Hammett wrote to worry me. But now, many years and many plays later, I know as little as I knew then about the conflict that would keep me hard at work in a world that is not my world, although it has been my life. I have had great benefits from the theatre, liked and enjoyed many people in it, count a few of them as my close friends, had pleasure in success and excitement even in failure, but I have wandered through it as if I were a kind of stranger. (Except when I was writing, or the plays were in rehearsal: then all the natural instincts are at work the way some people play a musical instrument without a lesson and others, even as children, understand an engine.) Maybe it happened because I started out wanting to write novels and didn't have much interest in the theatre or movies; maybe my own nature does not fit the rushing strong tones of the theatre, although certainly my own tones are often shrill; maybe because I am not good at collaboration, the essence of the theatre; maybe because I like fame, but don't like, and am no good at, its requirements; or maybe vanity of any kind other than my own seems to me at first funny and at last boring. But most of all, the theatre is not a natural world for those who question whatever is meant by glamour. One must, one should, pay fame the respect it demands, or leave it alone and find someplace else to go. I have not been able to do either and thus have often made myself and other people uncomfortable.

It was in those pre-Moscow Paris weeks that I had first met Ernest Hemingway, although his bride-to-be, Martha Gellhorn—we didn't know then that she was to marry him, and I doubt that she was sure of it, either—had crossed on the boat with Dorothy Parker, her husband Alan Campbell, and me. Martha spent a good deal of her time in the boat's gymnasium, where, Dottie said, all of Ernest's ladies began their basic training for the life partnership.

I liked Ernest. It would have been hard for a woman

not to like him if he wanted you to, tried for it. He had just come out of Spain—this was the second year of the Spanish Civil War—and had come up to Paris for a holiday before he and Martha returned to Spain.

And it was that same week that I first met Sara and Gerald Murphy, although I had heard about them for years. I suppose they were in their late forties, remarkable people who seemed to me as original and stylish as they had been described. Years before I met them the Murphys had moved to Europe with their three children to escape their rich, solid background. (Sara's sister, Hoytie Wiborg, was a kind of Henry James heiress in London and Paris society and a rather amusing irritant to the Murphys.) Gerald had become an interesting painter who soon ceased to paint for a high flown reason that everybody explained to me but that I no longer remember. In Paris and on the French Riviera, which they founded as a summer resort, they were the center of a brilliant world of writers and artists attracted by the originality of their style as people. The rules that the Murphys had overturned seemed to anybody of my generation interesting but not important, but they had attracted and influenced Hemingway, Fitzgerald—the Murphys had introduced the one to the other in a famous first meeting where Ernest told Fitzgerald that Zelda was crazy—Benchley, Dorothy Parker, MacLeish, Picasso, Stravinsky, Léger, and many others. Tales were still told of an apartment in Paris the Murphys kept almost empty so that they could redecorate it every month, or for every party, with junk stuff that nobody else had dreamed could be made to look beautiful; of the small dinners they gave in Antibes, one of which Fitzgerald described in *Tender Is the Night;* of the remarkable guests who came for a night and stayed for a summer.

I liked them both. Gerald was witty and almost self-mocking elegant. Sara was pretty and warm and hidden-shrewd. Not long before we met they had lost their two sons, and certainly that strengthened the bonds with their old friends Hemingway and Parker, who did not like each other but who in those weeks were trying hard to mask it from the Murphys. But it was Gerald's often overcivilized hand that kept Ernest and Dottie, when they were drinking, edge-polite, too polite. I think it was my first knowledge of people who dined and drank together and couldn't wait to talk about each other afterwards. Ernest would confide that Alan Campbell acted toward Dottie as if he were the manager of a movie actress or a prize fighter, and Dottie would whisper that Ernest was a God-damned snob—there were, indeed, a great many social names in his conversation, and once an American polo player, arrogant with money and little sense, joined us for an evening until Gerald rapped him away. And almost every night, starting with baklava sweetness, Dottie would try to get Ernest to admit that he'd knocked a few years off his age, or to get Gerald to pretend he'd read somebody she'd invented. It was witty, all of it, but I remember feeling awkward: my generation was perhaps all round duller and certainly less talented, but loyalty, or the rhetoric of it, had come back into fashion with the depression, and these four remarkable people—I don't remember that Martha Gellhorn joined us, perhaps she was not in Paris—came from another world and time.

One night after dinner, when we usually parted, the Campbells and I, led by Ernest, moved around Paris from whiskey to scrambled eggs to their old acquaintances at the Deux Magots or Lilas to a place with blaring, bad jazz. By that time I was drunk and headachy and left a note with a waiter saying goodnight.

I had been asleep for two or three hours when there was a loud pounding on the hotel door. Ernest was there with a bottle of Scotch and a package. He was in good humor and we had a large drink of Scotch from his bottle, a talk about my coming to Spain after Moscow, some conversation I didn't understand about the women in his life, and then he threw the package on my bed.

He said, "The proofs of *To Have and Have Not*. Want to read them? Right now?"

It wasn't that I was so young that year, it was that I was younger than I should have been about respected literary men and I had forgotten that I had told him earlier that evening that when I worked at Liveright's I had swiped the first copy of *In Our Time* as it came from the printer, sitting with it at the office through a forgotten dinner date, taking it home with me to read again that night, coming down to the office at eight o'clock the next morning so anxious to talk about the book that I had forgotten other people wouldn't be there at that hour, and had paced up and down the street, and then run up and down the stairs, until Horace and Julian Messner and Tom Smith finally arrived.

So I was pleased to be sitting up in bed, fighting a hangover, flattered that Ernest had brought his new book for my opinion. He sat by the window, drinking, looking through a magazine, mostly watching me as I read the book. I wanted him to go away and leave the book, but when it was good, which wasn't always, I forgot about him. And it was good, and then suddenly very strange, right before I rubbed my eyes and turned off the lamp as daylight came in the window. I went back and reread two or three pages.

"There are missing pages in these proofs."

Ernest said, "Where?"

He came to the bed and I showed him what I thought was a puzzling jump in story and in meaning.

"Nothing is missing. What made you say that?" His voice had changed, not to sharpness, but to a tone one would use with an annoying child or an intrusive stranger, and these many years later I can still hear the change. I tried to say why I thought what I thought, but I got out only half sentences and even those stopped when he kissed me on the forehead, picked up the page proofs and walked out the door. I was puzzled and hurt and, after a minute, angry. I followed him into the hall and stood staring at him as he waited for the elevator.

He came back toward me, pulled me within arm's length, and said, "I wish I could sleep with you, but I can't because there's somebody else. I hope you understand." He smiled at me, patted my head, went down in the elevator, and I was so surprised that I stood in the hall until it was too late to run down the steps and say—Say what? So I went to wake Dottie in the room next to mine. She shook her head at me for a long time.

"You mean I shouldn't have read it or I shouldn't have said anything?"

"Oh, who wouldn't? How were you supposed to know that Max Perkins persuaded him the book was too long and Ernest wouldn't let Max cut it so he made the cuts himself and they're bad, evidently, and you guessed it. And you've only just met Ernest and nobody told you, poor girl, that you're not allowed to think a comma could be in the wrong place, or that the book isn't the greatest written in our time although that's hard to follow, isn't it, because his previous book was always the greatest?"

I said, "What was that about not sleeping with me? Who asked him? Who the hell even thought about him?"

"Revenge, Lilly. Made him feel better. And if that's all he ever says or does you'll be lucky, because he's not a man who forgives people much."

The next day I left for Moscow, changing trains in Berlin. I had been warned that I might have trouble in Berlin—I had a four or five hour wait and a change of railroad stations—and a young Russian consular officer met me at the station. There was no trouble, or I didn't think so, until the second train was nearing Warsaw and then I went to look for my small trunk. It was missing, the Polish conductor claimed, but certainly, he said, I would receive it in Moscow, the Nazis were not barbarians, a mistake had been made, my name was German, and so on. When the trunk did arrive from Berlin two weeks later the insides had been slashed to pieces, every book had been torn apart, every bottle had been emptied.

Although I have long ago lost the diary of that trip, Dash was right: I did not enjoy the Moscow Theatre Festival, except for a production of *Hamlet* with the Prince played as a fat young man in a torpor. I went to one official party and saw no other Russians. (I had sent off a few letters of introduction, but when they weren't answered I put it down to the Slav habit of postponement.) I did not even know I was there in the middle of the ugliest purge period, and I have often asked myself how that could be. I saw a number of diplomats and journalists but they talked such gobbledygook, with the exception of Walter Duranty and Joseph Barnes, that one couldn't pick the true charges from the wild hatred. Most of them, our diplomats, certainly, were frivolous men who might have functioned well in the Vienna of Franz Joseph. Some of what they said in those days most certainly turned out to be the truth, but it is hard to understand fact from invention when it is mixed with blind bitterness about a place and a people.

I went back to Paris after a few weeks in Prague. My first night in Paris I had dinner with Otto Simon. Simon had been born in Prague as Otto Katz, gone to a German university and become a well-known journalist. When Hitler came in, he moved to Paris, compiled and wrote an interesting book, one of the first about Nazism, called *The Brown Book of the Hitler Terror*. He was a Communist who, the year I met him, was a kind of press chief for the Spanish Republican Government. He was a slight, weary-looking, interesting man who had moved in many circles. At dinner that night a famous and beautiful German movie star crossed to our table to kiss him and to speak with him in German. Otto took for granted that my German was good, and so when she left the table he said, "Please forget what you heard. We were in love with each other when she was young and I was not so *triste*."

He was a brave, kind man who stayed in Spain until the very last days of the Franco victory, when, in New York, a few of us found the bail to buy him out and to send him on to Mexico. After the war he returned to Prague, had an important job in the government, and was executed by the regime who thought up the insane charge of Zionism to kill his independent spirit.

But that was a long time later. That dinner night in Paris he persuaded me that I must go to Spain. It didn't take much persuasion: I had strong convictions about the Spanish war, about Fascism-Nazism, strong enough to push just below the surface my fear of the danger of war.

8

FROM a diary, 1937:

Valencia, October 13

It was a long, dusty trip. Valencia seems quiet and so
far I have not seen an air raid, although last night Steven
and Luigi, from the International Brigades, here on recovery leave, said I should ask the hotel to put me in another
room away from the glass skylight. I tried that this morning, but it got me nowhere so I ate a can of quenelles from
the box of mostly ridiculous canned goods from Paris that
Hemingway told me I must bring with me, but I am sure
he thought I'd have sense enough to buy meat or fish. I
have been nervous, and last night I dreamed of Amélie's
black dress without Amélie in it, floating in and out of the
Marais, speaking to Victor Hugo.

[1968—Amélie Bogeat cleaned and washed for me in
Paris. At this minute, twenty-eight years and two months
later, I am looking at a recipe for chocolate mousse that
she sent me in early 1939, with a letter saying she be-

lieved France was on the edge of war. I had left with
Amélie ten letters to be sent my father in New York so
that he wouldn't know, and worry, about Spain. But a few
weeks later he had to know because I did a radio broadcast from Madrid. In New York, Louis Kronenberger
went with him to the broadcast to help with the fears we
both were certain my father would have. Louis reported
later that my father's only comment was to tell him that
he knew a not too expensive tailor who would make Louis
the dinner jacket my father thought he needed. It might
have been his way of not showing anxiety; it might have
been that he had none.]

Steven and Luigi and a Spanish girl whose name I
never heard took me to a cafe and we drank a great deal
of warm beer. The owner said we could have a supper of
fried sardines. They didn't seem to mind, but the oil was
so rancid I couldn't manage, so I went back to the hotel
for another can of quenelles and everybody thought them
splendid. By midnight we were all tipsy and the girl was
telling Luigi in eight or ten mispronounced English words
that Steven mustn't worry so much because the part could
not mend with the head. I thought I was well out of that
conversation until Luigi shouted at her to quit and Steven
got up and left us. Luigi and the girl walked me to the
hotel and Luigi said I wasn't to worry. I wasn't worried:
increasingly I find myself most comfortable with conversations I don't understand.

October 14

I get up early and go to the dining room for coffee.
Everybody bows and I bow and I can't remember any of
their names or what they are doing here. I know some of
them are journalists, some of them are working for the
government, and most of them are foreigners, but they
swim as one except for a tall, pale young Frenchman and
a German couple who shake hands with affection as they

part each morning in front of the hotel. I have done nothing since I am here and I recognize the signs. I have presented my credentials, as one must, gone once to the Press Office where I was pleasantly welcomed by Constancia de la Mora, had two telephone calls from her suggesting I come back to the office and meet people who might like to meet me, and have not gone. This is nothing new: part the need to make people come to me, part not wanting to seem important. But then why have I come here, what will I see, or do, what good will I be to these people as I eat their food or use their cars or lie on a bed reading Julian Green? I settle it by going for a walk.

A few blocks from the Press Office, where I tell myself I am certainly going this morning, there is a flower market. I stop to buy flowers and some green leaves I have never seen before, and go around a corner and down a strange street and another one. By now I have lost my way and can't get to the Press Office and feel better walking in the hot sunshine watching a cat that is about half a block ahead of me. I didn't hear anything until I saw the cat sit down in the street, its head raised at a queer angle. Then suddenly the cat took off under the grating of a store as a woman with a market push-cart picked up a little girl, threw the girl in the cart, and began to run down an alley. Maybe the child's screams kept me from hearing the sirens, or maybe I had heard them earlier because a long-sensitive tooth made me know that I had clamped my jaws very tight. Two women ran past me and called out something I couldn't understand, and then I began to run toward a square I had never seen before, telling myself that as long as I heard the sirens the planes had not arrived. In the middle of the square I saw a policeman gesturing toward people I couldn't see. I slowed down hoping to figure out what he meant, but I couldn't, and so I ran on toward an open treeless stretch. The policeman was shouting at me now, but I didn't know enough Spanish to understand him. He was angry as I waited for him. I said, *"No sé donde lugar voy."* He pointed under a bench, shoved me, and ran on. As I crawled under the bench, the sirens had stopped. I was lying face down into the heavy smell of my flowers. In the distance I heard a great, swelling sound, as if a storm wave had finished its move into shore. And then another, this time further away, or so I thought. I don't know how many minutes I stayed under the bench, but I knew that being alone there frightened me more than it was worth. I stuck my head out, tried to figure what streets I had crossed, and made a dash across the square. All streets were empty now and I knew that I was acting as I had been warned not to act in an air raid, but I desperately wanted that shabby hotel room because in it were a few dresses, a toothbrush, a raincoat, a few books. It was all that belonged to me in this strange land. It was home.

When I got to the corner of the hotel, I had come to the end of running. I stopped at the convent wall next to the hotel, too troubled with breathing to notice immediately that now the planes were overhead, flying fast. Two Spanish soldiers stood in the door of the convent and one of them was eating from a bunch of grapes. He nodded to me, pointed with his grapes, and said in English, "Italian bastards." As he spoke, one plane dropped down and from it slowly floated what looked like a round gift package. The soldier with the grapes stepped into the street, shook his fist and screamed into the air as the bomb, and another, exploded. Then he turned, called to his friend, and began to smile as he pointed south to four planes coming toward us.

He came toward me. "Ours." He pulled off some grapes, wiped them on his sleeve and handed them to me. "O.K. Now. O.K."

But it wasn't O.K. In the section around the port, about five minutes later, the Italian bombers killed sixty-three people.

October 17

I have been to the Press Office, I have met La Pasion-
ara and paid a visit to Rubio, the Press Chief, who gave
me some candy, and I have dined with the charming and
witty del Vayo and some other government people. A
great many people have told me a great many things—
atrocities on one side and the other; nuns and priests torn
by the limbs in Republican villages; peasants and intellectuals burned alive on Franco's side; why what government
fell when; the fights among the Anarchists and Commu-
nists and Socialists; who is on what side today who wasn't
yesterday—but this is not the way I learn things and so I
have only half listened, although my head will soon come
off from the polite up-and-downs it has been making, and
the fixed smile might grow into a tic. If I have anything to
do here, anything to say or write, I am better off by
myself.

Two days ago, I discovered a pleasant square near a
building that has a large amount of bomb-scarred statuary
in its courtyard. I was staring at the statuary, wondering
how I'd find out about the house, when a man and a
woman in black came either from it or from around the
side of it. The man stopped and looked at me and then
they both moved on. A few steps further, he stopped
again and turned. Then the woman turned and they both
stood watching me. I thought, I've intruded on their house
and I'll go say I'm sorry, but as I moved toward them I
knew I couldn't say that in Spanish. As I got near them,
the woman turned sharply, pulled the man by the sleeve,
and they moved off. I went on toward the pleasant square,
sat reading for about an hour, walked back to the hotel.
As I passed the house with the statuary the man and
woman were standing in the courtyard. The man came
toward me, the woman moved behind him. When I smiled
they stood still, and after a minute the woman said something to the man, who put his hand to his head in a salute,

75

clicked his heels and marched behind a broken statue of a horse and peered from behind its injured head. They're having a nice time about me, I thought, but why?

October 19

Last night Steven and Luigi, the girl and I walked down to the bombarded port area. (The planes had been around all afternoon and the mess was new and looked hot.) The filthy indignity of destruction, I thought. is the real immorality, as I slipped and turned my ankle. Steven said he would take me back to the hotel and wouldn't allow Luigi and the girl to come along.

When I had wrapped my ankle in a torn pair of pants, I sat on a chair and Steven propped my foot up on another chair, and gave me a pain-killer from his pocket. Then he told me what the girl had meant the other night by the mind not healing the part: he had been wounded in the penis, the wound repaired, but the future unknown. He said he didn't have a regular girl, didn't want one now, but would want one when he got back to Kansas City and didn't yet know if he could ever have one again.

I said, "I never thought of anybody being wounded in the penis. How little I know about any of this. Just feeling and jabber."

Steven smiled. He borrowed Julian Green and said goodnight.

October 20

I went up to Benicasim this morning with Gustav Regler. Regler had been a captain in the German army during the First World War, had become a fairly well-known novelist after the war, and had left Germany when Hitler came in. Now a high-ranking officer and a hero of the German section of the International Brigades, he had been badly injured here, in what was called "the little war," when his car was bombed to pieces going up to the front lines. Driving fast toward Benicasim, we talked about writers and writing and I was sorry when we reached Benicasim at dinnertime. This safely based recovery hospital is mostly occupied by the International Brigades wounded and some of their wives have been allowed to join them here.

They obviously respected Regler and when, in a sad little after-dinner meeting, he made me and my visit too important, one man, with a huge scar on his face, rose to say that they were sure that now many other intellectuals would come to Spain and go home and write the truth and Mr. Roosevelt would then send the guns and planes to a people who were fighting for freedom. Before he finished, an older man got up and said didn't my people have sense enough to know that it was here that Fascism would live or die, no charity was needed, just enough to let them kill it here, save American lives later on, and would I please tell that to Roosevelt? When I didn't answer, he repeated the question slowly and carefully, adding that if the United States sent supplies, the Spaniards and the International Brigades would do the job, were willing to do the dying, I must say that immediately. He choked and coughed and waited for an answer. I said that wasn't the way things worked, it didn't matter what people like me said or thought. They were silent for a second and then a woman applauded politely and everybody went off to bed.

I was given a straw bed next to the Prague-born wife of a Yugoslav officer. Lying there, with a small candle between us on the floor, we talked of my recent weeks in Prague. I told her about the famous doctor and his wife with whom I had stayed, their friends, the visits to the opera, and concerts, and my shock when they spoke of Hitler's domination of Czechoslovakia as almost certain, and seemed so resigned and passive in the face of it.

She said, "I have not lived in Prague for many years.

Goodnight." She gave me the candle for my side of the bed and turned away from me.

I could not read by the candle, so I smoked until the candle went out. Then the Czech lady said, "Of course, I know Dr. ——. He is a good man, a Jew, impressed with his fool of a wife. Who were the other people you saw?"

I told her about two brothers who owned a newspaper, and a music critic, and an educated divorced lady, friend to the doctor's wife.

She said, "Yes, I could have guessed. The brothers are related to me. Liberal pigs. Pigs. They will kill all the rest of us with their nothing-to-be-done-about-it stuff. They will save themselves when the time comes, the dirty pigs. There isn't a man in this hospital, if he lives, who will ever be all well again. Those dirty pigs. Goodnight."

I didn't sleep much that night thinking about what she said and how this war was like no other. Men had come great distances to fight here and when the war was over, if they came out alive, or with enough arms or legs or eyes to seem alive, there would be no world for them and no reward. They seemed to me noble people. Because I had never used that word before, it came hard to say it to myself even in the dark, and, as if I had had a vision of what I had missed in the world, I began to cry.

The next morning Busch, the American doctor, and Thomas, the political cheerleader, insisted I come on a round of visits to the wounded. The ward was large. Leading off it was a room with beaver board partitions for the very badly wounded and in one of them were two young men. One was a Canadian and the other was a New York boy with the small white face that is so common in poor people who live in cities. The Canadian had lost his left foot but he didn't know it yet. The New York boy was lying on his side, breathing hard, his face moving in pain. I was afraid to look at him, and when Busch went over to examine him I stood by Thomas, a fat little fellow who himself had just recovered from a bad wound in the spine. The New York boy cried out and then screamed.

I closed my eyes and Thomas said. "He was shot up. Kidneys, thigh, neck. Thigh wound won't close right."

"Isn't there any dope for him?"

Thomas nodded. "Sure. Busch will give him something. But the kid's a hypochondriac."

October 21

Last night I went looking for Luigi and Steven, but they are not to be found and I guess maybe they've gone back to their brigades. The hotel clerk says Otto Simon came by and will come again. I didn't know what to do with myself most of today, so I took a notebook to the pretty, small square and wrote about Benicasim.

I looked up from my notebook. The statuary-courtyard man and woman are on a bench opposite me. She is knitting something small and ugly brown. He is intently poking a cane into the bush in front of him. As I see him, he looks up at me. The staring has gone on long enough. I bow, he bows, the woman bows, he bows again, the woman bows again, I go back to my notebook.

In a minute he is standing over me. His voice is a loud boom. "*Madame, faites-vous un croquis?*"

"*Non, monsieur.*"

He peers down at the notebook. "Ah, you are English," he says in a British accent.

"No, I am an American."

"What a miracle."

The woman has put down her knitting. As he sits down beside me, she half rises. But she settles back as he speaks severely to her.

"Lita!" He turns to me. "That is not her name. What is not your name?"

"Pamela Gigglewitz."

"*Madame* Gigglewitz?"

79

"Once upon a time."

"You are wise."

I thank him and shift on the bench. He pokes around with his cane, frowning, thoughtful. Then he points to the woman.

"She is a nun *fanée*. But still of the blackest faith. She will ask me if you are Catholic."

The non-Lita said in an unexpectedly deep voice, in good English, "Return please to your bench."

He rose to his feet, laughed, and suddenly bellowed so loud that two men a distance from us stopped and stared. "Answer on demand."

I was so startled by the noise that I didn't know whether he was speaking to me or to the woman.

I said, "No, I am not a Catholic. I was born a Jew," at the same minute that she shouted to me, "Are you of the faith?"

The man said, *"Bon.* O.K. Ssh." Then he moved rapidly out toward the street. The woman followed. When they got near the exit of the square they both turned and stood staring at me. I realized they were the first people I had ever seen who were of no age that I could guess because something had happened to their faces.

October 22

Luis and I first met at seven o'clock this morning when he arrived two hours late, to tell me that he was my official government guide and protector on the trip to Madrid. (He meant he was the chauffeur.) At four in the afternoon, coming down the long hot stretch of road to Aranjuez, I was tired of him. I was tired, too, of the sun and the road and the warm, squashed grapes lying between us on the seat. We had talked too much: of the war, of automobiles, of my passport, of the long, purplish plus-fours that he had bought from a hotel clerk in Valencia. I had been polite about the plus-fours but had not been polite about his driving, which was based on a personal relationship with the car—sometimes he loved it and gave it frightening freedom, and sometimes he punished it with twists and curses, and once he beat the hood with his foot. He had been polite about my cigarettes, but had not liked my English. He said over and over again that I was the only American he couldn't understand. He said I talked like a Swede, which isn't true, but ever since early morning when he peered over the first road guard's shoulder to look at my passport, he had wanted to make a mystery of me. He liked it that way.

We had talked of Brunete. Luis said he had been there as the chauffeur of a General. He said the General thought him brave and he thought the General brave but the General, like all Spaniards except himself, knew nothing about automobiles and, therefore, could not appreciate good driving. That was very smart of the General, who is fighting around Huesca now but who would not be if Luis were still driving his car.

But by four o'clock we were too tired and hungry to bother with each other anymore. The mountain road was winding down and Luis dozed from time to time. It is not a good idea to sleep on the Madrid-Valencia road, and when we came too close to an army truck, I shoved him angrily with my elbow. He woke up, put his hand on the horn and kept it there. The truck didn't move because there was no place to move to, and our back wheels scraped the mountain fence as we speeded up to pass it. We passed it and Luis twisted the wheel violently, ignored the next curve to shout back at the truck, to explain to me once again that all Spaniards are brave soldiers and bad drivers.

My head had hit the side of the car as we careened.

"For God's sake," I said, "let me drive."

He said, "A woman could not drive this road."

We had been over this several times during the day and

my voice was angry now because my head hurt and I told myself I hadn't come to Spain to die in a car with Luis.

I said, "I've been driving a car since I was fourteen years old."

He said, "All right. But the automobile change too much in all that time. The picture in the passport book look older than it says there. You lie in passport book, yes?"

I laughed too long and too loud. I was sick of the remarks about my passport. When I stopped laughing, he looked at me.

"You need to eat."

I said I didn't need to eat. It has been hard to eat. I can't get used to the smell of the rancid olive oil. Most of the time I feel light and pleasant, but I guess the bad part of hunger is setting in because the last four or five days I have felt weak and irritable. Luis said I could do what I wanted, but he was going to find a place to eat. I said there wasn't much to get from these people along the road, they needed the little they had, so why didn't we wait until we got to Madrid?

He looked at me. "If they have nothing, they will say it. If they have something, they will give it. That is Spanish."

We rode on for a long time without passing a house. Then suddenly, as we came out of the shadows of a hill, the inevitable church appeared, high and handsome above the miserable village.

Luis laughed. "Where there is a church that high, there are people that poor. They will give us something."

We wheeled off the road, went bouncing into the ruts of the little square around the church. This village was like all the rest: the fine church in the dusty square, a few heavy-laden mules, a few children in doorways, dogs sleeping in the gutters, one store that maybe before the war had things in it, the sun that gave no light to the dark houses.

An Unfinished Woman

Nobody paid much attention to us except the starving dogs. They moved to the car and stood looking at us. Hot and aching, I groaned my way out of the car and sat down suddenly on the running board. Luis was already across the street eyeing the most likely house, and when a group of soldiers came out of a house and spoke to him, he disappeared. I sat on the running board and stared at the ground, hoping the dizziness would go away. A little girl came along, leading a donkey towards a high hill facing me. I watched her, and it was only when she was halfway up the hill that I saw where the bombs had been on another day. Two houses were mostly gone, and the child turned her head away as she passed them. I patted a dog whose bones were out beyond his frame, and a very little boy, unaccountably fat, came close and said, *"Salud."*

I said, *"Salud, niño,"* but he said *salud* so many times that I stopped answering him. He was funny standing there, singing it, pleased with himself.

I fell off the running board and a man came towards me from a basement near the car. He had a glass of wine in his hand and he pushed it at me and smiled. I was afraid that it would make me even dizzier, but I drank it. It was raw and bitter and hard to manage. When Luis came bouncing back, looking like a fool in the purple plus-fours and army cap, the man poured him a glass of wine.

Luis was pleased with himself. "It is as I tell you. One hundred O.K. Two eggs and she give a potato for you. I escort you."

We went up a flight of whitewashed steps into a room so dark that I had to wait at the door before I could see my way in. There was a stone fireplace, a bed, a chair, a table, a brilliant red vase. Four women stood around the table as if they had been part of a ritual that was momentarily suspended. They bowed to me. Another woman, sitting at the fireplace, holding a pan, rose and shook hands with me. She was a plump, youngish woman with

83

very bleached hair, black for two inches at the roots. She motioned to the chair, indicated the pan.

I said to Luis, "Please tell her that I do not want any food. Say that I thank her very much, but she must not waste it on me because I am not hungry—"

He looked at me with such contempt that I stopped speaking and sat down. But the blonde woman had understood me. Her English was heavy with that almost German accent that Spaniards so often have.

"It is an honor to share with a friend of the Republic of Spain."

Luis had found a *bota* of wine and was drinking it fast through the funnel as he chatted with the ladies. I didn't understand much of what he said, but I knew he was talking about me because the country women looked at me with shy interest from time to time. The bleached lady paid no attention to Luis, except once when she turned her head and told him to lower his voice, obviously because he interfered with her hospitable monologue to me: she was from Madrid, she therefore knew about American ladies; she did not like this country village, but she had brought her children here for safety, which had been a foolish decision because they were bombed almost every day; her aunt was one of the women at the table and was a bastard Fascist because of the bastard priests; she liked American shoes, how much had mine cost, someday she would have such a pair; her husband had left her when she was nineteen, but who cared; did I have information about Chile where she had a cousin with whom she had been in love; it was for him she had first dyed her hair, but no good had come of that except a pregnancy which she had fixed herself, and now all she had for the passion were two postal cards from Chile. She had scooped the potato from the pan, put the egg on top, decorated it with saffron leaves. It was the first thing I had eaten with pleasure in many weeks, and when I told her that she kissed me, and then turned to listen to something Luis was telling the four women.

"So. He says you write. What do you write?"

Luis said, "On the stage, write, write, write." He took a pencil from his pocket and wrote on the table and made faces with his mouth to imitate acting, and then rose to imitate actors taking curtain calls. He did it for so long that I sighed and the blonde lady laughed.

Luis was annoyed. "So. O.K. Laugh. It is written in the passport that she write. Also, she say that she makes writing in the cinema, but yet she do not know the favorites I name to her. But—" He seemed to have a change of mind, because he now began to speak in Spanish and I heard the name of Charles Chaplin.

The blonde lady said to me, "What an honor. You bring here his family greetings."

I said to Luis, "What are you saying about me?"

"I say you say you are cousin to Charlie."

"And I say I did not say I was cousin to Charlie. I've met Mr. Chaplin and that's all."

Luis said, "There is a saying in Andalusia from where I was born. Goes like 'Do not make yourself so small because in doubt you are so big.'"

"There is a saying in Louisiana from where I was born that you are sometimes a foolish man."

The blonde lady was amused. "He did not say you were cousin to Charlie. He said you were sister to Charlie."

"O.K.," said Luis. "So I gave pleasure to old women here." He saluted. "Come. My orders say Madrid before the night."

The blonde lady was leaning over my head. Now I felt her part my hair at the top and then on the sides. "You do something to your hair?"

"Sometimes I have it bleached."

"What color you born with?"

"I've forgotten. Something like this, I guess."

She patted my hair back in place. "Soon you will need

bleach. That was the work I do. That is where I learn the English. Go to the Calle de Isaac, Maria's. She work good on the hair. Tell her—" She stopped and her face grew sad. Then she smiled and said, "Tell her nothing but do good job for my American friend."

We kissed each other and the four ladies of the table followed us downstairs. I had left my shoes for the blonde lady under the chair. She found them as Luis was making a wild swing around the square, and the last I saw of her was from a window as she shouted for me to come back for my shoes and then, as I waved no from the car, she clapped her hands in applause.

[Four or five days later—I tried to find Maria's. But almost every house in the three or four blocks where it should have been had been bombed away.]

Madrid, October 23

It was after eight o'clock last night when Luis and I got to Madrid. He said I was not to take any wooden nickels and certainly we would meet again. There was a note from Hemingway at the hotel desk telling me where he was eating dinner and inviting me to join him. But I was very tired and fell asleep immediately, only slightly conscious of rumbling sounds in the distance, not thinking much about them until the next day, and even then forgetting to ask what they were.

Early this morning, a young man from the Spanish Press Office came to tell me that Columbia Broadcasting had agreed to give them radio time for me that night and the government people were very pleased because they hadn't had much luck getting air time in America. I wanted to see University City, but I got tired before I got there, and when I came back to the hotel Ernest was in the lobby with a bottle of whiskey for me, and an invitation to have dinner that night at the apartment of an English newspaper correspondent. Madrid bullfight people had given Hemingway a piece of beef. He said I'd better come and share it because I wouldn't see beef again.

[1968—My diary does not have the name of the English correspondent where I went that night for dinner, but he was a large man with that overknowing air that journalists so often have, and most British have, whatever they are.]

When I arrived Ernest was already there, and Martha Gellhorn, looking handsome in her well-tailored pants and good boots. I took along two cans of sardines and two cans of pâté, and Ernest said he was glad I had brought in canned goods from Paris because John Dos Passos hadn't brought in any food but had eaten everybody else's, and he and Dos Passos had had an ugly fight about that.

The beef from the bull was tough, but the wine was good. I began to hear the noise during the English sugary pudding. I dropped my spoon and Ernest told me that I was hearing my first bombardment.

The Englishman, Ernest, and Martha went out to the balcony to watch—every night at almost the same hour the Franco people bombarded the telephone building— and I sat on the couch in the living room with my head bent low and my eyes shut, hoping I could control the panic I felt. Several times Ernest called to me to come out on the balcony, it was a beautiful sight, he said, and once Martha called, and once the Englishman came to the door and stood looking at me and went mumbling back to Ernest. Ernest came to the door, stared at me, opened his mouth as if to speak, changed his mind, and went back to the beauty of the shelling. After a while the phone rang, and the Englishman said the man at the radio station said the station itself was being hit, it would be too dangerous for me to come there, so would I tell the chauffeur who was already on his way to take shelter somewhere?

About ten minutes later the doorbell rang, a servant

admitted the chauffeur, and I went down the stairs with him.

When I was a few flights down, Ernest shouted at me, "You can't go into that shelling." He ran down the steps toward me. "Come back here."

I said I wasn't going to come back, it was important for me to do the broadcast, they probably couldn't get the time on another night. Ernest was holding me by the arm. Then he dropped my arm and said softly, "So you have *cojones*, after all. I didn't think so upstairs. But you have *cojones*, after all."

I said, "Go to hell with what you think."

When the broadcast was over and I was back at the hotel, Ernest knocked on my door. We had a few drinks and I kept wanting to tell him that I would have gone into far more dangerous places to get out of that apartment that night, but I didn't tell him.

[Although I saw Hemingway often in Madrid and a number of times in the years after, I don't think he liked me ever again, and I'm not sure what I felt about him, either.]

October 28

Last night I packed a jewelry case—what a ridiculous thing to have brought to Spain—with a few things I thought I would need for my trip to the front lines. I took a bath, washed my hair, and was drying it when Otto Simon came to see me. We took a long walk. Madrid is a sad city, particularly at night. Otto said all great cities look plague-like in a war, much worse than small towns or country villages.

He said, "Why are you going up to the front?"

I said the Press Office had asked me, I thought I should go, I didn't really know.

"Have courage enough not to go. It is a foolish, dangerous waste."

"I don't want to go, but I haven't guts enough to tell them that."

"I'll tell them in the morning. Don't worry. I'll say I ordered you not to go."

I thanked him and felt much better. We were standing now in the terrible rubble of University City. He sat down on a pile of rock.

"You don't look well, Otto. Is something the matter?"

"Ach. I've been sick for years. In my forties I am an old man."

"It must be hard to be a Communist."

"Yes. Particularly here."

"How long have you been?"

"I can't remember, it's so long ago. A young boy, almost a child."

He got up and took my arm and pressed it hard. "Don't misunderstand. I owe it more than it owes me. It has given me what happiness I have had. Whatever happens, I am grateful for that."

[1968—When I read of his execution in Prague, in 1952, I remembered the passion with which he spoke that night and hoped that it carried him through his time in jail, his day of death.]

November 3

There doesn't seem to be any sense staying here longer. I have done all the dutiful things—spoken to a group of International Brigade people, made three recordings which will be translated, gone to a nursery and two hospitals, made a speech to be broadcast to Paris, had the forever sardine dinners with government people who said that I and all like me must explain, write, plead that the United States and France must send arms immediately. God in Heaven, who do they think I am, any of us?

November 4

I am going back to Valencia tomorrow so I went around to get my coat from the woman who was fixing the lining. I took her a can of beef soup and she gave me a little green bottle in which there must once have been perfume. Walking back to the hotel, I was shocked to see that a whole block was almost entirely destroyed since I had been past it a week before. I stopped in front of what had been a fine nineteenth-century house converted to apartments, and asked a woman who was standing in the broken doorway when it had been destroyed. She said that the night before twenty-seven people had been killed and nine wounded. I asked her if I could go inside. She shrugged and said she had nothing to do with the house, she came from another neighborhood.

I was careful, I thought, about climbing the broken stairs, but as I got to the second floor, a step crashed under me, and I leaped past it for the landing. Directly in front of me a door was open. The floor seemed safe, but the pleasant center room was a tangle of overturned furniture, and the smell of scorched material was fruity and sour. I called out but nobody answered. I had seen many bombed houses from the outside, but I had never before been inside one and I stood there thinking that the thrown-about objects made their own formal design: a woman's hat was lying next to three daguerreotypes in a triple frame; an unbroken blue tile was on the edge of a table; a couch cover was burned and wet; a bowl of limp lettuce was sitting in a chair. On the burned couch were two small china bottles, with roses painted on one side; a book, printed in French, *La Vie de Mireille*, was open on the floor and on top of it was an overturned kitchen colander with a few grains of cooked rice at the bottom; the skirt of a print dress was on a fallen ironing board; next to it were a white table napkin and a large key. All around my feet were pictures of people in the clothes of other times, other places. I picked up the china bottles with the painted roses, and a daguerreotype of a young girl, and started down the stairs, jumping past the bad step onto what I thought was a good step. I went crashing to the bottom. The noise was very loud and a man came into the hall followed by two children. They stared at me as I struggled up from the broken wood. The bottles were not harmed, although the top of one was badly chipped.

I said to the man, "Where are the people who lived in the first apartment?" He shook his head.

I held up the bottles. "I would like to have something to take back to America"—but the man moved away.

I said to the children, "Where are the people who lived in the first apartment?"

The younger boy said, "Two ladies. They die."

"In the bombing?"

"I don't remember."

[1968—Transcribing these notes from the diary of that day in Spain, I cross to the fireplace mantel and look at the china bottles and the picture of the young girl. I have carried them with me to many houses for many years.]

Valencia, November 6

It was nice to come back to Valencia, maybe because air raids frighten me less than the nightly bombardments in Madrid. The people in the hotel dining room seemed like old friends and I eat now at the same table with the handshaking German couple, a nervous, minor aide from the Press Office, and an English doctor who has come here to supervise the medical supplies sent down by English organizations. I can't understand much of what the English doctor says, but then he doesn't say much. Foreigners here are not as famous or as important as the ones in Madrid and so there is no big talk and one doesn't have to know or listen to everybody's history.

Last night Constancia took me to a political meeting of

about fifty people. I don't know why she asked me because I was the only foreigner there. A dour-looking young man was appointed my translator, but he didn't translate much except the occasional sharp gibes and the one impassioned fight. An elderly Spaniard made an elaborate speech of thanks to two Russians sitting in the back row. He said the Russian planes and guns were of excellent quality, splendid products of socialism, but, unfortunately, that could not always be said of the advisers and technicians that came with them. A young man rose to deny that, another rose to shout him down, there was a great deal of easily understood carryings-on about who was entitled to the floor, and it was finally taken by the man with the deepest voice. He said ingratitude made his ears sharp with pain, but what else could one expect from a Spaniard who had spent his early life in the conservative great houses of England and his later life in the cafes of Paris? He apologized to the Russians, which was amusing because they had long before left the room.

November 8

Rubio has arranged a place for me on the Thursday plane to Barcelona. I have twice put off my departure: each day I tell myself that I will stay until the war is over and be of some use, but at night, when I don't feel well, dizzy and weak, I want very much to leave. I am not hungry anymore, except early in the morning, and this morning I took out my last Paris cans—flageolets, anchovies, brandied peaches. I began to wolf the beans. Without knowing that I did it, I had locked the door of my room, and maybe that was why I felt sick after the first large spoonful. I put the beans aside, bought a withered orange from a street stand, and took my notebook to the pretty square. I must have been there a couple of hours when I saw the strange couple—the nun *fanée* and the man in black—sitting opposite me, and I knew I had come to the square because I wanted to see them again. The woman was knitting on the same ugly brown affair and the man was playing with an abacus.

As I looked up, the man bowed and held out the abacus. "I count the days of my life. Then I count my father's money. What do you read?"

."Good morning. Good morning, madame."

He rose. "Madame? Hah! Answer my question without fear."

"Did you ask me a question?"

"Most certainly. Trust me."

I said I would trust him, but I didn't remember the question. Very patiently, speaking the words by over-shaping his mouth, he said, "What do you read?"

"I am not reading. I am writing."

"So." He went back to his abacus. After a second he rose and leaped toward my bench.

"Do you approve of Ralph Waldo Emerson?"

I laughed.

He said, "You find him amusing?"

"No. I find your question unexpected."

"Is it your habit never to answer?"

"No," I said. "It is rather my habit to answer too readily. I've never read much of Emerson. Some of what I've read I like, some of it seems to me pompous."

" 'Pom-pousse'? I do not know the word. Perhaps it will come back to me at bedtime when I eat." He suddenly pointed at the woman. "A greed, she is a greed."

The woman said something to him in Spanish, he answered, then he crossed to stand in front of her and shouted down at her. She went back to her knitting and he sat down next to me.

"My father is very rich. Bottles and many other matters. We were sent away here when they departed." He leaned close and whispered to me. "Very rich, very. Do you know where you are? You are in Valencia. Often I do not know where I am, but I prefer to be on the country estate. She mounted upon me first when I was at the age of twelve, the nun *fanée. Elle m'a monté quand j'avais douze ans. Triste, n'est-ce pas?*"

The nun *fanée* got slowly to her feet and moved down the path toward the exit. The man rose immediately and began to run toward her. He ran past her, left the square, and I could see him running very fast down the boulevard.

Tonight I took the peaches, two cans of anchovies, a box of crackers to the dinner table. I asked the handshaking German to open them, but he put his hands in his lap and smiled. I passed them to the young man from the Press Office, but he shook his head. I was puzzled and thought I had offended all of them until the English doctor wrote something in his address book and passed it to me. "They are shy about taking other people's food. Open the cans yourself and pass them around." I started to open the anchovies, but the key got stuck. The doctor opened the cans, and gave them back to me. Nobody would have an anchovy, but each passed the can to the next person with great politeness. When the can came back to the Englishman, he kicked me under the table and said, "You are leaving tomorrow. You have brought these down to have a kind of party. You will be unhappy if we don't share your party, yes?"

I liked him very much as he rose and served each person one anchovy and a cracker. Everbody ate very slowly, and there was no talk. I served the peaches and they stared at their plates, almost as if they were frightened to eat. There were still a few anchovies and so I gave one to the German lady, one to her husband, one to the press attaché. There wasn't any for the doctor or for me. The German immediately put his anchovy on my plate and the German lady leaned over to give hers to the doctor.

The doctor said, "No, thank you. In England we eat them as a savory and I don't like them. Miss Hellman told me that she doesn't like them, either."

I said that was true, I was sick of anchovies, and suddenly both the doctor and I were talking at once. It was a long time before they finished their anchovies, and when the oil of the can was passed around, I heard the German lady make a sound of pleasure. I didn't want a peach, but there was such disbelief when I said so that I ate part of one. This small party had taken an hour and had acted on my table companions as if they had drunk a case of champagne. For the first time in the weeks I had known them they chatted and laughed, and the German told an elaborate joke that everybody pretended to understand. As we left the table, we all shook hands. At the door, I turned to speak to somebody and saw that the German lady was wrapping my half peach in a piece of paper. She handed it to her husband. He shook his head and gave it back and she gave it back to him and this time he took it and kissed the hand that gave it to him. The doctor had waited at the door for me and had seen what I had seen.

In the hall he said, "My God. Hunger is awful."

November 11

Rubio telephoned at five this morning to say that for security reasons the plane, scheduled to leave at noon for Barcelona, would take off in an hour. I was still packing in the airport, and writing farewell notes that I will mail from Paris. Barcelona looked lovely and Rubio said he would show me the city before the train left for France, but after we had walked for a while I got so dizzy that we sat down on a bench until an army car passed us and Rubio asked for a ride to the station. As I got on the train, Rubio introduced me to the tall young French journalist I had sometimes seen in the hotel dining room. As the train pulled out, I knew I would probably never see Spain again, and Rubio's sad, owl face, staring up as the car window went past him, seemed to me a symbol of his country's defeat.

The Frenchman and I, in the same compartment, were as concerned as strangers usually are that they will be bored with each other. I read a book, he slept, he read a book, I slept, and when I woke up he was staring out the window with an empty wine bottle on his lap. He told me he was leaving Spain after a year and a half because he had tuberculosis and was going straight into a hospital in Paris. I said that a friend—I was talking of Hammett— had had tuberculosis, was now cured, it wasn't the disease it had once been, and so on, cheery, but he didn't answer and we didn't talk again until the train pulled into Toulouse.

It made me uncomfortable to arrive in Toulouse, so safe, so untouched by war. The young Frenchman and I wandered around the railroad station long after our bags were cleared. We both wanted to leave immediately, but there wasn't anything but a milk train for Paris, so we decided to spend the night in Toulouse and made a booking for the morning train.

He found us a hotel near the station, good enough to have a bath down a long hall. I stayed in the bath so long that I came out staggering, as if I were drunk. The Frenchman was sitting in my room as I half fell through the door. He helped me to the bed and I tried to light a cigarette but I couldn't hold the match steady.

I said, "It's like being drunk."

He said, "Too little food, and other feelings. Rest a bit."

After a while, I said, "What's your name? Rubio told me but I often can't remember names."

"Pascal. Centuries ago, which is where my family lives, such a name was a road between reason and the Church. I know Toulouse very well. My grandparents lived here. There's a fine restaurant. Let's go and have cassoulet and good wine. We will feel better and sleep well."

It was, indeed, a good restaurant, nineteenth-century rich in dark walls and bright chandeliers, the customers so nice and fat. Pascal ordered Marennes oysters and nothing ever tasted better. We toasted each other in wine and his long, sick-sour face began to have color, and sometimes he would smile to himself.

"Each Sunday my grandparents would bring me to this restaurant. My grandfather supplied it with geese and chickens. They are both dead now from tuberculosis. My mother, too, in Paris later. What did your family die of?"

"My mother and aunt from cancer. I don't know about the others. Everybody dies from something."

"No, they don't. I had two friends who died because they wanted to. I am going to be homesick for Spain. There people are dying for a reason. I tried to be a soldier, but they wouldn't take me in the Brigades. So I am a not good journalist. I bore you."

"No. It's that I don't know what to say that is sensible. How old are you?"

The waiter said, "Pascal has twenty years," as he popped the lid off the cassoulet and brought the dish down for us to see and smell.

Pascal laughed. "Twenty-five. And you, Cowboy, have two hundred."

The waiter laughed, "Not until next year."

The first taste of the cassoulet was wonderful, but on the third taste I began to sweat and knew I was near to vomiting.

In the waves of vomit that were coming close to my throat, I heard Pascal's voice say, "I am sorry. I am sick."

When I had choked back the waves and knew I wouldn't be sick at the table, I looked up and saw Pascal on the sidewalk, his shoulders rising and falling as if he were in pain. Cowboy was standing at a distance from him, but when he came close and put his hand on Pascal's arm, Pascal moved away. I sat at the table for a long time, and when I was ready to leave Cowboy said the check had been paid, not to worry, and maybe cassoulet wasn't a proper dish "to reenter civilization." Back at the hotel, I knocked on Pascal's door, but he didn't answer. I went to bed sure that I would see him on the morning train.

But he was not at the station and was not on the train. Two days later, in Paris, I called his office. Three telephone calls later—I didn't know Pascal's last name—a very irritable man told me that he was in a hospital and gave me the address. That afternoon I went around to the hospital, almost opposite the hotel on the Rue Jacob where my husband and I had once lived. My French has always been bad, sparse and timid, the accent still patois New Orleans, and the French enjoy not understanding me. The nun at the desk had a good, long joke with me that day until she finally said that my friend was, indeed, in the hospital, but was too ill to see anybody. I left him a note with my address, asking if I could come and see him soon again, but I did not hear from him. A week later I went back to the hospital and an older nun told me that he was dead. She said that he had refused to see his father, had often, in the final days, thought he was in Spain, had died alone, had refused the last rites.

9

MOST people coming out of a
war feel lost and resentful. What has been a minute-to-minute confrontation with yourself, your struggle with
what courage you have against discomfort, at the least,
and death at the other end, ties you to the people you
have known in the war and makes, for a time, all others
seem alien and frivolous. Friends are glad to see you
again, but you know immediately that most of them have
put you to one side, and while it is easy enough to say
that you should have known that before, most of us don't,
and it is painful. You are face to face with what will
happen to you after death.

I had, from so short and relatively safe a visit to Spain,
little right to such feelings, but I had them, and the few
weeks I spent in Paris when I came out were unpleasant.
But Paris was never my city, and at the time I told myself
that was in part my reason for depression over the pieties
of Léon Blum, the fashionable parties being given for
Spanish orphans, the sad chatter among intellectuals as

they assured one another that the Republic of France would never allow the Republic of Spain to be defeated. I crossed to London.

On my first night in London I went to dinner at the house of an old friend. Louise and I had grown up together, and if she had married for money and nothing else, the money boy never did anything worse than laugh in the wrong places. The people at the table were, I thought, intelligent enough to eat with, which in those days in London didn't have to be very intelligent in exchange for a French chef.

Louise told the table that I had just come out of Spain. A man to her right said the English version of "Really" several times and then, "I've never been able to fathom the issues."

Louise, nervous, said, "Perhaps Lillian will tell you."

The man said, "Which side did you choose to visit, Miss Hellman? Each has an argument, I dare say."

I said, "I chose Franco, of course. He's got more money."

Louise's husband said, "Now, now, no harm intended, I'm sure—" and a lady opposite me, hurrying in, said, "I'd love to go to Spain again, the Prado, Toledo. Is it very interesting there now?"

After a minute a titled gentleman sitting next to me, in an accent as clear as can be managed with a mouth constructed of hot gruel, said, "You didn't answer my wife's question."

It isn't easy to be ruder than upper-class Englishmen, although I told myself that wasn't any reason for not trying, but as I opened my mouth to say, "Who could have guessed you had a wife?", I thought, My life, all I felt in Spain, is going out in drip-drops, in nonsense, and I suddenly was in the kind of rampage anger that I have known all my life, still know, and certainly in those days was not able, perhaps did not wish, to control. I left the table so fast that I turned over my chair, left the house so fast that I forgot my coat and was not cold on a winter night, threw myself down so hard on the hotel bed that I slipped to the floor, had a painful ankle and didn't care.

If I have remembered that unimportant evening in London, it's because I had broken my ankle and was in bed, or a chair, for the next few weeks.

Nothing, of course, begins at the time you think it did, but for many years I have thought of those days in the lonely London hotel room as the root-time of my turn toward the radical movements of the late thirties. (I was late: by that period many intellectuals had made the turn. So many, in fact, that some were even turning another way.) It saddens me now to admit that my political convictions were never very radical, in the true, best, serious sense. Rebels seldom make good revolutionaries, perhaps because organized action, even union with other people, is not possible for them. But I did not know that then and so I sat down to confirm my feelings with the kind of reading I had never seriously done before. In the next few years, I put aside most other books for Marx and Engels, Lenin, Saint-Simon, Hegel, Feuerbach. Certainly I did not study with the dedication of a scholar, but I did read with the attention of a good student, and Marx as a man and Engels and his Mary became, for a while, more real to me than my friends.

In 1939, soon after *The Little Foxes,* I bought a Westchester estate, so called—large properties were cheaper in those days than small ones—and turned it into a farm. Hammett, who disliked cities even more than I did, came to spend most of his time there, and maybe the best of our life together were the years on the farm. At night, good-tired from writing, or spring planting, or cleaning chicken houses, or autumn hunting, I would test my reading on Dash, who had years before, in his usual thorough fashion, read all the books I was reading, and a great many more. They must have been dull and often irritating questions I threw at him—my father had once said that I lived within a question mark—but Hammett used to say he didn't mind the ragging tone I always fall into when I am trying to learn, because it was the first time in our life together I had been willing to stay awake past ten o'clock.

But this time the ragging, argumentative tone came for a reason I was not to know about for another ten years: a woman who was never to be committed was facing a man who already was. For Hammett, as he was to prove years later, Socialist belief had become a way of life and, although he was highly critical of many Marxist doctrines and their past and present practitioners, he shrugged them off. I was trying, without knowing it, to crack his faith, sensed I couldn't do it, and was, all at one time, respectful, envious, and angry. He was patient, evidently in the hope I would come his way, amused as he always was by my pseudo-rages, cold to any influence. I do not mean there were unpleasant words between us. None, that is, except once, in 1953, after he had been in jail and gone back to teaching at the Jefferson School. I was frightened that his official connection with the school would send him back to jail and was saying that as we walked down 52nd Street. When we were a few steps from Sixth Avenue, he stopped and said, "Lilly, when we reach the corner you are going to have to make up your mind that I must go my way. You've been more than, more than, well, more than something-or-other good to me, but now I'm trouble and a nuisance to you. I won't ever blame you if you say goodbye to me now. But if you don't, then we must never have this conversation again." When we got to the corner, I began to cry and he looked as if he might. I was not able to speak, so he touched my shoulder and turned downtown. I stood on the corner until I couldn't see him anymore and then I began to run. When I caught up with him, he said, "I haven't thought about a drink in years. But I'd like one. Anyway, let's go buy one for you."

A few years after I bought the farm, the United States declared war. It was useless now to say yes, many of us knew it was coming; during the war in Spain, Hitler and Mussolini could have been stopped, the bumblers and the villains led us into this. (I had tried to write some of that in *Watch on the Rhine*.)

When the war came I thrashed around trying to find something useful to do, but all the jobs offered were official, tame, bound to high-sounding titles enclosed by office doors. Then Hammett disappeared for a few days and reappeared having enlisted as a private, although he'd had a tough time convincing the doctor who found the old First World War tubercular scars on the X-rays.

After he left Pleasantville, I felt lonely and useless, jealous of his ability to take a modest road to what he wanted. I spent the next year or so doing what I knew to be idle lady stuff: I wrote a few speeches for people in Washington, I planted a granite field that broke two plows, I made speeches at rallies for this or that bundles for something-or-other, I watched other people go to a war I needed to be part of. And then, suddenly, I was invited to go on a cultural mission to the Soviet Union.

I was invited because a month after we declared war William Wyler, the movie director, and I, both under contract to Samuel Goldwyn, had agreed to make a documentary film of the war in Russia. (Wyler and I had made a number of pictures together by that time and were old friends.) I no longer remember exactly how the plan started because its origins were kept from us, but Harry Hopkins, without involving President Roosevelt, had set it in motion. The Russian news was very bad that winter of 1942, but all of America was moved and bewildered by the courage of a people who had been presented to two generations of Americans as passive slaves.

Both Wyler and I were wild to do the picture and so Goldwyn flew East to consult with us, and the famous cameraman Gregg Toland agreed to come along. Wyler and I went to Washington to see Ambassador Litvinov, whom I already knew and liked. But Litvinov said our plan was impossible, wouldn't work without full cooperation from the Russian government, and that they were too hard pressed to give it. When Litvinov described the horrors of the German sweep through White Russia to Moscow, Leningrad and Stalingrad, we felt like young schoolchildren who had heard of *Oedipus* and thought it excellent to stage in their lunch hour.

But the next afternoon, Litvinov telephoned to ask me to come immediately to the embassy. Molotov had arrived that morning in Washington, Litvinov had mentioned our movie, and to his surprise Molotov thought it a fine idea and said the Russian government would guarantee a bomber, camera crew, and whatever else we needed for however long we needed it.

It was a wonderful day. Wyler went to see Hopkins, I made long-distance telephone calls, Wyler knocked down a drunk who was making anti-Semitic speeches in front of our hotel, we ran around in circles missing each other at the airport, and arrived back in New York that night for a meeting with Mr. Goldwyn in his apartment at the Waldorf Astoria Towers. Something about the Towers, the ill-proportioned apartments, the carefully guarded guests, has always depressed me as I enter the lobby, and so it is possible I was looking for trouble when the conference began. But Goldwyn was as pleased as we were, and we quickly agreed—a rare occurrence in Hollywood circles—that we would leave as soon as possible, that no script or outline could be made until we saw what Wyler could photograph, that we would make a full-length picture that would, of course, have a regular commercial release. Because of the enormous American admiration for the Russians in those days, we were an almost guaranteed success before we started. Goldwyn recognized that, of course, and knew that a large part of the cost of the picture— planes, camera crew, extras—would be supplied by the

Russians. The three of us were, for a change, in complete accord on all details. (This had not always been so. Once Mr. Goldwyn had fired Wyler for twenty-four hours because he claimed Wyler made the set of *Dead End*, a picture about New York slums, look dirty, and I had quit in sympathy.) But this was a most pleasant meeting until Wyler said that while he was in Russia he'd like his salary paid in monthly installments for the support of his wife and children. This simple request caused Goldwyn's face to change, and I remember knowing immediately that something was going to happen. (I had, by this time, worked for Goldwyn for seven years.) I had nobody to support, but I thought I'd better do something, so I said I'd like my salary paid half on the day we started photography, half on the day I arrived home, even if I came back in a coffin. My attempt to lighten the air was a failure: we were in for the silent staring that always precedes a Goldwyn shocker.

Finally Sam spoke. "You say you love Russia. You say you are radicals. So you say."

Wyler said, "I don't know what you mean. Who is radical and who says they love Russia? What's that got to do with anything?"

It was as if he had not spoken. Goldwyn's tones were now very soft, an old and ominous sign. "You say you love America, you are patriots you tell everybody—"

"What?"

"Everybody. Everybody, you both go around saying. Now it turns out you want *money* from me, from *me* who am sacrificing a fortune for my government because *I* love my country."

Wyler turned to look at me and I knew he didn't understand the purpose of the conversation. It was, indeed, often hard to understand Sam's shockers, but I had been at it for longer than Willy.

Wyler said, "I don't understand what you're saying, Sam. This picture is being made for commercial release and you intend to profit on it as you profit on any other movie. You're not putting up a nickel for 'your government.' The Russians, as a matter of fact, are giving you most of a free ride."

I said, "We'll be paid as we are paid on any picture, so let's cut out the nonsense and go home to bed."

Sam rose to his feet. "*Nonsense?* You call it *nonsense* to take money away from your government?"

Wyler was walking slowly toward Sam as if he were coming out of a dream. "Are you really suggesting that we take no salary, you take the profits, and that makes you a patriot and us hypocrites?"

The anger was now ready. Sam kept it in a properly blessed tin box, with a touch-spring top. Reason would, from now on, have no further place and words no meaning.

So before the box could be opened, I said, "Sam, you think you are a country with rivers and mountains and cities, inhabited by people who will, of course, risk their lives to protect the riches of the country called Samuel. Two of your citizens, servants called Wyler and Hellman, doubt that you are a country. Therefore we are traitors. So off with our heads and let's take them home to bed."

Wyler laughed and we went home. We would, of course, have won that ridiculous argument—Sam never intended not to pay us, he only hoped we'd reduce our usual fee—but by the time relations had been mended, other things intervened: Wyler enlisted in the air force and I didn't want to make the trip with anybody else.

But Goldwyn and I—and Washington, behind the scene—went on talking about a Russian picture and finally came to what seemed like, and could have been, a sensible solution: we would do a simple, carefully researched, semi-documentary movie to be shot in Hollywood. I have, during the last year, read again my script for *North Star*. It could have been a good picture instead of the big-time, sentimental, badly directed, badly acted mess it turned out to be. Halfway through the shooting, Mr. Goldwyn and I parted company. (The picture, now called *Armored Train* when it is shown on television, has printed titles explaining the Russians were once our allies but haven't turned out so nice. If apologies were needed, and they were needed for the silliness of the movie, then the picture should have been scrapped. But the convictions of Hollywood and television are made of boiled money.)

But I think the picture was one of the reasons why the Russians invited me on a cultural mission in 1944 and why Washington—acting with faceless discretion—wanted me to go. (True, that when I got to Moscow I found they thought *North Star* a great joke, but I guess outside Moscow there were some simple peasant folk glad to find themselves so noble on the screen.)

In September of 1944, I flew to Fairbanks, Alaska, where the Russians were to pick me up for the journey across Siberia. I am glad I was too ignorant to know what Robert Lovett, Assistant Secretary of War and an old friend, told me on my return—that it was so dangerous a journey that he would have forbidden it if he had known I was going that way.

The trip was made in a C-47, a two-engine plane capable of a maximum speed of 240 miles an hour. It carried cargo, a full crew, few instruments, and a nineteen-year-old boy called Kolya, a Russian mechanic stationed in Alaska, who had conned a ride home by convincing the top Russian brass in Fairbanks that he spoke English, and was therefore a fit escort for the lady guest. His English consisted of "and," "so," "O.K." "Hell"—I was known all through the trip as Miss Hell—"lie up," which he used to mean lie down or sit up, "stockings" and "Betty Grable." The Russian commanding officer wished me a happy trip, said I would be in Moscow in three days, and gave me a fine sleeping bag.

The trip took fourteen days because the crew had been instructed to take no chances with their guest. Those two

weeks were, physically, the hardest time of my life. Kolya
and I sat, or lay, on packing boxes in the rear of the
plane, where the heating system ceased to work on the
second day. (When it got so cold we couldn't stand it any
longer, one of us would go into the pilot's compartment,
and the radio operator would move out.) We flew only
when the weather was good and that meant that for days
at a time we were lodged in log cabins on Siberian
airfields. The crew, unfriendly at first because I was the
reason for their long, cautious journey, soon came to understand that I didn't like the command delays any more
than they did. None of them talked English, but Kolya
and I spent four hours a day teaching each other English
and Russian, and while I can never really learn any
language by the time we were halfway across Siberia he
could understand almost everything I said and translated
for me with remarkable intelligence. His bright, round,
child's face, his hands shaking from the cold as he held
my dictionary, is still with me. I owe a dangerous pneumonia to his overconfidence about the English language.

We had come down in Yakutsk. The first night there
was pleasant: a spinster schoolteacher who spoke excellent
English had met the plane, the sleeping quarters were less
rugged than usual, and the teacher had spent dinner hour
through 3 A.M. reading and translating for me the poetry
of Yesenin. (She was as in love with him as earlier ladies
had been with Byron after his death.) But on the second
day I turned my once-broken ankle in the ice ruts and
Kolya, convinced that I would be crippled, and anxious to
show off Soviet medicine, insisted I go to the clinic. The
clinic was a long way in a jeep riding on ice, and when we
arrived there the doctor was absent. Two nurses, understandably, were bewildered by Kolya's insistence that I
"had been crushed by ice." The twisted ankle was diag-
nosed as just that, but I made the mistake of asking for a
laxative. Kolya was carrying our English-Russian pocket
dictionary and he and the nurses turned many a page

before they seemed to find the word. One of them shook her head over the word but the other one seemed convinced and Kolya, pounding his chest in some kind of show of military authority, made firm demands. I was presented with a small bag of salts in rough, large chunks. Kolya, with gestures, explained that I must dissolve them in water and all would be "excellence," his now favorite word. I don't know why I believed any of it, but I drank most of the filthy stuff that afternoon.

I was too sick for the next few weeks to make entries in a diary, but, between hours of sleep or passing out, I remember certain scenes, although I am not always sure where they happened, or if I have remembered them in their proper order. I remember crawling through the fifty below zero cold of Yakutsk to an outhouse, the sweat pouring into my eyes; two visits from a doctor who seemed dead drunk; a yellow liquid that Kolya and the pilot poured down my throat; being carried up the icy ramp of the plane, then strapped down with ropes to keep me from falling off the packing crates; Kolya lying on a cot outside my door at each night's lodging; hot milk which made me sick and a sour pickle that I wanted very much as Kolya shook his head and said it was not fit for a lady who had not eaten in five days; no longer wanting to go to the pilot's compartment for warmth and fighting with Kolya and the radio operator who carried me there; endless miles of pine trees seen from the window; and once, coming out of a long sleep into a fit of laughter—I was composing, dreaming, a death prayer—and then into a fit of crying that scared the crew so badly that they turned the plane back to the place where we had stayed the night before; and another doctor; and then a day when Kolya said, "Urals. Look down, Miss Hell"; and another day, soon after, when a woman in uniform came on our plane and Kolya said, "Now, all O.K., Miss Hell," and when I said I didn't know what he meant, he explained that the co-pilot had been bad, very ignorant, would not be allowed to fly again, but this lady was famous and would "bring us good into Moscow." On the fifteenth day, about two in the afternoon, Kolya woke me up because he wanted to open one of my suitcases. He took out a toilet bag, handed it to me with a mirror. I shook my head, either because I didn't understand or didn't care.

He said, "All good now, Moscow soon, maybe one hour."

I said that was nice and tried to go back to sleep. But he propped me up and made disapproving faces and then fiddled in the bag and wiped my face with cream, combed and brushed my hair, smudged lipstick on my face, wiped it clean, tried again, until I laughed and managed it myself. Then he pulled a dress from the suitcase and said, "Take off pants. No good Moscow committee. Fix nice dress. Stockings not O.K. now. I fix." He took from his bag an ugly pair of brown stockings he had bought in Fairbanks and gave them to me. He unlaced my boots, smoothed out the dress, pulled me to my feet.

"I go now there," he said, pointing to the pilot's compartment. "Please fix nice for people."

I said, "Kolya, I wish you had been born to me."

He laughed. "I tell this to my mother."

An hour later we were in Moscow, and there were men and women carrying flowers who ran toward the plane. But I remember only Sergei Eisenstein, who said in perfect English, "We know you have been ill. I have insisted there be no speeches. You must come to the hotel now and rest for a long time."

But I thought I felt fine. I was excited about being in Moscow, and soon after Eisenstein left me an embassy man came around and we went off to dinner and a long talk afterwards. After that, for the next five days, I remember nothing. When I came to, I was in a bedroom at Spasso House, Ambassador Harriman's Moscow residence, because George Kennan had moved me there. The embassy navy doctor told me I had had a bad pneumonia, so bad that he had decided to chance the first shot of penicillin he had ever given. He said the penicillin had worked like magic but that he needed a vacation. Months later, when I told Eisenstein that the sickness had begun in Yakutsk and seemed to be connected with a dose of rough salts, he took my dictionary home with him and came back the next afternoon to say that there was no word for laxative in the Russian language and that the salts had been meant to soak my ankle in. He said, "Lilishka, is there something the matter inside your head from time to time?"

I stayed in the Soviet Union for the next five months. I lived most of the time, through the generous invitation of Averell Harriman, at Spasso House, but I kept my rooms at the National Hotel for work, or for bad nights when the snow made it hard to get back to the Arbat district, or when the rather heavy atmosphere of Spasso made me want to eat alone.

In those five months I kept diaries of greater detail and length than I have ever done before or since, but when I read them last year, and again last week, they did not include what had been most important to me, or what the passing years have made important. I know, for example, on what date I went to Leningrad, and there are many pages about a terrible evening during which Olga Bergholz, the poet, and four other people told me about the siege and famine of their city, but I see and hear more clearly a woman and a boy of about seven or eight walking close behind us on the Nevsky Prospect.

The mother said, "The sausage is better lately. Not so much grain in it."

The child said, "Why doesn't he stand up the way he used to?"

"He can't stand up."

"But why?"

"Because he can't."

"But *why?*"

Leningrad translator turned to face the woman and
y. The woman spoke directly to her. "My husband.
We had one pair of valenki between us." (Valenki are
long, felt boots.) "He went across Ladoga to help bring in
the first food after the siege. The valenki froze to his legs
and when he tore them off, to save them for me, his skin
came off, too. I wear the valenki today."

When my translator had finished telling me all that, the
woman and the boy moved on. My translator began to
cry as we went past Pushkin's house—closed during the
war—and when we stopped to look at the house she
raised her hand to make the right-left Orthodox cross. She
said, "It was like that with all of us. During the siege my
boy ate a little piece of candle every day."

And my notebooks tell what people I saw, what the
usually glum dinner conversation at Spasso was about, the
bad plays that the Russians were convinced I wanted to
see, my impatience with the foreign colony's ill-humored
complaints, and then my own increasing ill humor in the
gray, terrible Moscow winter of 1944-1945, but nowhere
is there a record of how much I came to love, still love
Raya, the remarkable young girl who was my translator-
guide. Nor how close I felt then and now to a State
Department career man whose future, seven or eight years
later, went down the drain for no reason except the brutal
cowardice of his colleagues under the hammering of Joe
McCarthy. And there are many entries about Sergei
Eisenstein and our almost daily cup of tea, but I didn't
know, couldn't know, that twenty-one years after his
death he is more real than many of the people I saw last
week. And I know the name, because it is written down,
of the three-year-old fat, blond orphan who threw himself
at me the first time I ever saw him and who, when I went
to see him twice every week, would sit on my lap and feel
my face because the lady who ran the orphan school said
I looked like a picture of his mother, but I couldn't know
then that I would think about him for years afterwards,

and dream as recently as last month that I was riding with him on a toboggan.

But the most important few hours are not even recorded in the diaries. I had gone to a hospital for the severely wounded and was making the handshaking, false-smile clown-sounds that healthy people make when they are faced with the permanently injured, when suddenly a man came into the room. I think he was in his late twenties, I think he was blond, I think he was tall and thin. But I know that most of his face had been shot off. He had one eye, the left side of a piece of a nose and no bottom lip. He tried to smile at me. It was in the next few hours that I felt a kind of exaltation I had never known before.

10

FROM a diary, Moscow, 1944:

The Kremlin is the political heart of the Soviet Union and the geographical heart of Moscow. The city grew up around the great thirteenth-century walls that enclose the buildings of the Kremlin and has continued to grow away from them into what is called the A Circle and the outer B Circle. The A Circle includes the Kremlin, the important government buildings, the main shopping district, many of the theatres and the big hotels. The National Hotel faces St. Basil's Cathedral and the main gate of the north Kremlin wall. Between the cathedral and the wall is that famous cobblestone passage which has seen so much of Russian history: in the seventeenth century a czarist massacre of friendly petitioners; in the nineteenth century it was here that Napoleon turned loose his cannons on the burning city; in 1917 the Bolsheviks and the White Guards fought until the cobblestones were slippery with frozen blood, the passage blocked by bodies.

I am told that to the pure in art, St. Basil's is one of the architectural freaks of the world: to me it has the daring self-assurance of a great work. It is true that within one lifetime it would not be possible to see all that is of it or all that is on it. It is not a large church, but it has no lonely half inch. Maybe the architect-churchmen omitted the sculptured eye of a toad or a mandrake root, but you cannot be sure that if you looked again they wouldn't turn up. The cathedral rises to violate all rules, and maybe it reflects the nature of the people who move past it today as truly as it reflected the sixteenth-century men who built it for Ivan the Terrible.

The Germans never came closer to Moscow than the airport, which, of course, was close enough, but the city was spared the horrors of Stalingrad and Leningrad. But now, December 1944, the people here look tired, cold, shabby and exhausted-sick in this, the easiest,* winter of the war.

Russians are so accustomed to cold that they seldom speak about it, but when they describe the first winter of the war they speak about it even before they tell you of the evacuation of women, children and Jews, the resettlement in the Urals when families were lost to each other for months, the strange diets in places forced to feed refugees—a friend of mine, her mother and child ate nothing but caviar and milk for seven weeks—the arrival of the Siberian army that is credited with saving Moscow, and the young student army that fought the Germans at and near the airport. The students had been in classes the day before, they had no training, many of them had no guns, there was no air cover, no large artillery. They were volunteers and most of them were killed in the first week.

---

* This was the word used in 1944. In 1966, three Muscovites told me it had been the hardest winter of the war. I think this conflict of memory came about because in 1944 they knew they were on the way to victory and an end. In 1966 they remember only the deprivation and the misery.

When they tell you about the students somebody, maybe two people, start to cry, and the others are silent. Almost everybody by this year of 1944 has lost a husband, a father, a son, and usually more than one man in a family has been killed. But it is for the students that they cry or start to cough until the crying stops. I think they cry, in part, for their own endurance during these last awful three and a half years, in pride for that endurance.

Russians have always had a deep love of their country, but now they are in love with each other. They do not say they like bread: they say, "All Russian people like bread," as if liking bread was a medal won in a school of high morals. They no longer say, "Pushkin wrote . . ." but "Pushkin, one of the greatest poets who ever lived"—and a few days ago, a woman said to me, "We have no bald men in Russia." It's a kind of national coming-of-war-age pride. They don't boast about the Red Army or the near starving civil population, but they hurry to tell you about the millions of books sold last year, the forty theatres that are filled at every performance, the people who wait in line through the freezing nights to buy tickets for a ballet or a concert. The Russian intellectual has had a hard life. If he is now in his late thirties, forties, or fifties he has gone through the revolution and the hunger, privations and upheavals that followed the revolution. The 1930's were the first promise of something better, but the promise was soon followed by the hurricane of the 1937-1938 purges that sent him whirling, looking for the protective walls that were not there. The accusations against his friends or his heroes were only half understood and were, therefore, more frightening. Such men and women tell you that one day they knew a criminal charge of treason or disloyalty could not be true, the next day felt uncertain, and within a short time were half convinced that perhaps their country, their revolution might have been betrayed. Great honor must and will be paid those who did protest the criminal purges. It is hard to judge those who tossed about in silent doubt and despair, but it is even harder to believe that they did not understand what was happening.

Those years of struggle from the dark centuries of ignorance and poverty, then famine, then hope, then nightmare ideological upheavals, and, finally, war on a scale that has never been seen before, have made deep marks on all of them. The least important scar, perhaps, is a chip-on-the-shoulder feeling toward foreigners that often takes the form of looking for the insult. Last week a woman I like came to see me. She is in her forties, a pleasant lady who translates French and English poetry. Her face was tense and twitchy. She began almost in the middle of a sentence, "Last night he said across the table, 'Where is Akhmatova? Gone, gone, with so many others.' What do you think of that," she asked me, *"What do you think of that?"*

I said, "Is it so terrible? You told me only last week about the trouble Akhmatova has had—"

She ran toward me, pulling up her sweater as she came. "There are scars here," she shouted, "although they were not made with a knife. All over me, all over all of us. But I don't show them to strangers, I don't sip cognac at tables and lift my clothes to show the long scar called Akhmatova, my friend Akhmatova, or the scar called Mandelstam—You will not hurt my scars. But *he* wanted to put his fingers in them so they would bleed again."

Russians puzzle us, we puzzle them. Their pride is the pride of poor people, the manners they require from others must be more elegant than ever could have been known at Versailles. And in so many ways their recent social customs have run counter to ours: they are, for example, romantic and dawn-fogged about sex, and I often find the talk about love and fidelity too high-minded for my history or my taste.

But it is easier for me than for most foreigners. Two plays, *The Little Foxes* and *Watch on the Rhine,* are in rehearsal. (Rehearsals have been going on for six months.)

Certainly there are other foreigners who have good relations with Russians, but most of the journalists, diplomats,
military and trade commissions live on islands of each
other, cut off from all Russians except waiters, cooks,
translators, and various forms of bribe takers such as
whores and telephone operators.

The largest of these islands is the Metropole Hotel,
teasing close to the walls of the Kremlin. It was built in
the nineteenth century, and while it is often referred to as
run-down elegant, it could never have been more than
large and ostentatious with the carved gewgaws and mar-
ble that the Russian rich liked so much. (It was in the
Metropole that the last holdout aristocracy of Moscow
barricaded itself during the revolution, but that story has
too many versions to believe any of them.) Now the hotel
is in a state of disrepair and smells of cabbage, but its vast
corridors burst with the kind of international high jinks
that should attract a magazine novelist, except that the
high jinks are not very high and always have an aimless,
frivol-out quality.

Most of the foreign journalists live at the Metropole and
they have a long list of understandable grievances: the
press censors are suspicious, irrational, arbitrary; they
have never been allowed to visit the front lines, seldom
been allowed to travel anywhere; they see few important
government people and must get information out of Russian newspapers or on the rumor circuit; there is nothing
to buy with money they would like to spend; Moscow
winter weather is terrible and darkness comes depressingly
early in the afternoon and moves into lonely nights.

Journalists cannot, therefore, do a proper job and it is a
bad life for them, but with the exception of Alexander
Werth, John Hersey and a few others, they are men used
to bullying their way around the world and their daily
defeats turn dinner into a sour stew of complaints unless
one turns off the ears and plays the game of who is that at
the next table or across the room?

Who is that, on a recent evening, was a trade commission from Iceland; two unidentified men from Mongolia; a repatriated Russian tenor and his family who had been living in Shanghai; an American who is here to sell farm machinery and who plays the piano very well; part of the English military mission whose chief had been a spy in the First World War and author of a famous book about his experiences as a foreign agent—but who considers it unjust, or pretends to, that the Russians think he is possibly still spying; and four young, and one not so young, whores, accompanied by a very small Russian man. We were joined at dinner that night by a magazine writer who had arrived only a week before and had just been through his first rough days of Russian press censor officials. When he had had enough to drink he talked very loud about all Russians being savages, and when I had had enough to drink I said I didn't think so, and he said he did, and I said what difference did that make, and he said something else, and I said lots of people who had just learned not to sleep in their underwear thought that other people were savages, and it was all high-class talk like that until the American farm machine gentleman got up to drown us with the piano.

I can't seem to stay away from the Metropole: it is a highly colored small station in the somber world of the embassy where I live, and a relief from the painful world of my Russian friends. It's a grubby joint but it's lively and I have taken to dropping over almost every day to listen to the stories about the night before, or the ones that Alex Werth remembers from the first year of the war, or Henry Shapiro remembers from even further back. Then I wander up and down the corridors, looking for people to talk to.

The third floor is the most interesting: two Turkish diplomats who never seem to be at home have the rooms opposite the elevator; across the hall from them are two

Japanese military attachés and, in an adjoining cubicle, their Japanese chauffeur. Next to him is a journalist of a neutral country who is very proud that his mistress was once the mistress to a group of Uzbeks. This lady laughs too loud and too much and is the reason why the repatriated Russian tenor, who lives next door with his family, spends his mornings demanding a new suite of rooms. Next to the Russian tenor is a recently arrived middle-aged American who works in our consulate. He is disturbed by the almost nightly arrival of a big Russian girl who pushes into his room, looks around, and screams. The American knows no Russian, the big girl no English, and nobody will tell him that the girl is called Dempsey because she once, when hitting a man, reminded somebody of Jack Dempsey. Now she mourns the former occupant of the room who left Moscow without telling her and she thinks the middle-aged American had something to do with her lover's disappearance.

Across the hall lives a lady called Miss Butter Fingers, radical in the politics of her own country and most sympathetic to the Soviet Union, except on the day, long before my arrival, when she stole an icon on a visit to a German-destroyed monastery near Moscow. Her journalist colleagues were disturbed and forced her to return the loot with the threat of a kangaroo trial in the lobby of the hotel. Since then she does not often appear in the dining room.

Yesterday the Russian tenor spoke to me. Shanghai had taught him a little English, I knew a little French, but I did not know until the end of our half hour that he greeted me so warmly because he thought I was Australian and had been sent by the British Embassy to help him arrange a larger and quieter hotel apartment with what he called *un piano propre*. I have no idea why he thought the British would be willing to tangle with anything like that, but by the time I got around to asking, the tenor had given me up as an impostor. In any case, he loves his homeland with all his hearts, he wishes to sing once again for his peoples but how practice without *un piano propre* and with four children? I tried, occasionally, to speak, to ask why and how he had come back to Moscow, but his handsome wife appeared about that time and he introduced her, adding the information that she was his first wife and his fourth wife and his cousin.

Down the hall from the tenor, in two apartments, live the fur buyers. The fur buyers are three men of no age except vague middle age, interchangeable in color and size. They interested me more than anybody in the hotel and so I tried to do a little research on them. But any research was limited because they have been in the hotel so much longer than anybody else that nobody is sure of anything about them except "the trouble."

The fur buyers are American by citizenship. This was established by the embassy, and so Mr. Harriman invited them, along with all other Americans in Moscow, to a Christmas party. I did my best to speak with them, to bring them food and drink, even to ask one of them if he would dance with me. We did dance for a few minutes, but I got nothing more than nods and what I guess were smiles, and my attempts at conversation produced little except an occasional half-recognizable sound in English, and other sounds in a language I could not identify. (Russians say the fur buyers speak very little Russian, but seem to understand the language.)

Some of their hotel mates claim they are Latvians, others insist they are Bessarabians, but the information at our consulate is that they were employed by United States merchants as experts on the raw fur pelts that were, before the war, sold at giant auctions. Evidently, they used to spend six or eight months a year traveling around the Soviet Union and were caught in Moscow by the outbreak of the war. But none of this explains why they are still here: they are American citizens and they could have gone home long ago. When I asked Alex Werth about this he said, "Where's home for them?" I guess that's the answer, although another man I know feels that they wish to stay here in the belief that the war will end any minute and they will be the first on the scene to bid for the valuable wild minks and chinchillas who, unlike the hunters, must have grown fatter and more beautiful during the war.

"The trouble" involved the transshipment of a Russian prostitute. (Each fur buyer has a girl, but they are men who believe in class distinctions, because the girls never appear at their dining room table and nobody has ever seen them with the girls in the lobby or in the corridors.) I first heard of "the trouble" from a British Third Secretary, but the very mention of it caused him to choke with giggles and I could make little sense of what he was saying. Last week I went to a large official Russian party and spent most of the evening talking to Maxim Litvinov who had recently returned to Moscow. [1968—I knew Litvinov first when he was Ambassador to Washington and liked and admired him. Mrs. Litvinov had been the very British Ivy Low. I found Ivy—a combination of Bloomsbury and Russian Revolution—charming, but Hammett didn't. She had come for a weekend visit to the Pleasantville farm. On the second night Dash didn't appear for dinner. I went upstairs to find him reading on his bed. He shook his head. I nodded mine. He shook his and I knew that no amount of arguing would bring him to dinner. Angrily I said, "Why?" He said, "Because she's the biggest waste of time since the parcheesi board."] Litvinov and I sat at a table watching the dancers, who were mostly diplomats. Maxim doesn't think well of diplomats and spoke of them as buyers and sellers of world herring. One passing dancer was, he said, "the highest-ranking pederast" in Moscow, and when another gentleman, too tall and too handsome, went by Litvinov laughed and said, "It was the custom in his time to choose for foreign service on the basis of length of body and bone in nose, as with butlers. You can imagine their surprise when they first saw small, fat me." Then he raised his finger, pointed to a young, very blond man and said sharply, "That one tries too many tricks. We think he managed the girl in the trunk for the fur buyer. But why did he do it?" Before I could ask about the girl in the trunk, Litvinov was called to the phone and did not appear again that night.

The next day I pinned down the British Third Secretary who had had the giggles. There had been a long box in the lobby of the Metropole marked, in Russian, COFFIN OF A CHILD FOR TRANSSHIPMENT. The box carried whatever are the proper papers for a coffin and a Stockholm receiving address. It got through the Leningrad customs until a train official got curious about some odd-looking holes in the box. He poked into them with some kind of poking instrument that went, unexpectedly, through to another series of holes. Strange sounds began to be heard, and when the coffin was broken open there was a trunk inside the coffin and a Russian girl in whatever form of hysteria you get from being in a trunk that is in a coffin. The investigation turned up the news that the trunk belonged to one of the fur buyers and so did the girl. The girl was released, returned to Moscow, and no further action was taken. That seemed odd because the Russians are very severe about exit visas, but when I asked my British friend why, he shrugged and said, "Maybe they are giving everybody enough rope. They don't like the embassy Swedes, but they can't seem to get anything on them."

"But what about the fur buyer who shipped her?"

He said, "I don't know. He says he didn't ship her. He says she stole his trunk and made her own coffin."

Last month came the good news of our naval victory in the Philippines. But on the third floor of the Metropole the news got mixed up: the Japanese radio announced it as a victory for *their* navy and so the Japanese military attachés decided to celebrate with a refined, small party, where, according to the Russian tenor, tidbits were served, classical music came from the phonograph, and the guests were in their own beds quite early. But the Japanese chauffeur, in his cubicle, only got going about three in the morning with the noise of crashing glass and muffled female sounds. A half hour was not enough to worry his corridor mates of the Metropole, but when the female sounds became screams of fear, a few of the more humane rose from their beds. Sleepy, annoyed figures gathered in the hall. Out came the Turks, out the Mongols, out the ex-mistress of the Uzbeks, out the tenor and his children, out, even, the fur buyers to the edge of the gathering. Although the screams were now steady and agonized, the observers seemed reluctant to move. A reason was found that had not before occurred in the tolerant international life of the hotel: nobody wanted to mix himself into the affairs of a country at war with the United States, particularly since it had now been firmly established that it was our naval victory and not the Japanese. But a solution was finally reached: one of the Turks—a neutral—would not go directly to the chauffeur's room, but agreed to knock at the door of the strangely absent Japanese attachés and bring the screams to their attention. This was done, and the Japanese attachés, evidently awake and prepared for the summons, padded down the hall in Bond Street dressing gowns carrying a long pole used for opening windows and several smaller implements. They broke open the door. On the floor, in a corner, were two crouching women, one of whom had her leg stretched at an odd angle. (It was later found that she had a broken foot. She told the police that she had fallen over her girl friend during a game of tipsy hide and seek.) Several windows were smashed, all mirrors were broken, and an overstuffed chair was slashed to pieces. At this moment, the hotel manager pushed his way through the crowd, entered the room, held up his hand for silence and said in English, "I wish to say that this is simply not nice."

There are, of course, many quiet days at the Metropole. Last week very little happened. A journalist returning from London brought a girl he knew three pairs of nylon stockings. She thought them a mingy, unloving gift, so she wrote a short account of their life together and sent one copy to his newspaper and a carbon to his wife. A code clerk in a minor embassy slapped the oldest child of the Russian tenor and the Russian tenor says that he regrets his return from Shanghai into the company of barbarians. One of the fur buyers received a box of eggs that exploded in the main lobby with such force that the manager had him frisked for a gun.

The night the child got slapped John Hersey and I went to the opera. The streets around the Bolshoi were as crowded as they always are on the night of any performance. The Tchaikovsky-Pushkin *Pique Dame* was being performed. The cold, tired, hungry audience seems to feel at home with the lush nineteenth-century aristocrats on the stage. Maybe they would enjoy the comedy dramas in the Metropole across the street.

11

A FEW weeks after I arrived in Moscow, the Foreign Office invited me around for a visit. I met with two cordial gentlemen who each made the same formal speech of welcome. The Soviet Union was my host and in their tradition, a guest was to be honored and trusted. (There was a hint here that lesser people did not always act with such courtesy.) Would I, therefore, tell them what I would like to see, where I would like to go. They could promise nothing definite at the moment, but they could promise that I would move with as much freedom as war conditions allowed because I had come to them not only as a "cultural representative of my country" but because my plays were deeply admired by the Russian people (This was, indeed, odd: *Watch on the Rhine* and *The Little Foxes* were still in rehearsal and were to stay in rehearsal so long that I never saw a public performance.)

High-class official visits have never been up my alley. I am ill at ease, prefer another kind of flattery, and after a short time cease to hear what is being said. That would always have been true, but pneumonia had left me tired and foggy that day in the Foreign Office, and so it took me a long time to understand that thank you so much, but I don't want to go anywhere, I've hardly seen Moscow, was causing the older of the men to sigh, twist in his chair, and finally to rap on his desk.

He said, "Thank you very well. Now we proceed to make list of your desires."

Would I like to go to Leningrad? Would I like to go to Kiev? Perhaps there was a chance, very doubtful to be sure, that I would be allowed to join the army at the front lines. Now. With whom would I like to meet? I said I didn't ever think about meeting people, but maybe later on, I'd come back another day. The older gentleman was once more rapping on his desk.

"Madame Hellman, offers have been made for your pleasure that are not usual. Yet you reply that there is no person in the Soviet Union with whom you wish to meet."

I tried to say that wasn't what I'd meant, was sorry if it sounded that way, but before I finished the younger man rose and said, very sharply, "Comrade Stalin does not give interviews, although of course we will inform his secretary of your request to see him."

That night, and in the next days, I told Mr. Harriman and a few friends about my visit, but they all said not to worry, I wouldn't be allowed to go anywhere, it was all a lot of official palaver. I felt better and forgot about the whole thing until late October when Raya came to the hotel to say that we had been granted permission to go to Leningrad the next day. This didn't seem to me very special, but it caused a good deal of interest in the foreign colony. I no longer remember whether I was the fourth or fourteenth foreigner to be allowed to visit Leningrad after the siege was lifted, but the visit was still rare enough to make me, on my return to Moscow, more interesting than I had been to foreign embassies. Dinner invitations came thick and fast, one enclosed in a leather edition of *The Kreutzer Sonata*, one nestled in a large bouquet of flowers —hard to find in Moscow—and one tied to an electric heater, more desirable that winter than the return of youth. The gentleman who sent the heater was the head of his country's military mission and had, during the Russian Revolution, been an adviser to the White Armies. Shortly after, he coauthored a book about his experiences as a spy. The day after the gift of the heater, the spy grown older—he was now a brigadier general—arrived carrying a bottle of fine prewar vodka and a tin of fresh caviar. I remember that when we had exhausted ourselves on the vodka and caviar, we moved on to the strange color of my hair, the need for bleach, then to praise for a suit I was wearing and straight into how chic were the women of Leningrad when he first knew them. From then on the conversation was extraordinary: the loaded questions would alternate with the innocent as if he were a metronome and I a child at the piano. When the child took to staring out of the window, and no sound came, his teeth clamped together, the mouth pulled back, and then, as if this were an old habit he worried about, he put his hand over his mouth and coughed for a long time. The child said she didn't much like questions, was weary, uncomfortable. He said he understood, none of us got enough sugar, he'd go and fetch me some candy from his rooms. I guess he came back, but I don't know, because I left the room immediately after he did and sat for a long time on a bench in the Gorki Street subway station wondering whether shabby jobs made people insensitive and arrogant, or whether arrogance doesn't usually lead to stupidity. The next day I returned the electric heater and the general never spoke to me again.

On December 20 I was to have the second proof that the gentlemen in the Foreign Office had meant what they said. Raya came to see me, her pleasant, overstrained young face in a happy grin, all weariness gone, with what she called "the greatest possible good news." When she had teased me for a while, and I couldn't guess, she kissed me and said that permission had been given for a trip to the front and we would leave within the next few days at any hour we were notified. It was not good news to me. I saw no point to the trip. I was not a journalist and didn't wish to report on the war, I was uncertain I could take the hardships with any grace, I was frightened, and when I told her I would not go, she shook her head and said I must sleep on it, please not to decide, it was of great importance. I slept that night at the hotel, not anxious to face the occupants of the embassy. By morning I was more than ever certain that I must not fake, or test myself where I knew the test would fail and make a permanent scar because it had failed.

I don't remember why I changed my mind. Probably because everybody was in a state of shock that this amazing, unprecedented offer was being turned down. I don't remember anybody putting pressure on me, but in a few days I was packing and unpacking and repacking a small bag, borrowing a padded army coat from General Deane, mending woolen underwear, knitting myself a new pair of socks, doing the fussy things I have done all my life to avoid facing the turmoil that any decisive travel movement sets up in me.

On December 27, in the early afternoon, a tall, blond major met Raya and me at the railroad station. When he had bowed, paid compliments, saluted too many times, he gave Raya instructions to be translated: I must not ask the route of the train; I must not ask our final destination; I must ask no questions upon arrival "with the army"; I must not ask questions "upon exit"; all arrangements, decisions, "tours," were entirely at his discretion, and Raya would serve only as translator. She said it was cold standing in the station and would he pick up our luggage and give the rest of his orders on the train?

The first car moved out with only Raya, myself, and the major. There were two cars behind us, but the mayor pulled down our shades so that we couldn't see who boarded the train. This primitive blackout was ignored by the pleasant lady attendant-conductor who, as she set up a samovar at the end of our car, told us that we were headed for Kiev, that the car behind us was "full of Polish people" and the one behind that "full of other strange foreigners." Toward night, when the train stopped at what had once been a station and was now a total ruin, we got out to buy hot sausages from two old ladies who were selling them from baskets. "The foreigners" turned out to be Moscow journalists, many of whom I knew and was happy to see. But I was treated rather coldly and I did not know why until years after the war was over, when John Hersey told me that they were all understandably resentful that having asked to go to the Russian front in letters unending, they were now being sent to the Polish front while I, who didn't want it, was being allowed the journey they had all been begging for. The "car full of Polish people" turned out to be members of the Polish government in exile, going home to declare itself in Lublin because the Germans were still in Warsaw.

It was a long, roundabout journey. I was, of course, sorry that I had come, but there I was, grotesque of costume, unwashed, cold, less frightened than I had been because I was no longer in my own hands. (As others grow more intelligent under stress, I grow heavy, as if I were an animal on a chain.) There were endless cups of tea, nights in the train when I kept Raya awake reading to her from Mann's essays on Wagner and Freud; the boredom and stupidity of the Moscow major; a stop in Kiev, a walk down the destroyed Kreshchatik, which must have been a street of great beauty, and a night there when Raya and I wandered around the city long after the curfew, and then ran back to the hotel through the black, empty streets, stumbling over bricks and wood and beams, being too tired to care where the long running steps would take me.

The train moved up to Lublin. Major Kazakevitch was at the station to meet us. He was a charming young man. (I was told many years later that he wrote a good novel after the war and died in the 1950's of cancer.) I liked him immediately because he turned on the Moscow major and said, "Spare us the punctilio of the Moscow desk officer."

The hotel in which we stayed that night was a strange place: it was empty, it was heavily guarded, the rooms were warm, the windows were barred. (Two weeks later I was told that it was the quarters of Marshal Zhukov, the commander of the First and Second White Russian Armies facing the Germans across the Vistula.) All through that night there were shots in the distance and twice during the night there were the sounds of many men in heavy boots running by the hotel. (There were still pockets of trapped Germans in the city and the suburbs.) At seven o'clock the next morning I opened the steel shutters of our room. The day was brilliant with sun on clean snow. Across the street was a little girl in a fine squirrel coat and hat, and gray suede gloves that matched her boots. She was with a woman in a full English nanny costume and cap. They were a strange pair, moving quietly past the rubble of a destroyed apartment house, and I leaned far out on the balcony to watch them turn into a church two blocks away.

That morning, that afternoon, that what of time, did not have then, does not have now, any measure of hour-space or land-distance as I ever knew it before. We had driven to the concentration camp of Maidanek, taken from the Germans only a short time before. I was down in the blackness of deep water, pushed up to consciousness by monsters I could smell but not see, into a wildness of lions waiting to scrape my skin with their tongues, shoved down again, and up and down, covered with slime, pieces of me floating near my hands. A diary written six months later tells me that an elderly Polish couple were our guides, that the smell of iodoform was sickening, that I was in an enormous rectangular cement chamber filled with bins that held thousands of shoes arranged by size and color, that I touched a pair of red shoes, that as we moved around that endless, wired horror of flat earth, we came to the death ovens, large for men and women, small for children, that smoke was still faintly puffing from a large brick center structure whose purpose was variously translated as "for burning bones," "for waste," "for fire to heat the ovens," so that to this day I do not know what it was, that we moved again and there were trenches with human bones, that, turning now, we faced a building that had a long worm crawling up the wall, that I asked myself how a worm could survive in the terrible cold, that I chewed on a piece of gum to keep from vomiting and then did vomit, but not food, something yellow with red spots, that I repeated so many times, "I don't believe it, I don't believe it," meaning the worm—since there was nothing else that day to believe or not believe—that the Polish old lady was annoyed with me and said to the translator, "Hellman is a German name, isn't it?", that I went to sleep in the car riding back to Lublin and have no other memory until the car, the next day, the day after, whatever day, was approaching a river.

Major Kazakevitch said, "We are almost there."

The Moscow major said, perhaps for the tenth time, "Please do not inquire where you are, please do not ask number of men, guns, planes, present battle action, location of villages, forests—"

I said, "How often can you go on saying the same thing? How often can I tell you I don't give a damn, and wouldn't know a platoon from an army corps or maybe even a gun from a plane?"

The Moscow major said, "That is difficult to believe," and when Kazakevitch stopped laughing he said, in English, "I am looking forward to his meeting with the General."

The meeting took place a few hours later when we went to join the General and two of his officers for dinner. (The General was, I think, the tallest man I have ever seen, or maybe the handsome high fur hat made him seem that way.) We had not finished shaking hands before the Moscow major said, "I salute you, sir, as a great hero of the Union of Soviet Socialist Republics. Now I report to you my orders from Moscow. This foreign lady has been allowed by our government the enormous distinction of a visit to your front lines. Carrying with such permission goes the order that she must ask no questions of location of men or villages, numbers of soldiers, planes, guns—"

Kazakevitch was grinning with pleasure as he translated for me the General's interruption: "I dare say somebody will bring you a message when and if you are ever needed."

It was a good dinner, the best I had had in Russia. Meat and bread, cucumbers, tomatoes, Georgian wine, fine beer, with a beat-up phonograph playing from a chair. They were healthy men of good spirits, good manners. We made awful jokes which got worse in translation and one of the colonels did a kind of jig, and the General and I waltzed to something that wasn't a waltz, and everybody sang a song of their region, but the beer made me forget most of the words of "Dixie" or maybe I never knew them.

From a diary:

January 3, 1945

I am sitting in a pine forest, propped against a tree. Not a sound can be heard, although there must be three thousand men spread out in the forest and a thousand horses, resting or being fed. It is a scene from another, long ago war, or the background for an opera. I put down my notebook to stroke the face of a horse who is pushing his nose into the snow and I am back in Pleasantville on another winter day, sitting in the snow, hot from the sun, patting the heads of a pony and a poodle. I want to be where I am. I want to stay in this forest.

Later that day

An hour or so later, we arrived at Divisional Headquarters, and as we sat around General Chernov's fine, two-room dugout, he asked me what I would like to see. I said I wanted to go back to the pine forest and live there for a while. He laughed and said that was O.K. with him, they'd build me a pine room and come back for me after the war. We drank tea and spoke of his past: he had been a lieutenant in the czarist army, then had fought with the Red Army for three years in Siberia and had taken Vladivostok. He said, "In this war, I was the man who had to surrender Kovel and retreat to Stalingrad. But God has been good. I lived to take back Kovel and I will live to help with Warsaw. Would you like to see the German encampment?" He carried his binoculars to a small glass opening in his dugout wall, focused the glasses, moved me into his position, putting my hand over the top of the glasses. I suppose the Germans were five hundred feet from us and I was so shocked at their nearness that I dropped my hand. There was an immediate answer of grenades and heavy guns as Chernov pushed me to the floor. Lying there I saw the major pressed against one wall and Chernov against another. The major said, "Stay where you are. You moved your hand from the glasses and they caught the reflection."

"I'm sorry. That was so foolish—"

General Chernov laughed. "They'll stop. What they are doing is useless. But for a minute I thought I might not get to Warsaw."

January 7

I sat up all last night a safe distance from the glass of the windows, watching shells explode into the heavy snow, the river brilliant with signal flares. Once the house shook so hard that I was thrown against the table, and that shell must have caused a fire, because I saw high flames from a building and heard shouts of running men. At four this morning Kazakevitch stuck his head in the door, said not to worry, none of it amounted to much, he'd send over some hot tea. It occurred to me then, and only then, that I had not been frightened. Did I lose the fear on the train or at Maidanek? I take out my diary and decide to write about Maidanek, but I cannot make the second sentence—the first doesn't seem to be in my hand-writing—and know that I can't write about it now or maybe ever.

It had been a busier night than I knew. At breakfast we are told there had been heavy firing along the whole Vistula line, Russian patrols had brought in large numbers of prisoners, and nine S.S. men had deserted and were about to be questioned. Did I want to sit in on the session? I didn't understand why the nine desertions seemed so important until somebody told me that S.S. men were the élite troops of the German army and these were the first men ever to desert from it.

General Kusmean said, "There is never a first in a war. All we know is that they are the first ever to desert to us. I would guess the S.S. are now taking slobs and none of this means much." He waved to the two colonels and Kazakevitch and left the room, passing a tall, thin, sick-looking German who jumped to get out of his way.

The German gave his name as Techler, 61st Regiment

of the 5th Tank Division, former worker in an aircraft factory until it had been destroyed by American bombers in August of 1944. He had been conscripted immediately and moved to the Vistula front five days ago.

Colonel Zeidner said, "Why did you desert?"

Techler answered in a polite, tired voice, "We tried to desert the first day. We hear your offensive is going to start and we don't want to get hurt."

The other colonel said to the table, "The General was right. Waste of time. They've put men like this in the front danger spots to divert the first blows from the good S.S. troops. Get out."

Techler went out of the room slowly, as if he were sorry to leave. As he passed the hot stove, he put out his hand to touch it. Watching him, I did not see another man come into the room. Now I heard his voice.

"Max Makosh, 7th Platoon, 70th Regiment, 73rd Infantry Division. I do not believe in the ideals of the Nazi party—"

"Keep your ideals to yourself. Where born and so on?"

"Yes, sir. Born in Ruda, Poland, a mine worker, my wife is going to have a baby. We have no fight with the Russians, but the Germans came and took me—"

The major said to me, "Upper Silesia. Germans who emigrated to Poland and are solidly Nazi. This one understands a little Russian, of course, and it's making him feel good. Too good."

Zeidner said, "How many coal mines in or near Ruda, what quality coal, are Germans in charge of the mines?"

Makosh thought for a long time. "Yes, sir. But I know only about where I worked. Germans run the office so that a man down in the mines, like me, doesn't see them much and doesn't know—"

Zeidner leaned across the table and pushed Makosh's right hand with his left hand. "You are not a miner. Stop lying."

Makosh put his cap over his hands and coughed. "I used to be a miner sometimes."

Zeidner said, "There is a prison camp in Ruda. Describe it."

"I don't know about it, sir."

"When you do know about it, come back. In the meantime—"

"I know, of course, what I was told. The prisoners are mostly Poles, some French and Russians—"

"Are the Russian prisoners treated in the same way as the other prisoners?"

Makosh said, very softly, "I have heard they are treated bad. My mother's uncle works in the place and he said the Russians get only half food rations and sleep in a filthy place. Many die, he said, and have green feet. He told us all that and we said a prayer."

The other colonel had been scratching the table with his penknife. Now he threw the penknife over the head of Makosh into a door, crossed to the door, pulled out his penknife, spoke very angrily in Russian, and left the room.

Zeidner turned to look at me. "Do you wish to write about this, have you anything to ask?"

I said, "Ask him about the Jews in Ruda."

Makosh said, *"Pana,* I knew two nice Jew boys when I was young. But you know how it is with Poles. They do not like Jews, *pana—"*

"Please stop calling me *pana.* I am not a Polish lady."

The soft voice said, "I am a religious man. Therefore, I do not lie. The Jews were taken away to be killed. I did not help the Jews."

He bowed his head. When nobody spoke he moved toward me. "No, I did not help them. I am a small man who does not know what is outside his village. I don't even know how many men in a regiment, or a brigade."

Zeidner leaned forward and pushed him away from the table. Then he looked down at a paper on the table. "You have been a member of the Nazi party since 1931. You told your friend Techler that you killed three Russian prisoners." Zeidner rose now and shouted. "You're wearing Russian boots from the green feet of the men you killed. Get out before we kill you."

We walked over to join the General for dinner. The colonel was already there, slumped in a chair. When a soldier brought in the food, he said the General was busy and would not be joining us. (The Moscow major was, for the first time, at dinner with us.) The talk was listless and gloomy.

Zeidner said to me, "The first Nazi is hard for everybody. Drink some wine."

The colonel said, "It is our sad duty to say goodbye to you, Miss Hellman. We wish you to know that your visit has been valuable. A plane will take you back to Moscow tomorrow morning."

I said, "Oh. Have I done something?"

The Moscow major wagged a finger. "No questions, madame."

The colonel turned to look at him, turned back. "We are going into Warsaw."

There was a gasp and rattle from the Moscow major and the colonel laughed. "The offensive will begin in a few days and we will either take Warsaw on the sixteenth or seventeenth or we will surround it and continue on. General Zhukov says that he has learned many a lesson from your Civil War." He turned his head to the Moscow major. "The Civil War took place in the United States of America. Please report that I have given this secret to Madame Hellman."

After dinner, as a farewell present, I think, it was arranged that Raya and I were to have a steam bath. We were pouring water on each other's hair when a sharp rapping was heard at the door. The modest old man who presided over the stove came out from hiding and shouted that two ladies were bathing and officers would have to wait. But Zeidner's voice could be heard demanding that Raya come to the door immediately. He and Raya talked over each other as she said she couldn't, she was wet and naked, and he said to get unwet and unnaked immediately, he had a most important piece of news.

We made a strange pair going up the steps of the General's house into the small room where we ate each night, shivering from the extremes of high heat and night cold, no guns heard for the first time, our wet heads wrapped in towels, my American army coat looking even worse with nothing under to pad it out, a scarf holding the front together. Raya said, "You look like a poor czarist widow come to collect her husband's pension, wearing his coat to prove her poverty."

The penknife colonel was there and Zeidner and, a few minutes later, Kazakevitch. The colonel said immediately that although the plane was ordered for eight the next morning, the General wanted me to know that I did not need to go back to Moscow, I could move with the army into Warsaw, and stay with it on the march to Berlin, which might, would, take six months or more, but was certain of its destination.

Zeidner said, "Certain?"

"Yes, certain. Maybe five months, maybe seven, but certain. There comes a time when an army cannot be stopped. We know it and so does the German General Staff."

Raya, who seemed smaller than usual, her face bright with excitement but clouded with something else, said, "But Moscow has ordered us back——"

"Moscow has nothing to do with it. It is the General's decision and Miss Hellman's."

When I did not speak, Kazakevitch said, "Your head is wet, you're cold. Go to bed now and I will come at seven."

I did not want to go to bed. I thought: I will not sleep
tonight, whatever I decide, or the next night or the next,
until I will feel too sick not to sleep, and after that will
come, as it always has, a hatred for the side of me that
either falls into action or avoids it without thought, aimless, giving in and over to people or places, or slamming
doors in anger or fear, all the same coin. But it was not
like that. I fell asleep immediately, woke up at six o'clock,
tore a sheet from a notebook, thanked the General, said I
would remember the offer all my life but I hadn't the
courage for such a journey, not in fear for my life, but in
fear of my nature, and hoped that we would both live long
enough for me to understand myself and be allowed, if
that should happen, to explain it to him.

The major came at seven and I gave him the note to
read. He smiled and went off with it and we got ready for
the plane. At eight-thirty he reappeared with the Moscow
major and a small box. I still have the gift. It is a cigarette
lighter made from a gun barrel. Carved on it, in awkward
Latin letters, are the words: *From the First White Russian
Army as pleasant memory of your visit, January, 1945.*

In the late afternoon of January 17, the Russian who
operated the switchboard at Spasso House rang my phone,
mumbled, disconnected the phone, rang again, mumbled
something else and then announced, "His Honor wishes a
line to you."

His Honor was a pleasant voice who said he was secretary to Prime Minister Stalin and that the Foreign Office
had informed him of my wish to do an interview. (The
Foreign Office, if it had learned nothing of what I wanted,
had certainly not forgotten anything that it wanted.) I said
no, I'd never said that, certainly not, it would be an
imposition, no, indeed—

The voice said, "Because of the important events of
today, it is impossible for Comrade Stalin to see you on

the date you proposed. However, we are prepared to make an appointment on February second or third, if that is convenient for you."

I said I was sorry, so sorry, but I was leaving Moscow in a few days en route to England to make a war documentary, but how courteous, how gracious, how other-things-or-other I thought the invitation. The voice sounded pleased with the news of my departure and we exchanged elaborate good wishes for the future of his country and mine.

The Russian telephone operator and I had never liked each other. (He listened in on all conversations, even in languages he said he didn't understand, and sometimes he made a point of coughing into the phone to let you know he was there.) I went out in the hall, guessing what he would do. He was already half up the stairs to report my call to Mr. Harriman.

One of his pretenses was deafness, so I shouted at him, "Know what Chekhov said? He said to hell with the great of this world."

As I turned back to my room, the first big gun went off, then the second and the tenth and the fiftieth in the loudest salute of victory I had ever heard. I ran downstairs to find out what it meant and bumped into General Deane, who called out, "They told you the truth. They took Warsaw today."

I stood in the hall thinking that I could have been there and then told myself to shut up, I couldn't have been there, and must not have such fake regrets again.

But I often thought about the General, and when the Russians took Berlin I wanted to send him a cable but was too lazy to find out how to do it. In any case, he wouldn't have received it. When I returned to Moscow many years later, I tried to find him. He had been killed two days after Warsaw.

12

Twenty-two years later, the same week in October when I had arrived during the war, the plane lowered for the Moscow Airport. I put out my cigarette, took off my glasses, closed my book and was shocked to find that I was crying. All women say they do not cry very much, but I don't because I learned long ago that I do it at the wrong time and in front of the wrong people. The two young English commercial travelers opposite me stared and then turned their heads away, but the German in the next seat made no secret of his interest, and a Russian across the aisle shook his head at me. I shut my eyes on all of them. What fragment at the bottom of the pot was the kettle-spoon scraping that it had not reached before?

I told myself that maybe I was worried about seeing my old friend Raya: it is not easy to see an old friend after so many years, and certainly not women because they change more than men. But I knew the tears were not for Raya: they were for the me who had, twenty-two years before, been able to fly across Siberia for fourteen days in an unheated plane, lying in a sleeping bag on top of crates, knowing the plane had few instruments even for those days, starting to be sick in Yakutsk, unable to explain in a language I didn't know, not caring, thinking that whatever happened the trip was worth it, although when the pneumonia did come, I changed my mind about that. The tears had to do with age and the woman who could survive hardships then and knew she couldn't anymore. I was sorry I had come back to Moscow.

The pretty, fat young stewardess said in Russian and then in English, in a singsong voice, "And now we have come to the end of the road and we must take our parting. A good journey to you, ladies and gentlemen."

I laughed, and the tears stopped, or so I thought, until I came down the long ramp toward the visitors' gate and saw Raya before she saw me. I leaned against the wall, knowing that I did not want to greet Raya until the weariness had passed.

The fat young stewardess came past me, stopped, turned and said, "Madame, we have come to the end of the road and now we must take our parting."

I said, "Thank you, but that is a mournful sentence in English and you must find another."

She was annoyed. "My teacher was English from England."

That is, or was, a favorite sentence of Russians, and as I shook my head her face became the big face of a fat girl named Martha Judge who used to hit me when I was six years old in New Orleans, and I said to myself, "To hell with this memory nonsense," and moved down the ramp.

I had no need to worry about seeing Raya again. She was twenty-four or twenty-five when I last saw her, a girl with a sweet, gentle face, a small girl, now a small woman, but very little changed. Her first husband had been killed, before I met her, in the famous student defense of Moscow when raw boys with guns that had to be shared marched out to the airport to hold back the Germans. By the time I met Raya the daughter of that marriage was four years old. (The daughter is twenty-six now and has a baby of her own.) But neither Raya nor I talked about the past for five whole days except in an occasional, shy sentence, but when the memories did come, they came pell-mell strong.

In the immediate postwar years after I left Moscow in 1945, we had written many letters, but after a while I no longer heard from Raya and put some of it down to Slavic putting-off-until-tomorrow, but knew, also, that some other wall had gone up for both of us. Now, in wanting to explain, she was shy, stumbling, finally saying that she did not know how to write about herself or her country in the postwar Stalin years, and so had postponed the letters until it seemed too late to take them up again. I felt my own kind of pain in this mishmash summary of the years that had passed: I was also shy and stumbling when I tried to talk about the McCarthy period which had changed my life, and when Raya asked me about the farm in Pleasantville, I had a hard time telling her that I had sold it in 1952, guessing what the future would be for Hammett and myself. I tried to explain why Hammett had gone to jail and why I, who offered to testify about myself but not about other people, had not gone to jail, but that was tough going with a foreigner, the legal complications, and the personal—Hammett and I had not shared the same convictions—and so I gave up, saying finally that I guessed you could survive if you felt like it, but you only knew that after you had survived.

We were in a restaurant, Raya and I, when we talked of those years. Neither of us said any more than was necessary, both of us soon fell silent. When I got back to my hotel through the cold November rain, I fell asleep, and for the first time in many years dreamed of the farm in Pleasantville: a dream of the walnut trees and the weeping beech, of November pig killing, of spring scilla, and pickerelweed and skunk cabbage when it is purple, and the lovely mush that was spring. I woke before curtain time for the Bolshoi and canceled the tickets because I didn't want to move from the room. The dreams had brought back a time of me and I needed to spend the evening with it, knowing now that the tears from the day on the plane would come back again if I continued to bury this period of my life. I would not have chosen the gloomy National Hotel in Moscow for the digging up of frozen roots, but there I was.

The night was confused. I felt as if I had a fever, and it is possible that I was half drunk during the night because sometime that evening a waitress brought me bread, caviar and a small bottle of vodka, and there was no vodka left the next morning. The sessions of sweet, silent thought were not always silent: that night in the hall, somewhere near my door, a man and a woman were having an argument in French about Intourist food tickets; and downstairs somewhere somebody was playing the piano and singing in German; and my bathroom pipes clunked as the heat faded; and during the night I knocked over a large china figure of a Greek athlete and crawled around the floor trying to find his hand; and after that I washed my hair and fell against the tub and bruised my arm.

The memories mounted with the cigarettes and, I guess, with the vodka. They were not bad memories, most of them, and I was not disturbed by them, or so I thought, but I knew that I had taken a whole period of my life and thrown it somewhere, always intending to call for it again, but now that it came time to call, I couldn't remember where I had left it. Did other people do this, drop the past in a used car lot and leave it for so long that one couldn't even remember the name of the road?

The road had to be to the lake in Pleasantville. But at first, I could only remember the last day I had ever walked it. After the moving vans had left the house, I had gone down to the lake remembering that we had left two turtle traps tied to a tree. I climbed up and around to bring in the traps, and then wondered what to do with them, how to ask the storage people to keep turtle traps safe for the future. Then the memory of the turtle traps brought back the first snapping turtles Hammett and I had caught, the nights spent reading about how to make the traps, how to kill the turtles, how to clean them, how to make the soup; and the soup brought back the sausage making and the ham curing, and the planting of a thousand twelve-inch pines that must now be a small forest; and the discovery of the beaver dam, and the boiled skunk cabbage and pickerelweed for dinner, in imitation of American Indians, that had made everybody sick but me; and working late into the night—I had written four plays at the farm and four or five movies—and then running, always with a dog and sometimes four, in the early summer light to the lake for a swim, pretending I was somebody else in some other land, some other century. And then back again to that last day: I had carried the turtle traps back to the house, forgetting, until I got to the tree nursery along the lake road, that I didn't own the house anymore. I stopped there to look at the hundred French lilac trees in the nursery, the rosebushes waiting for the transplant place they would never get, the two extravagant acres of blanched asparagus, and standing there by the road that May afternoon of 1952, I finally realized that I would never have any of this beautiful, hardscrabble land again. Now, in the Moscow room, I was glad it was gone, but sorry that the days of Joseph McCarthy, the persecution of Hammett, my own appearance before the House Un-American Activities Committee, the Hollywood blacklist, had caused it to be gone. There could never be any place like it again because I could never again be that woman who worked from seven in the morning until two or three the next morning and woke rested and hungry for each new day.

From a diary, 1966:

Tanya came to see me this afternoon after a long journey from the country. What had been a sharp, unhappy young face is now charming-plump, and her laughter is as deep as I remembered it. When Tanya was young she knew a man, liked him, didn't think much about him until she met him again in 1955 when he had just returned from ten years in a Siberian camp. She had divorced a drunken first husband but was full of happy stories about her life with Alex. She wanted me to like him, she said, because she likes him so much. We had dinner together. He is the head of a provincial art institute, a decent scholar, I was told, and I liked him immediately. (It is always pleasant to find an intellectual who looks like a peasant, instead of the often weak-handsome and the more often stunky-meek.) During the next days I found that their Moscow friends referred to Alex as the Saint, a man who gave anything to anybody, a man who, in the words of one of their friends, "did not care to be afraid." Alex and I got along fine although we had an argument last night about the Germans. His defense of Germans seemed to me odd for a Jew who fought with the Russian armies all the way to Berlin, and I might well have gone too far with the argument had Alex not risen to speak to a friend who passed our table in the restaurant. The man sitting next to me explained fast that Alex had been sent to the Siberian camp in "eternal banishment" because he had protested the behavior of Russian troops in Germany. When Alex sat down again, I think he knew that somebody had told me his history. Gently he said that he knew my ancestors had been Germans and maybe that made me less forgiving. I said maybe, I didn't know, but that Harriman, when he was ambassador, had told me that he had called on Stalin to relay a request from Roosevelt that all the Allied armies be instructed to act with care and decorum as they entered Germany. Stalin had laughed and said he would so instruct the Russian armies, but he didn't believe that men who had been fighting for years could be kept from rape and loot. But Stalin is not a good man to quote these days and Tanya and Alex and their friends were silent.

Moscow was always an ugly city except for the Kremlin Red Square and a few rich merchant sections, but now it is much uglier, as if Los Angeles had no sun and no grass. The city sprawls around, is inconvenient and haphazard with brash new buildings pushing against the old, as if bright mail order teeth were fitted next to yellowed fangs. There is a brutality about modern architecture in America, but in Moscow the brutality is mixed with something idiot-minded, as if their architects could loll about, giggling, poking at each other at a tipsy party given in honor of nothing.

There are still some fine nineteenth-century houses in Moscow—it has very few from the eighteenth century—and while they never could have compared to the great houses of London or Paris, now they seem lovely and soft, often in pinks and fading yellows, next to the new shabbiness on the next block. More churches are open, more have been restored since I was last here during the war, and St. Basil's, opposite my window at the hotel, is a wonderful building, as if wild bands of children had painted the brilliant onion domes and put the cheerful blocks into rounded shape. The light comes up late in Moscow in November, but there is never a morning that I don't want to walk across Red Square to look at St. Basil's. But you can't walk across Red Square anymore: I guess it was smart to allow no dangerous foot traffic in the giant spaces of the Square, but it is a tiring nuisance to go down the subway steps through the long corridors, up again and down, pushed and shoved, simply to find yourself across the street. True, it is very nice when you get there: nice to see the crowds all day, every day, waiting to look in religious reverence at Lenin's body, nice that the grounds of the Kremlin are now open to the public, wonderful to be able to go inside the exquisite small churches. Greek Catholicism, Russian form, has a warmth and coziness unlike other architectural church forms, as if God needed only brilliance of color and carving to feel praised.

The Palace of Congresses, the new building inside the walls of the Kremlin, is less bad than most, but it was vanity to put it so close to the wonderful old Kremlin buildings and ask it to compete. The new apartment buildings, spread out in all directions in the flat, ugly land, have no color and no form. The new hotels are imitations, I guess, of Abramovitz, or maybe men of the same time share the same vulgarities. The Danes and the Swedes have done some decent modern design, but the Russians have ignored their close neighbors and seem to be intent on imitating the mess we have made of our cities. But then everybody who has been in the Soviet Union for any length of time has noticed their concern with the United States: we may be the enemy, but we are the admired enemy, and the so-called good life for us is the to-be-good life for them. During the war, the Russian combination of dislike and grudging admiration for us, and ours for them, seemed to me like the innocent rivalry of two men proud of being large, handsome and successful. But I was wrong. They have chosen to imitate and compete with the most vulgar aspects of American life, and we have chosen, as in the revelations of the CIA bribery of intellectuals and scholars, to say, "But the Russians do the same thing," as if honor were a mask that you put on and took off at a costume ball. They condemn Vietnam, we condemn Hungary. But the moral tone of giants with swollen heads, fat fingers pressed over the atom bomb, staring at each other across the forests of the world, is monstrously comic.

Today Frieda Lurie, an official of the Writers Union, and I went to a shabby old building, climbed a lot of steps, came into a room where twenty women were working at desks, and told a scrawny lady that we had come to collect my royalties. (Not for the performances of the plays, although I don't know why, but for the publication of the plays.) The scrawny lady had known for a week that we were coming, and why, but she had a few minutes of pretending she couldn't quite place my name or the title of the book. Then she handed over ten bundles of rubles and I stuffed them into a paper bag that held some toys and a jar of caviar. She angrily pushed at the paper bag and told Frieda that this was most irregular, I must count the rubles before I signed the release papers. I said I wasn't going to count them, I didn't like to count money and didn't do it very well. The lady said that it was a necessary legal requirement. I said not for me and we were about to have trouble when I said, "Tell her I like what money buys, but I don't like handling it, and won't, and that's that." She understood English, because she smiled suddenly, nodded, and handed over the papers that had to be signed. On the walk back, I wondered why I had made such a fuss, if my dislike of counting money could have started at my grandmother's Sunday dinners where they spoke of things in exact dollar amounts—the rug had cost two thousand four hundred three dollars and seventy-four cents, the chauffeur had used up four dollars and thirty-two cents of gas on a drive of two hundred and two miles—or whether it came much later, from the opening night of *Another Part of the Forest*, when my father counted crisp bills throughout the performance, throwing the actors and causing angry mutters in the audience around him. My father, who had little concern with money, had never done anything like that before, although he had been acting odd, speaking odd, for many months before that night. At the party after the performance, I was angry with my father until Gregory Zilboorg, the psychoanalyst, said to me, "Your father has senile dementia. You must face it and do something about it very soon." The shock of that sentence is still with me now, over twenty years later, but I didn't do anything about it for another six months, and then only when the terrible crack-up came that sent my father to a hospital. He blamed me for his being in the hospital and thus I lost my father, as he lost his mind, for two years before his death.

A few days later, at dinner again with Tanya and her friends, one of the women said the scrawny lady, who was her cousin, had been amused that I refused to count my royalty money. She said it was Russian of me, not to care about money. I said I did care about money, cared so much, in fact, that I pretended not to care, and maybe that was the reason I had always been so attracted by Russians, who are nonsavers, noncomputers, generous about sharing and giving, no middle-class calculations about what you take or give back. My hosts were pleased, but assured me that Russian openhandedness had nothing to do with Socialist theory, they had always been like that, maybe because Russia had skipped the middle-class revolution, maybe because the poverty had been so great, maybe even religion; and so we batted all that around for a while and finally got to Dostoevsky's *The Possessed,* and had an argument about the book because I liked it more than they did. By this time we had all had a lot to drink and, of course, we ended the evening with somebody reciting Pushkin, long, long, long. That's the way I remembered many nights during the war, somebody reciting Pushkin, long, long, long.

In 1945 I had met a young captain who was home from the front, just out of the hospital after a bad leg wound. Captain K was in his middle twenties then, his graduate degree interrupted by the war. He had been doing his thesis on modern American novelists and wanted to use his recovery leave to work on it. We had talked a lot in those days: Hemingway wasn't well published in the Soviet Union, but the captain was hungry for knowledge of him. I tried hard to sell him on Faulkner and Fitzgerald, but although he had heard of both men, he knew nothing of them. Russians are extra dogmatic about what they don't know, and so he was sure they were not as good as Hemingway.

Now, on this trip, I asked about Captain K, but nobody knew what had happened to him. Toward the end of my first week, he telephoned me from the lobby of the hotel. I opened the door to a man I would not have recognized: the face had become too large, and folded around itself; the blond hair was now a darkish red; the manner, once eager and sharp, was now so withdrawn and quiet that he didn't answer my greeting, but moved directly past me to the table and sat down. At the end of ten minutes of forced chitchat from me—I don't like myself when I do that and often end up not liking the person who forces it on me—he said, "I am glad to see you, Lilishka. The rain is not coming now. Shall we make a walk?"

We walked in silence, going past the old building of Moscow University. Then he stopped, turned, went back to the building and stood in the courtyard, staring at it.

He said, "I have not seen it for years. I do not now come to this neighborhood. The last time I came down that staircase, I held my thesis in large bag. I was to go to front lines that night. I think there will be much time to finish my thesis at front in the long nights."

I said, "Is that the thesis on American novelists that you used to talk about?"

"Yes," he said, "but by the time I knew you I had long lost it. I did not want to tell that. I was not wounded that time, by the fence that was mined, but I was thrown a distance and my thesis was gone. In the army they called me Comrade Thesis and then later Captain Thesis. No, I did not resume to work on it again." After a long silence he said, "You were O.K. right. Faulkner is fine writer, best. You have Faulkner books with you?"

I said I didn't, but I would send them to him.

He said, "Tell me about the book *Sanctuary*."

I don't know how to tell about books, and I thought he meant just good or bad, but he wanted the characters and the plot. It's a complicated book, *Sanctuary,* and there was something ridiculous about describing Popeye on a cold Moscow day when, for me, Popeye is the South I knew, full of vines and elephant ear leaves, heavy with swamp air and Spanish moss, home and frightening land, so I told him instead about the time in the early 1930's when Hammett and I had first come to New York together. I think we had just met Faulkner, and for the length of Bill's visit in New York the three of us would meet each night, sometimes early in the evening, sometimes very late, usually at Dash's place, arguing about books and drinking through until morning, when I would fall asleep or pass out, and they would eat breakfast or start another bottle. I told the captain that Faulkner was on a kick then about *Sanctuary*—I am told he stayed on the kick throughout his life—claiming that it was a potboiler and he had only written it for money. Hammett used to be irritated by that and would answer that nobody ever deliberately wrote a potboiler, you just did the best you could and woke up to find it good or no good. Usually, by the time of such talk they were both too drunk to listen to each other and each would speak at the same time, or to me, or in space. The captain said he didn't know much about drinking, he had skipped his youth, did I still drink a lot? I said no, not as much, I couldn't, but I'd like a drink now in the cold drizzle that had started. We wandered around looking for a place, and by the time we found it I realized that we were in the Arbat section. The neighborhoood has changed a great deal since I lived in Spasso House during the war. Spasso, which had once belonged to a nineteenth-century sugar millionaire, could never have been a beauty, and during the war it was a seedy kind of embassy, but now it looks spruced up and prosperous-gay. Standing in front of it I remembered all the dinners, sometimes pleasant and homey with Harriman, his daughter, and the few foreign career officers who lived in the house, sometimes just aimless off-tempered, a table of people living in a place they didn't like, waiting to be cheered by anything, even by my discovery of fresh onions in the cellar. And I remembered a small, crazy dog that lived in the room next to mine; and the visits to the house of the great dancer who, wherever she sat, always faced a mirror, her eyes unwavering; and siphoning off gasoline from the embassy car to clean my hair, and falling over and over again in the courtyard as I practiced walking in flat, high felt boots; and Prokofiev urging me to leave a chamber music concert because he didn't like music "played"; and the nice kid from Kansas City who ran the army P.X. and gave lectures about the possible state of my liver, and a hundred other faces and voices from so long ago.

I was looking now for the miserable, state-owned antique store where so often I had tried to find something, anything with color, to cheer me in the cold, gray misery of wartime Moscow. The store is gone now and a brassy department store has taken its place, but I laughed as I remembered the day when John Melby and I had found two nineteenth-century children's picture books and were on our way out to the street. Then he touched my arm and pointed to a high shelf. On the shelf was a large photograph of the real faces of Garbo and the director Rouben Mamoulian, with crudely faked bodies arranged in one of the poses of love. Both Melby and I advanced toward the picture in movements evidently so furtive that the two ladies who attended at the store came toward us. I put out my hand to take the picture but John shook his head and pulled me to the door. When we were on the street, I turned to go back, but he held my arm and said that of course some joker had put it there, but as foreigners we would never be forgiven for buying it. He only got me back to Spasso by promising that he would get one of the Russian employees at the embassy to go around and buy it for me. But two days later, the Russian messenger said the picture was gone. Maybe, maybe not.

Captain K knocked at my door a few mornings later. Again he went immediately to the table. picked up a magazine, read it for a while without speaking to me. (I like people who refuse to speak until they are ready to speak.) I went back to reading Malamud's *The Fixer*.

After an hour or so. I said I had to go out for lunch. He immediately picked up *The Fixer* and asked if he could stay on and read it. When I came back in late afternoon, he had finished the book and was lying on the couch, his right leg propped up on two pillows. I was not meant to see that, because he jumped to his feet and put the pillows into place too fast.

He said, "I came this morning to speak with you about Eisenstein. After he died, we found engraved little box with greeting from him to you. I had the intention to mail it to you. But time went by and then I cannot find it."

"All of you," I said.

"All of us?"

"Slavs," I said. "I would like to have had something from Eisenstein. You must have known that."

Eisenstein had been at the airport to meet me when I landed in 1944, and after that we met three or four times a week during the months I was in Moscow. We would often walk in the afternoon darkness and, in the early days, I would suggest that he come to Spasso for tea, but he would smile and say goodbye. Perhaps because I asked no questions, he finally told me that it was dangerous for im to be seen at our embassy. (He did come, finally, to my farewell party, but that was the only time, and then so many other Russians came that I guess he felt it no great chance to take.) Eisenstein was, during that winter of 1944, cutting the first part of *Ivan the Terrible;* he would talk about the picture, and his other pictures, and his Baltic youth, and his studies of the human eye, and German literature and English poetry, and music. And sometimes we would go off to rehearsals of *The Little Foxes* or *Watch on the Rhine*. He would be amused at my muttered complaints which he made worse when he translated for the actors and directors. One day an actress in *Watch on the Rhine* broke into tears at an objection I made to the heavy ornamentation she was giving the part. Eisenstein said, "What shall I tell her? I've worked with her many times and the tears will go on all night unless you give some foolish praise, or cry with her."

I said, "I don't want to cry with her so tell her she's wonderful and let's get out of here."

He translated that into "Miss Hellman says to tell you that you are wonderful in the hope that we can get out of here immediately."

Eisenstein was one of the most forceful and brilliant men I have ever met, and one of the best to be with. Neither of us ever talked about ourselves, although once he asked me if I was married to Hammett and then he spoke vaguely about a wife. (I had heard from other people that she was not and never had been a wife, but a devoted friend and housekeeper, and some of his friends denied even that.) It is considered a political and social sin in Russia to print news about anybody's personal life. I don't know the origins of this taboo, but it operated as well for the life of Stalin—one remembers that until Svetana Alliluyeva emerged under Western eyes one did not know how many times he had been married, or what child came from what lady, or what happened to the ladies—as it does for the life of the men now in the Kremlin or the

poet or the scientist. It is puzzling, however, because
Russians gossip among themselves as people do every
where, except they know more about each other than my
neighbors on the tight little island of Martha's Vineyard
Eisenstein was, at the time I knew him, both in and out of
government favor: in enough to be making a large, expensive movie, out enough to be worried about whom he saw.
where he went, what was going to happen to his work
Among intellectuals, however, even those a generation
younger, he was still a great figure—he has become an
even greater figure because of his new published collected
work—but nowhere did I hear any gossip about his life
although I was always conscious that caution set in when
people talked about him.

One day, a few weeks before I left Moscow in 1945
Eisenstein phoned to say that he had finished a rough cut
of *Ivan* and had borrowed the apartment of a friend to
show the picture to a few people. The next night Averell,
Kathy Harriman and I went to the only luxury apartment
I had seen in Moscow. It was flutey and crowded with
nineteenth-century bibelots, shawls, and carved furniture.
The large piano was draped with six or seven young men,
nibbling on sandwiches, who looked as if they were posing
for a winter picnic. Surrounding the young men were three
or four older men who offered candies and lit cigarettes
with the attention of elderly valets to young royalty. *Ivan*
was a turgid, dull movie—I think Eisenstein already knew
it was—and it was not a pleasant evening.

I said to the captain, "It made me sad, that evening.
That great man, the bad movie, the pretty boys—" forgetting that he didn't know what evening I was talking
about. "I wrote to Eisenstein when I got home. I wrote
several times, but I had no answer. Then I got a cable
that said, 'I am ill. Please airmail thirteen mystery stories
to bring me luck.' I knew it was a joke but I sent the
thirteen mysteries, anyway. Long before they could have

eached Sergei I read in the newspaper that he was dead.
t was a strange joke for a sick man, wasn't it?"

The captain turned to look at me. "It was not a joke. It
was most serious."

"You can't mean that. How could it be serious?"

"Eisenstein was a most superstitious man, of such pro-
portions that he would not speak again in his lifetime to
an old friend who once laughed at his misery over salt
spilled on a table. Perhaps he hide this from you because
you are Western woman. Now tell about writer Norman
Mailer."

I was about to say that this telling about books and
people was no good for me, but the captain's face suddenly twitched and he leaned down to rub his right leg and
then to move it in a quick up-and-down exercise, turning
his head away from me. So I said that I had known
Mailer for many years, thought *The Naked and the Dead*
very good, had never much liked the other novels, but
now I admired *Cannibals and Christians*. It was not possible, not the time, to explain the affection and angry
teasing that have made the seesaw on which Norman and
I have sat out our relationship, but I tried to say, discov-
ering it as I said it, that *Cannibals and Christians* had
made me understand the growth of Norman as a man. If I
had not given full credit before it was not all my fault:
Mailer's growth has been mixed with so much foolishness,
his real powers so sprinkled with aimless errands, his true
sweetness so buttoned under the meanest-kid-on-the-
toughest-street in Slumsville, Harvard, Class of 1943. But
that was all too hard to say.

I said, instead, "Mailer is a wonderful writer, a natural,
the best kind, who wasted time being famous, but maybe
he won't waste it anymore. I don't know. You can't know
actors and Norman is an actor."

The captain said, "I like very much Mailer, a brave
man, I think. Did you hear ever of historian Smirnoff?"

I shook my head.

"Did you hear ever of the siege of Brest?"

I nodded.

"The Russian garrison fought against the Germans unti
most were dead. Those who live were taken prisoners, al
sick with wounds. Then, years in German concentratior
camp, bad. So there are not many who live when war i
finished. They go home. But no one of them arrive home
No one. Smirnoff, the historian Smirnoff, wishes to write
of Brest, so he begins investigation for his work. Where
are the men who make the fight at Brest? Nobody knows
So Smirnoff sets the task to find out. He find out: they have
gone in straight-line train from German prison camp over
Urals to Russian prison camp. This man, this Smirnoff is
hero, hero, not like in war when there is no other thing to
be. This man, this Smirnoff, began to make fight by
himself. All the time he go to the Kremlin, knock on one
door, knock on other door, day and day, month and
month, no fear for himself, day and night— He won. I
come back. Me and others." He laughed. "Now poor
Smirnoff is famous, like great judge or priest of old days
and nobody gives him rest. From all over people write
him about cows are not good, my science teacher is vodka
drinker and such, please speak with Kremlin."

I said, "What was the reason, the official reason?"

"The old crazy man Stalin believe that if Germans had
you prisoner, perhaps you wished to be prisoner, or perhaps you talk secrets to them. Do you not think Smirnof
is good story of a man?"

I said, "Do you still write?"

"No, I am now pharmacist's assistant. I learn it in the
prison camp."

"Are you married?"

"For six years. Then my wife go away with man from
hotel desk in Yalta. Last year she send me picture of the
house of Chekhov and said I should come look at it."

I said, "You will marry again."

He shook his head. "No. I have not the faith. I make

mistake so large I could make mistake more large." He rose. He was limping badly now. "I have brought a list of poets. I would be glad if you could send their books to me. Not thirteen, like Eisenstein. Four."

The list was Wallace Stevens, Auden, William Carlos Williams, and a man called James Senate. Weeks later, in London, I was on my way to buy the books when I realized I had no address for the captain and no way to find it.

13

Fʀᴏᴍ a diary, 1967:

Paris, April 23

For two days now I have asked myself why the French frighten me. I came here the first time when I was very young, lived here for four months, and have come back many times since. True, I am ashamed of the patois French that New Orleans taught me and won't take part in conversations with educated people, but waiters and taxi drivers think I talk just fine. I have felt more at home in Copenhagen in three days and more comfortable in a frozen outskirt of Irkutsk. I can't remember being frightened of the French when I was young and poor, so why should I be now when I am not poor? I stay at the best hotels, go to the best restaurants, can buy in good shops, can afford meals for those old friends who didn't share in the French boom. (Most intellectuals didn't.) And yet, in the last years, I am timid as I walk along the lovely streets. It's as if all of France had become a too thin lady.

Very thin ladies, any age, with hand sewing on them, have
always frightened me, beginning with a rich great-aunt
and her underwear embroidered by nuns. The more bones
that show on women the more inferior I feel.

I know my way around Paris and yet each day I get
lost and it's no longer possible, as it was even three years
ago, to say to hell with all that, today I go once more to
see Ste. Chapelle or to the Marais or to wander around the
Rue de la Université, trying to sort out all those houses
that Stendhal is supposed to have lived in, and then take
myself alone to a small place to eat and rest. I have, this
week, bought a dress and a bag, no better and no cheaper
than New York, have kept myself from the angry question
of why a dress should need four fittings, and have had
dinner or lunch with old friends. (I have written to Ara-
gon and Elsa but, for the first time, they have not answered
me, and yet I know they are in Paris. It is understandable:
they are growing old, they work hard, and who, after a
certain age, wishes to see anybody at intervals of two or
three years?) The dinners and lunches were not as good as
they used to be, but the talk is still good, or, at least, high
class. It may be the only country in the world where the
rich are sometimes brilliant.

April 24

We are at the Château Choiseul Amboise. It has been a
good day: I feel at my best when somebody else drives the
car, gives the orders, knows me well enough to see
through the manner that, as an irritated theatre director
once pointed out, was thought up early to hide the indeci-
sion, the vagueness. The hotel and gardens are charming,
the dining room high and white, the dinner of Loire
salmon is excellent, and I feel very close to the man
opposite me. The years we have known each other have
made a pleasant summer fog of the strange, crippled
relationship, often ripped, always mended, merging, final-

ly, into comfort. I am comfortable now. I feel young again on this journey that was his idea. We have a local marc in the garden, we have been talking as old friends should talk, about nothing, about everything.

R says, "I must say something to you. I should get married again. My feeling for you has kept me from marrying."

I have heard this many times before. I mumble that to myself.

"What did you say?"

"Nothing. Are you marrying a theory or a woman?"

"I met a girl in Berlin. We've been living together. I have been in a panic since she went home."

I push my chair back. I know now why this trip was arranged. It is not the first time he has done this. I go to my room, drink too much brandy, and the anger turns in against myself. The next morning we cancel the rest of the trip and drive back to Paris. I have a stinking hangover and don't speak on the ride back, don't even think much except to tell myself how much jabber there is in the name of love. The next day R sends me flowers just as the porter is carrying down my luggage for the plane to Budapest.

Budapest, April 30

Is it age, or was it always my nature, to take a bad time, block out the good times, until any success became an accident and failure seemed the only truth? I can't sleep, I have had a headache for three days, I lie on the bed telling myself that nothing has ever gone right, doubting even Hammett and myself, remembering how hard the early years sometimes were for us when he didn't care what he did or spoiled, and I didn't think I wanted to stay long with anybody, asking myself why, after the first failure, I had been so frightened of marriage, who the hell did I think I was alone in a world where women don't have much safety, and, finally, on the third night, falling asleep with a lighted cigarette and waking to a burn on my chest. Staring at the burn, I thought: That's what you deserve for wasting time on stuff proper for the head of a young girl.

Edmund Wilson's friends are nice people. Mrs. S is a bluestocking but handsome and with good manners. Her husband, much older than she, is an art expert. Bluestockings are the same the world over, but the European variety has learned a few graces: Mrs. S, of course, chose the table in the restaurant and ordered the dinner, but she pretended that her husband did and he was pleased. When I got back to the hotel I felt cheerful, for the first time in a week. I sat on the balcony outside my room and looked at the old church across the square. In the park the hotel night clerk was drinking something from a glass. I thought about Mrs. S and her husband, their age difference must be what mine was to Hammett. But Dash was not grateful, or ungrateful, either, for a much younger woman, and I didn't choose tables or food or anything very often. He used his age to make the rules.

One day, a few months after we met, he said, "Can you stop juggling oranges?"

I said I didn't know what he meant.

He said, "Yes, you do. So stop it or I won't be around to watch."

A week later, I said, "You mean I haven't made up my mind about you and have been juggling you and other people. I'm sorry. Maybe it will take time for me to cure myself, but I'll try."

He said, "Maybe it will take time for *you*. But for me it will take no longer than tomorrow morning."

And so I did stop for long periods, although several times through the years he said, "Don't start that juggling again."

Many years later, unhappy about his drinking, his ladies, my life with him, I remember an angry speech I made one night: it had to do with injustice, his carelessness, his insistence that he get his way, his sharpness with me but not with himself. I was drunk, but he was drunker, and when my strides around the room carried me close to the chair where he was sitting, I stared in disbelief at what I saw. He was grinding a burning cigarette into his cheek.

I said, "What are you doing?"

"Keeping myself from doing it to you," he said.

The mark on his cheek was ugly for a few weeks, but in time it faded into the scar that remained for the rest of his life. We never again spoke of that night because, I think, he was ashamed of the angry gesture that made him once again the winner in the game that men and women play against each other, and I was ashamed that I caused myself to lose so often.

And so I told myself that it was unjust to hold in contempt R, who is another juggler. Unjust. How many times I've used that word, scolded myself with it. All I mean by it now is that I don't have the final courage to say that I refuse to preside over violations against myself, and to hell with justice.

I have sent two cables to the Writers Union in Moscow, saying that I would arrive on Sunday night. A few hours ago, a call comes from Moscow, a man's voice makes sounds that I can't hear. I make sounds that he can't hear, I hang up, he calls again, and then Tomas comes on the phone to ask if I would like a picnic, free, no charge, with his children. I say yes, the man in Moscow goes on shouting through Tomas, an operator shouts at him in Russian, and he hangs up.

Tomas is a taxi driver whose cab I took my first day here. He speaks good English, is wry and funny, makes

An Unfinished Woman

fancy hints about his fallen station in the world. Every
morning he calls to see if I want to hire him for the day,
and sometimes I do.

Yesterday, when I left him, I said, "Thank you for
calling every day. It is kind of you to be so nice to a
stranger."

He stared at me. "That is not it, you do not count very
well. You have been giving me large amounts of forints."

"I have? How much?"

"That is for you to decide. For me, I would not like to
ruin the golden goose."

Now the golden goose is lying on her back in the hills
above Budapest. Tomas's two little girls are playing with
Tomas's shoes.

Tomas says, "They had different mamas. Both ladies
departed from me. But me, their papa was the same, or so
is my hope, who cares."

I close my eyes. A few hours later the sun is down, and
I wake up shivering. One of the little girls is running down
the hill and the other is crying. Tomas brings me the one
who is crying and I rise and walk with her as he lopes
down the hill to catch the older girl. That is what she
wants, because she turns, laughing, and waits for him. He
carries her back up the hill, looking very tired, shaking his
head at me as he speaks of his age and weight.

On the way back to Budapest he says, "The older one
gives trouble. She is like her mother, the one who departed from me, although the second departed from me also.
You know why she departs? I tell her that my rich uncle
in San Francisco will send washing machine because when
I am sixteen the rich uncle writes and says he will send
washing machine when I marry. You know what he sends
when I write and say now I marry? He sends ten-dollar
American bill. It is forbidden here, of course, to send
foreign money outside. Communism!" He turns his head
and speaks in Hungarian. The older girl fishes out from
her dress a last-century largish locket, opens it, shows me

a folded ten-dollar bill. The child is grinning, but when I smile back, her face goes cold and she slumps in her seat.

Later that evening, Mr. B, a literary politician in any country, arranges to have a young poet come to escort me to a reception for the president of PEN, an Englishman. I always find this kind of gathering difficult, but was made to feel rude when I said that I would like to skip it. Even when I was young, when we didn't know the good word square, we knew PEN was square, and for writers with three names. But it is explained to me now that the organization has become important because it arranges an exchange of visits between Communist writers and Western Europeans—only the Soviet Union has refused to participate—that might otherwise never take place.

The reception is unexpectedly pleasant and I speak for a long time with a tall, sad-faced man without knowing that he is Geza Ottlik, a novelist about whom I have heard. (On the way back to the hotel, my poet escort says that Ottlik is considered a "master" by the younger generation, but that he doesn't write novels any longer.) In a small group at the party—I have a bad ear for foreign sounds and thus for anybody's name—we sit talking of *Encounter*, and the CIA scandal, and the possibility, mentioned in the press, that the CIA paid for certain delegates to the last PEN meeting. A fat man says the CIA has ruined itself forever, it will not again appear on the cultural scene, don't I agree? I say no, I do not agree: what he calls a scandal is only a minor discomfort to be forgotten in a few weeks. The fat man bristles and says his American friends have told him otherwise. I do not like such arguments, seldom trust people who make them, and so I shrug and shut up. But the fat man is annoyed with me and demands that I explain what I mean. It is not easy to explain to a foreigner, maybe to anybody, that what you had thought was a small, primitive concept of dignity, the early voice that says nobody can buy me, became in our time so corrupted by anti-Communism that bribes were not thought of as bribes, particularly if they came in the form of trips to foreign lands, or grants for research, and were offered by Ivy League gentlemen to a generation of intellectuals who were jealous of the easy postwar money earned by everybody around them. Intellectuals can tell themselves anything, sell themselves any bill of goods, which is why they were so often patsies for the ruling classes in nineteenth-century France and England, or twentieth-century Russia and America. I try to say that and end up by saying, "Ach, I don't know." The fat man begins to talk about the English nineteenth century and after a while a young man says to me, "He talks of everything like an encyclopedia, on and on." Somebody laughs and people rise and move off. A lady takes my arm and moves me to the punch bowl.

"He is a spy, as you so quickly guessed."

"The fat man? No, I did not guess. A spy for what?"

She giggles and says, "The government," and pokes me in the ribs.

May 6

It has been ten days since I have slept more than a few hours or eaten more than one meal a day. I have lost eight pounds. That would usually please me, but I look tired, sad, and that does not please me. You can do and you can take almost as much as when you were young, but you cannot recover fast. I tell myself that I must forbid myself these upheavals because I can no longer afford them. But how often I have said all that before, what good does it do, how little my nature allows me to carry out the resolute wisdom of night. For a minute I wish age would strike with the bad health I have never had, then immediately frightened, superstitious, I jump from the bed, put on a coat, cross the park, and look for the first restaurant that might have coffee. On the way, I argue, I lecture, I determine. I am suddenly so sick of myself that I spit in the street. I stand staring at the spit, laughing.

I remember: Hammett and I are having breakfast with friends in the country, served on one of those ugly bar arrangements with high stools. Hammett is teasing me. He tells about a hunting trip when, in an attempt to aim at a high-flying duck, I had hit a wild lilac bush. He is saying that I have no sense of direction about anything.

I say, "Don't count on it. I could spit in your eye if I wanted to. How much says I can't do it?"

"The Jap prints," he says, meaning a rare set of Japanese art books he has just bought and loves, "fifty dollars, and anything you want to say to me for a whole week."

I spit directly into his eye and the daughter of the family screams. Hammett had a quiet laugh that began slowly and then creased his face for a long time. It begins now and is increased by the perplexed, unhappy looks of the others at the table. He says, proudly, "That's my girl. Some of the time the kid kicks through."

I turn into a restaurant, happy now at the memory of Dash's long, thin, handsome face at that spitting breakfast more than fifteen years ago. The place is crowded, the people at tables near the entrance stare at my fur-lined coat on this warm day. I move to the back and sit down at a table with two young women. I have coffee and try to order a boiled egg.

One of the young girls says in English, in an excellent accent, "The eggs are at the front bar. May I get them for you?"

She gets up and the other girl asks me in less good English if I am Australian. When her friend comes back we ask and answer questions. They are graduate students, one in English, one in French. Magda is the daughter of a history professor, Charlotte the daughter of a factory foreman. They are pleased that they know two of my plays, they ask if they can show me any part of Budapest or the countryside. I tell them I don't like gypsy music, am sick of hearing it, is there any place to hear jazz?

Magda claps her hands. "Indeed, indeed. My younger brother, if you can tolerate him, plays with a group every Saturday night. Will you come?"

It is past midnight. The apartment must once have been part of a solid private house. I am sitting in a broken chair, my back hurts. Around me are Magda and Charlotte, and Charlotte's beau Sandor, a tall young man of about twenty-four. I count the others, including the band, as eleven, and all eleven are younger, in their teens. The jazz band is not good, very imitative of us. They have been playing since nine o'clock, with few rests, but now they are tired and hungry, I guess, because two girls appear with coffee, pastry, and wine that is too sweet for me. The room having been blown with noise is now silent except for somebody who is whistling. Everybody eats or drinks and a few of them stare at me. Something is expected of me, but I don't know what, and I feel awkward. Finally, one of the younger boys says something and Sandor answers him. Then somebody else speaks and Sandor answers sharply.

He says to me, "They say 'Launch.' "

"Launch?"

"That is the translation. They mean you must have come to this country with a purpose. So launch the purpose here, now. Hungary is bad and poor, America is good and rich, et cetera, et cetera."

"Why would I do that?"

Magda laughs. "My brother says maybe you think they should enlist in Vietnam war against Communist aggressors."

I remember a Harvard seminar when two students wished to bait me. I decide on the answer I made then.

I say, "Tell your brother to go to hell."

Magda translates, and they laugh. She says, "They are young. We are not young, although there is only five or six years between us. We were the believers, they are not."

"Believers in what?"

"Socialism. We grew up believing. Now we are bitter."

Sandor, Charlotte's beau, says to Magda, "Speak for yourself, less for others. I am still a Communist. My own kind of Communist."

Charlotte puts out a hand and touches him. Timeless gesture, and timeless response when he pushes her hand away. She turns to me. "He stays with the workers. He is finding a new Communism."

He says, "Do not explain me. Not that way."

She says something to him in Hungarian. Magda whispers to me, "She is too *triste, éthérée.*"

Charlotte, as if conscious of me again, says, "My brother was to be an engineer, but now he doesn't want to be anything, except not to starve or ask favors of the government. Sandor tells him without work man is nothing."

I say to Sandor, "What do you work at?"

"I do not work." He moves about in front of me. "Something new must come, Marxism must advance. Now we leave it to the protectors of the state. It is too good for them. Something new must come."

Charlotte's brother laughs. "Lady foreigner, turn your ears away. Nothing new will come. There is nothing in this world but now for now."

Then he crosses the room, raises his arm, and the music starts again, for the first time in a kind of folk melody. The guitar player sings, and when the first verse is finished several others sing with him.

Magda brings me some wine. "The song says, 'Shut your heart against the past and the future. Now is for now.'"

After the rather sweet melody is over, the band goes back to jazz. It is two o'clock and I rise to leave. Sandor,

Charlotte and Magda walk me back to my hotel, a long
distance across the river. Sandor tells me that the new
socialism must come from the worker, I say that was the
old way, he says that's what people thought but things go
off the track, and for a few minutes it seems to me I am
young again and Sandor is William and Charlotte is Ger-
trude and the conversation is being held on the porch of a
house in the Berkshires. I ask Sandor too many questions
in order to hide my weariness with what he is saying, and
thank them for the evening too many times. We agree that
we will meet again before I leave Budapest, but the next
day it is raining and I decide to fly to Moscow that
afternoon.

Moscow, May 8

I should never have criticized the National Hotel. My
hosts, the Writers Union, have put me up at the Pekin
Hotel, built in the fifties, and already shabby. It may have
been comfortable then for Chinese visitors, but it must
always have been strange for other foreigners. (Since I am
already known as a difficult lady, I think it best not to
complain.) My translator is a gentle, friendly young woman called Maya, doing her doctoral work in English literature. Raya and Lev, dear, good friends, are hurrying back
from Tiflis, but Elena and her husband were at the airport
to greet me. Elena, who is about my age, looks very like
my father's mother—a fine, craggy face filled with life
that was and life that is. It is very hot in Moscow and
hard to recognize a city that I have known only under
snow or cold autumn rains.

Elena arranged for me to hear the Richter concert
tonight. As good as he is, the audience is better: old ladies
rise after each number, hand their drooping flowers to the
nearest young girl, who carries them up to Richter.
Richter bows to the young ladies, and the old ladies bow
and simper to him. There was a disagreeable crowd at the

entrance to the concert hall. The tickets are scarce and here were hundreds around the theatre trying to pick hem up at the last minute. Music lovers are a rough bunch, I tell myself, whether they are crowding the Beates or Richter. A man had pushed so hard around me that my left hand got hurt. I snarl at the man in English, he smiles, Elena scolds him, but she does not like my jokes about the manners of proletarian music lovers.

May 10

There is a large statue of Tolstoi in the courtyard of the Writers Union. They insist this is the house that Tolstoi described for the Rostovs. But during the war I was shown another place that was called the Rostov house and I still believe that is true not only because my guide then was a very old man, a distinguished historian, but because the Writers Union place could never have been big or rich enough for the Rostovs. Mr. Sirkov, the secretary of the union, is away, which is O.K. with me. I have tea with two other officials who tell me how glad they are I chose this time to come to Moscow because, in two weeks, the Writers Congress will begin. This is the first time I have heard that this twice postponed conference will take place at all, and I explain that it will be impossible for me to stay that long because Mike Nichols and I are casting a revival of *The Little Foxes* and I am due home. I am glad that is true because I heard in Paris that the conference will be run by the conservative faction of the Writers Union and that no protests about past or present censorship will be allowed.

May 12

Raya and Lev have returned to Moscow and we had dinner last night and a fine evening. Their pleasure in their new apartment—they have waited so many years to get it—is fun to watch, and the open way in which they live, people wandering in and out to talk, to eat, to borrow books, to sleep for a night or a week, is a way of life I envy, but for which I have no gift.

One of their friends told me that Robert Lowell is expected for the Writers Congress, but I don't believe it. I think Voznesensky has been asked to bring him to Moscow, but I have faith in Cal's instincts of where to go when. Tonight as Raya, Lev and I returned to the hotel, a large group of men and women were moving about on the sidewalk, half of them falling-stage drunk. One woman could not stand up. Three men were holding her as they tried to persuade a taxi driver to take them in the cab. The taxi driver didn't want them. We stand listening to the argument until the woman begins to vomit and the taxi drives away.

As we turn into the lobby, I see Captain K standing at the corner. I start toward him but he shakes his head and puts up his hand. I watch Lev leave the hotel, I wait for a few minutes and then go into the street. One of the drunks moves toward me. He is not smiling and his mumblings sound angry. A friend says something to him, but he shakes his head and follows me to the corner. I don't see the captain until the drunk is against a wall and the captain is pushing the drunk's friend with his other hand. They are the fastest, most efficient moves I've ever seen. Then the captain takes my arm and we run across Mayakovski Square.

He says, "I read in paper you come back. I am happy to see you. But you look not so healthy as last time. I am hungry. I do not eat because I wait for you to arrive at hotel."

We go into the subway. On the train, he takes out a small book and reads for the next twenty minutes. Then he rises and we get out. I have no idea where we are. We walk a long block, turn into a dirt road. We are now passing the small wooden houses that I remember so well during the war, with the pretty carved window frames and door ornaments, and the very small, hot rooms. The captain unlocks the door of what looks to be a pink house trimmed in black or dark green, and we go through the front room where a man is sleeping, and then into two small rooms, with a kitchen off one of the small rooms. He smiles, makes a gesture of welcome, moves into the kitchen. The light is dim but I see that books are piled high in corners, under the army bed, under a wooden stool. The room is military clean and there is no decoration except a small bust of Dante and a picture of what seems like a very, very tall man with his face half turned from the camera, holding in his hand a large handkerchief. There are no papers on a desk made from two wooden boxes, but it is piled with books and pamphlets in Russian, English, French and German.

The captain comes out of the kitchen carrying a bottle of vodka, tea, a jar of mushrooms, black bread, a dish of tomatoes. We silently toast each other in vodka. I don't want food, but I eat a piece of bread and have some tea.

I point to the picture. "Your father?"

"My uncle. I lived with him my life."

"He doesn't look like a peasant."

"A peasant?" He laughs. "A peasant? You remember little of what I tell you years ago."

"You didn't tell me much, except about the war and your thesis."

I pick up a worn, leatherbound English edition of Coleridge and suddenly remember the books he had wanted in November.

"I went to buy you the books, then realized I didn't have your address and that you wouldn't have wanted me to write and ask people to find you. I'll send the books immediately I get home."

He nods. "But you. With you something is the matter?"

"Age, maybe."

"Work?"

"I guess so."

"For a long time?"

"I guess so."

"The death of Mr. Dashiell?"

"No, I don't think anymore. Maybe just too much of myself. Or knowledge that has come too late, or wisdom I can't make use of now or don't want to. All kinds of things."

He pours us more tea, picks up a book, puts it down, picks up the magazine *Foreign Literature*. He has forgotten I am in the room.

Finally he mumbles, closes the magazine. *"Merde. Merde.* More polite it is in French, eh? Tell me of yourself. It is safe. I am hermit."

"This 'tell me,' 'tell me,' 'tell me.' How can one talk that way?"

I wonder why I have sounded so irritable and I want to say something friendly to make up for it, but I can't think of anything.

"So you go home from Moscow in 1945. Before you leave you tell me that G. Zilboorg is doing a psychoanalysis. I read *Mind, Medicine and Man* by Zilboorg. Did you return to his treatment?"

I nod.

"I would like to hear of such an experience."

"It was a long, painful business. Then it is over and you can't fit the pieces together or even remember much of what you said or what was said to you. But I no longer have headaches."

"It was good, then?"

"It was better than it was not. That's all, I guess." I have never said that before, never knew I thought it, but having put it into words, it seems mingy and not the whole truth. "I don't drink much anymore. I understand more of what was wrong. I don't know. When life doesn't go well, then it seems to me all that time and money should have done more for me. When things get better, I am grateful for what I learned, glad of the changes in me."

He says, "He is dead, G. Zilboorg. From one foreign quarter I hear that he was much respected." He hesitates. "But from another, I hear strange tales of his last years."

I wonder how, isolated from all others in this distant land, he has heard about Zilboorg in New York. Zilboorg had been a Russian, it is true, but— Then I remember that the captain had started as a medical student and that in the war years he had been reading Freud and Adler and asking questions.

"Yes," I said, "Zilboorg ended odd." But the story is too long, too complicated, too American. "But I respected him and was grateful to him. I went to him in his good years. After he died it took me a long time to believe the ugliness I was hearing. I guess people who mesmerize other people die absolutely on the day they die—the magic is gone."

He nods. "Like Stalin."

"Yes. And then it's hard to know whether the turn against them comes because the magic has gone or because they really were kind of crazy or—I don't think it was all venality with Zilboorg, although it looked like it to many people. He was an old-fashioned Socialist who hated inherited wealth as undeserved, and many of his patients were people like that. But I don't think you can milk the rich anymore."

He writes something in a notebook. "Milk? Milk. American? I like, make note of it."

I rise, move about, and then lie down on the floor. "I have a bad back."

"And something other is bad? Work? The theatre work?"

"I don't like the theatre anymore and yet it is what I do best. I have cut myself away from it, don't go much, don't learn, don't even want to. And I am getting old and I can't understand how that happened to me."

179

"Did you not marry again?"

"No. And there was a long, long time when I deprived myself of any man."

He smiled. "I did not think that when first I met you."

"It wasn't true then. It came with Joe McCarthy." That sounds so wacky that I sit up from the floor laughing. "Do you know about McCarthy?"

"I have read much, but I was in prison camp when he came to your nation."

"Well, I'm religious, I guess, although I don't like to think that. So I told myself then that if they didn't put Hammett back in jail, if he could be sick and die in peace, I would be a good girl, like a nun, and not ask for anything else—"

But now I am laughing so hard that I start to choke and the captain gets me a vodka.

Talking about yourself, when you don't do it much, is heady stuff, so I said, "So the years that are good for many women were not good for me. I didn't know that I wanted anybody, didn't even think about it much, but there, suddenly, was the wrong man, of course, as could be expected, as usual."

"As usual? Mr. Dashiell was not wrong."

"No, that turned out fine, just fine. But it didn't start fine, and maybe only came out fine because I was stubborn. I'm not making any sense. I'm sleepy."

We took the subway back to the Pekin Hotel and it looked more dreary than usual at five o'clock in the morning.

Leningrad, May 16

How good it is to come back here. My room in the Astoria Hotel must be directly below the one I had during the war. I open the old notebook: "It is as if this city had been built by another people who had no connection with Moscow or Kiev. It is a silent, lonely beauty." Now, so

180

many years later, it still seems silent except at rush hours, and people from Moscow don't like what they call its deadness, by which they mean nobody shoves or pushes or has to. The great sweep of squares and parks, the delicacy of the colors—Rossi Street must be one of the most charming streets in the world—the better manners of the men, the better dresses of the women, do not please the vigorous Muscovites.

I walk all day in the spring rain, up and down, up and down Rossi Street as delighted as I was years ago by the imagination that put the pale, delicate southern-yellow buildings in this cheerless, damp northern climate.

Last night we went to the Gorki play. Awful, just awful, decorated and ornamented with direction that can leave nothing unsaid, with actors who can leave nothing undone, including an exit. It was over at one A.M. but I walked the streets for the last half hour, waiting for Raya and Maya. As I left the theatre one usher told another that I was *nyet culturni*. Five hours is, evidently, more cultured than three.

May 18

We went to Pushkin's apartment this morning. It is a charming place, not too much furniture and that very good. It was fun listening to Maya and Raya, rivals in admiration, reciting Pushkin to each other as we wandered along Nevsky Prospect. They are as moved as if the poetry had appeared last month and they had carried tears to his grave yesterday.

Late in the afternoon we went looking for Dostoevsky's apartment. They thought they knew where it was, but they didn't, and it was hard to find anybody who did. But there it was, finally, a middle-class nineteenth-century four-story apartment building, curving around a corner, no plaque to mark it and no way of seeing his apartment because people still live in it. An old woman spoke to us, saying

181

she had lived all her life in the apartment above Dostoevsky's. Wouldn't we use our influence on the "authorities of government" to have the building declared a monument with a proper sign and proper words to mark "the bedding place" of so great a man? It is, indeed, strange that although Dostoevsky has been widely published again not even the most liberated talk about him as a great writer. You can get an argument any time you want about *Crime and Punishment*.

In the afternoon we go to see Olga Bergholz in a hospital. Her friends last night were mysterious about her ailment, and she herself gives it no name, maybe because it is no more, and no less, than too much life behind her, too much, perhaps, ahead. Bergholz is thought to be a good poet and Maya is delighted to come along with me. I am glad to see Olga again, although I was not easy with her when we met during the war, and am not easy now. She was a pretty woman, but the face has turned old-child peevish. The hospital people are affectionate with her as they come and go bringing her a cake, flowers, books. This is her birthday and she has made a small party for us. We have the cake and tea as she speaks of other birthdays spent with her good friend Akhmatova, how generous Akhmatova was to her when she was young. Then she talks of new poems she is writing, asks me what I am writing, but does not wait for an answer as she takes me to the window to look at the lovely hospital garden, and uses the garden, I think, to tell me that the gardener is her great admirer, isn't it wonderful about simple people? I want to go, I want very much to leave the room, although I know she doesn't want us to leave, because she goes with us down the stairs for another talk on the landing.

I feel guilty, so I make Maya find a florist where we buy a great bouquet, take it back to the hospital, and leave it with a nurse. I am conscious that Maya is puzzled about the visit, and so am I, until I realize that Olga has reminded me of Dorothy Parker, who is also sick, and to whom I have not always been a faithful friend these last few years. I go back to the hotel and write Dottie a story that I heard two nights before, knowing it is the kind of thing that will please her.

14

DOROTHY PARKER

I FIRST met Dorothy Parker in 1931, shortly after I moved back to New York with Hammett. She caused a wacky-tipsy fight between us. She had read *The Maltese Falcon* and *Red Harvest*, perhaps a year or two before, and she had written about them, but she had not met Hammett until a cocktail party given by William Rose Benét. I was already uncomfortable at this party of people much older than myself, when a small, worn, prettyish woman was introduced to Hammett and immediately fell to her knees before him and kissed his hand. It was meant to be both funny and serious, but it was neither, and Hammett was embarrassed into a kind of simper.

I had a habit in those days—there are still often hangovers of it on other levels—of making small matters into large symbols and, after enough cocktails, I saw the gesture as what New York life was going to be like for an unknown young woman among the famous. That night I accused Dash of liking ladies who kissed his hand, he said

I was crazy, I said I wasn't going to live with a man who allowed women to kneel in admiration, he said he had "allowed" no such thing, didn't like it, but if I wanted to leave right away, he would not detain me. I said I'd go as soon as I had finished my steak, but I guess by that time we were fighting about something else, because a few months later he said if I ever reminded him of the incident again, I would never live to finish another steak.

I was not to meet Dottie again until the winter of 1935 in Hollywood, and then, having glared at her for most of the evening in memory of that silly first meeting, we talked. I liked her and we saw each other the next day and for many, many other good days and years until she died in June of 1967.

It was strange that we did like each other and that never through the years did two such difficult women ever have a quarrel, or even a mild, unpleasant word. Much, certainly, was against our friendship: we were not the same generation, we were not the same kind of writer, we had led and were to continue to lead very different lives, often we didn't like the same people or even the same books, but more important, we never liked the same men. When I met her in 1935 she was married to Alan Campbell, who was a hard man for me to take. He was also difficult for her and she would talk about him in a funny, half-bitter way not only to me but given enough liquor, to a whole dinner party. But she had great affection for Alan and certainly—since she was to marry him twice—great dependence on him. If I didn't like Alan, she didn't like Hammett, although she was always too polite to say so. More important to me, Hammett, who seldom felt strongly about anybody, didn't like Dottie, and in the later years would move away from the house when she came to visit us. He was not conscious that his face would twist, almost as if he had half recovered from a minor stroke, as she embraced and flattered a man or woman, only to turn, when they had left the room, to say in the soft, pleasant, clear voice, "Did you ever meet such a shit?" I think the game of embrace-denounce must have started when she found it amused or shocked people, because in time, when she found it didn't amuse me, she seldom played it. But Hammett found it downright distasteful and I gave up all efforts to convince him that it was the kind of protection sometimes needed by those who are frightened.

I am no longer certain that I was right: fear now seems too simple. The game more probably came from a desire to charm, to be loved, to be admired, and such desires brought self-contempt that could only be consoled by behind-the-back denunciations of almost comic violence.

If she denounced everybody else, I had a right to think that I was included, but now I think I was wrong about that, too: so many people have told me that she never did talk about me, never complained, never would allow gossip about me, that I have come to believe it. But even when I didn't, it didn't matter. I enjoyed her more than I have ever enjoyed any other woman. She was modest—this wasn't all virtue, she liked to think that she was not worth much—her view of people was original and sharp, her elaborate, overdelicate manners made her a pleasure to live with, she liked books and was generous about writers, and the wit, of course, was so wonderful that neither age nor illness ever dried up the spring from which it came fresh each day. No remembrance of her can exclude it.

The joke has been changed and variously attributed to Mischa Elman and Heifetz, but it is hers, because I was there when it happened. We were knitting before the living room fireplace in the country house that she and Alan once owned in Pennsylvania. Upstairs, Alan was having an argument with his visiting mother. The afternoon grew dark, it began to snow, we made the fire very large and sat in silence. Occasionally, the upstairs voices would grow angry loud and then Dottie would sigh. When the voices finally ceased, Alan appeared in the living room.

He said, immediately, angrily, "It's hot as hell in here."

"Not for orphans," Dottie said, and I laughed for so long that Alan went for a walk and Dottie patted my hand occasionally and said, "There, there, dear, you'll choke if you're not careful."

Once she said to me—I quoted it at her funeral and found to my pleasure, as it would have been to hers, that the mourners laughed—"Lilly, promise me that my gravestone will carry only these words: 'If you can read this you've come too close.' "

Long before I knew her she dined in Paris with a group of Lesbians who were seriously talking of the possibility of legal marriage between them. Dottie listened most politely, clucked in agreement. They expected her friendly opinion and asked for it. The large eyes were wide with sympathy. "Of course you must have legal marriages. The children have to be considered."

But for me, the wit was never as attractive as the comment, often startling, always sudden, as if a curtain had opened and you had a brief and brilliant glance into what you would never have found for yourself. Like the wit, it was always delivered in a soft, clear voice; like the wit, it usually came after a silence, and started in the middle. One day she looked up from a book: "The man said he didn't want to see her again. That night she tried to climb into the transom of his hotel room and got stuck at the hips. I've never got stuck at the hips, Lilly, and I want you to remember that."

Dottie was very fond of the Gerald Murphys, but fondness never had anything to do with judgment. The Murphys had been in Europe and she had not seen them for six or eight months. We met to walk to their apartment for dinner. Dottie said, "Make a guess who Gerald will have discovered this time, what writer, I mean."

I said I couldn't guess, I didn't know Gerald as well as she did.

She said, "O.K. Give me three guesses and if I hit one right, will you buy me a drunken lunch tomorrow?"

I agreed and she said immediately, "Madame de Staël, Gerard Manley Hopkins or Philippe de Swarzberger."

"Who is Philippe de Swarzberger?"

"An Alsatian who moved around Tibet. Born 1837, died 1871, or so it's thought. A mystic. Most of whose work has been lost, but two volumes remain in Lausanne under lock and key, and Gerald invented him this afternoon."

We had a fine dinner at the Murphys and were drinking our brandy when Gerald produced a small book and asked if he could read a few poems from it. It was, indeed, a volume of Gerard Manley Hopkins.

It was Gerald who told the story that always seemed to me to sum up the contradictions in the Parker nature. Long before I met her, she had an affair of high tragi-comedy with a handsome, rich, wellborn stockbroker, getting extra enjoyment from it because Elinor Wylie had also had her eye on him. Murphy said that one night he called to take Dottie to dinner. She appeared as neat and pretty as usual, but with a black eye, recently caked blood on the mouth, and nasty bruises on the arm. She explained to Gerald that the wellborn had beaten her up the night before, that even worse cuts and bruises were concealed by her dress.

Gerald, horrified, said, "How can you bear that man, Dottie? He's a very dirty cad."

Dottie turned to stare at him, opened the door of the taxi, said softly, "I can't let you talk about him that way," and fell from the taxi into the middle of Park Avenue traffic. (The cad, many years and a wife or two later, was to fire a gun into his mouth in the Martha's Vineyard airport.)

Her taste in men was, indeed, bad, even for witter ladies. She had been loved by several remarkable men, but she only loved the ones who did not love her, and

they were the shabby ones. Robert Benchley had love
her, I was told by many people, and certainly I was late
to see the devotion he had for her and she for him. Sh
had had an affair with Ring Lardner, and both of thes
men she respected, and never attacked—a rare mark o
feeling—but I don't think she was in love with them
because respect somehow canceled out romantic love. (Sh
talked far too much about how men looked—handsome
well-made, and so on.) But then her relations with lovers
and with her husband, were always a mystery to me—
perhaps because I had missed the early days of the at
tempted suicides, the long, famous tape of the broke
heart. There is no question she wanted it that way—sh
wanted the put-down from everybody and anybody, an
she always resented it and hit back. The pride was ver
great, although she never recognized that she so ofte
pleaded for the indignity that offended it.

But she was, more than usual, a tangled fishnet o
contradictions: she liked the rich because she liked the wa
they looked, their clothes, the things in their houses, an
she disliked them with an open and baiting contempt; sh
believed in socialism but seldom, except in the stick
sentimental minutes, could stand the sight of a workin
radical; she drank far too much, spent far too much tim
with ladies who did, and made fun of them and hersel
every inch of the way; she faked interest and sympath
for those who bored her and for whom she had no feeling
and yet I never heard her hit mean except where it was, i
some sense, justified; she herself was frightened of bein
hit, being made fun of, being inconvenienced, yet whe
she was called by the House Un-American Activitie
Committee and I went to say that I would come with he
she said, in genuine surprise, "Why, Lilly?" I don't thin
it occurred to her, or to many of her generation, that th
ruling classes were anything but people with more mone
than you had. She acted before the committee as she acte
so often with their more literate, upper-class cousins a

dinner: as if to say, "Yes, dear, it's true that I'm here to observe you, but I do not like you and will, of course, say and write exactly that."

But she wrote it too often in sentimental short stories about the little dressmaker or the servant as they are patronized by the people Dottie had dined with the night before. It was her way of paying back the rich and powerful, and if it is understandable in life it is too raw and unshaded for literature. The good short stories, like "Big Blonde," are her imaginative projections of what she knew or feared for herself, and have nothing to do with vengeance on the rich. Her put-them-in-their-place stories are often undigested, the conclusions there on the first page. The other stories, and much of the light verse, I think, are a valuable record of their time and place.

But I am not an intelligent critic of those I like. It is not that I am overgenerous or overloyal, it's that their work, from the very best to the not very good, is too close to what I know about them, or hope to find out, and thus I am so occupied by the revelations of the author in the work that I cannot be cool about the work itself. This has been of value: it has made it possible to be good friends with writers who, in the end, do not require extravagant praise if you make clear that you have little interest in extravagant analysis. A book is good, bad or medium for me, and I usually don't know the reasons why. Years later, I will often think the good was not as good as I once thought, but on the record, my inability to know the why, my rather lumpish, incoherent acceptance or rejection, has often been less mistaken than those who care more or know more of what literature is made.

And so it was with Dottie. I never gave her all the good words she got from so many others, and I always cut off her praise of my work, never sure that she meant it, never really caring. We were polite, we were reticent, but very little fakery was given or required, although certainly we both lied now and then about each other's work and we

both knew it. I once wrote a short story, my first since
was very young, and gave it to her to read. She had warr
words for it, but the fact that she picked up a phrase—
no longer remember what phrase—and kept praising it
originality and delicacy, worried me. A few months late
she asked me what I had done with the story. I said I hac
decided it was a lady-writer story, not about anything. Sh
protested, she quoted the phrase again, she said how mucl
impressed she had been, and she tripped over a group c
poodle puppies that we had brought along on our walk
As she stooped down to console them, I said, "God is no
just. He punishes puppies for the lies of pretty ladies te
their friends."

She said, "Lilly, I *do* like the story"—but I had walkec
ahead of her.

In a few minutes she caught up with me and we went ir
silence to the lake. It was a cold spring, but Hammett anc
I had decided to set the snapping turtle traps earlier thar
usual and I was anxious to have a look at them. I haulec
up one of the long, wire cages and there was our firs
turtle of the year. As I put the cage on the ground to look
at him, his penis extended in fear.

Dottie said, "It must be pleasant to have sex appeal for
turtles. Shall I leave you alone together?" She had paid me
back and all was well.

After Dottie married Alan Campbell for the seconc
time—she had phoned me from California immediately
after the wedding reception with "Lilly, the room wa:
filled with people who hadn't talked to each other ir
years, including the bride and bridegroom"—we did no
see each other as often as in the years before. But there
would be periods when she moved back to New York anc
would come to stay with me in Martha's Vineyard. It wa:
in those years that Dash would pack and leave the house
to return only after Dottie had left. But there was the las
painful summer of his life when he couldn't leave any
place anymore and I had to lie to Dottie about the reasor

for putting her up in a guest house down the road. I would sit with Dash as he nibbled on his early dinner and pretend to eat from my tray. Almost immediately he would sleep from the weariness of eating, and Dottie would come soon after to have dinner with me. I never ate a whole dinner that summer, partly because the pretend eating had spoiled my appetite, partly because I was so often silent angry with Hammett for making the situation hard for me, not knowing then that the dying do not, should not, be asked to think about anything but their own minute of running time. Dottie stayed about a month that year without ever seeing Dash, and the measure of her tact was that she never asked a question about a situation she must have understood.

Hammett died that next winter, I sold the Vineyard house, and built myself a new house. The first telephone call in the new house came from Dottie to tell me that Alan was dead from an overdose of sleeping pills. She was very sure that the overdose was not intentional—she believed he had had too much to drink and had forgotten how many pills he had taken. I believed her. Alan was the first person I ever knew to take sleeping pills and I remember a trip to Europe the three of us made on the old *Normandie*.

One day I said to Dottie, "What happens to Alan every afternoon, where is he?"

"Takes a sleeping pill. He hates to toss and turn from four to six."

Less than a year after Alan's death, Dottie moved back to New York. We saw each other, of course, but after the first few times I knew I could not go back to the past. The generation difference between us seemed shorter as I grew older, but I was irritable now with people who drank too much and Dottie's drinking made her dull and repetitive, and she made me sad. I had money again but no longer enough to give it without thought before it was needed, which is the way it used to be between us; but mainly, plainly, I did not want the burdens that Dottie, maybe by never asking for anything, always put upon her friends. I was tired of trouble and wanted to be around people who walked faster than I and might pull me along with them.

And so, for the next five years of her life, I was not the good friend I had been. True, I was there in emergencies but I was out the door immediately they were over. I found that Dottie's middle age, old age, made rock or much that had been fluid, and eccentricities once charming became too strange for safety or comfort.

Dottie had always, even in the best days, clung to the idea that she was poor. Often she was, because she was generous to others and to herself, but more often it came from an insistence on a world where the artist was the put-upon outsider, the *épaté* rebel who ate caviar from rare china with a Balzac shrug for when you paid. I had long ago given up trying to figure out her true poverty periods from the pretend-poverty periods, and the last sick years seemed no time to argue. She had, many years before, given me a Picasso gouache and a Utrillo landscape, saying as she gave them that she was leaving them to me anyway, so why not have them now? It was her charming way of paying off a debt and I remember being impressed with the grace. A few years after the gift, when I thought she was short of money, I sold the Utrillo and sent her a check. (She never told me that she had received the check, we never spoke of it at all.) Now, in 1965, she needed money and so I decided to sell the Picasso. It was a good, small picture, sold immediately for ten thousand dollars, and I took the check to Dottie the day I got it. Two days later, a woman unknown to me phoned to say that Dottie was in the hospital, sick and without money. I said that couldn't be, she said it was, and would I guarantee the hospital bills? I went to the hospital that day. Dottie and I talked for a long time, and as I rose to go I said, "Dottie, do you need money?"

"She's been calling you," she said, "the damned little

meddler. She's called half of New York to make me into a pleading beggar."

"She meant no harm. She thinks you're broke."

"I *am* broke, Lilly. But I don't want people, not even you——"

"You're not broke. I gave you a check two days ago for ten thousand dollars. Where is it?"

She stared at me and then turned her face away. She said, very softly, "I don't know."

And she didn't know, she was telling the truth. She wanted to be without money, she wanted to forget she had it. The check was found in a bureau drawer along with three other checks. It had always been like that, it always would be. After her death, and nobody ever left fewer accumulations, I found four uncashed seven-year-old checks. She never had much, but what she had she didn't care about, and that was very hat-over-the-windmill stuff in a sick lady of seventy-four.

What money she had, she left to Martin Luther King, a man she had never met. I was the only executor of the will. I was, I am, moved that she wanted it that way, because the will had been dictated during the years of my neglect. But I had always known and always admired her refusal to chastise or complain about neglect. When, in those last years, I would go for a visit she always had the same entrance speech for me, "Oh, Lilly, come in quick. I want to laugh again." In the same circumstances, I would have said, "Where have you been?"

And in a little while, we would laugh again, not as often, not as loud as in the old days, but enough to give us both a little of the old pleasure. Her wit, of course, was delicate, clear, and sharp. I don't know what mine is, but it isn't that, and I never knew why it amused her. But we were affectionate about each other's jokes, even when they weren't very good, and would endlessly repeat them to other people with the pride of mothers. (She never in her life repeated her own witticisms, perhaps sure that other

people would do it for her. I was one of the many who
did.)

Among the small amount of papers she left were odds
and ends of paid or unpaid laundry bills, a certificate of
the aristocratic origins of a beloved poodle, a letter dated
ten years before from an admirer of her poems, and the
letter from me sent from Russia about six weeks before
she died. This is the letter:

Dearest Dottie,

Leningrad is a beauty, Moscow is not, but I think you
ought to know that once upon a time not so long ago there
was a man called Beria, Stalin's police boy, who liked very
young girls. Then there was Madame Comrade Gigglewitz—I was told her name but I can't remember it—
whose second husband was a minor GPU official, but not
so minor he didn't know Beria's tastes. Madame Gigglewitz waited until her beautiful Natasha, the child of a first
marriage, reached the age of fifteen and then, putting
Natasha in her baby carriage, she wheeled her over to
Beria. You will remember that the sexual act does not
necessarily take a long time, particularly when your Mummie is there to help. So clipclop and Natasha is pregnant.
Beria likes that and sets Natasha up in an apartment with
a curly fur coat, an elderly cleaning woman, a car and
chauffeur, and when he isn't too tired from sending people
to Siberia he comes around to coo at the baby.

But Stalin, Beria's friend and admirer, ups and dies.
For three days Natasha hears nothing from her lover and
nothing from the chauffeur who has always taken her on a
daily nice drive. On the fourth day she is indignant, as you
would be, too. So she calls Beria's secretary and asks when
the car can be expected.

The secretary says, "I think never," and hangs up.

Most of us go to our mummies when a secretary i
rude, and that's just what she did. Madame Gigglewitz i
brighter than Natasha—who wouldn't be?—so in a few

hours they are sitting before a judge swearing to a document that accuses Beria of traitorism whispered to Natasha through the years, or bed. Natasha's Ma had guessed right, of course: Beria had been arrested, was tried and condemned, and Natasha's testimony helped to shuffle him off. A year passes—do you remember once asking me what else a year could do?—before Madame Gigglewitz and Natasha thought it wise to petition for the support of Beria's child. They are sentimental here about the sins of the father shall not be visited, so they give the child a nice allowance and Natasha goes to live with Mummie, share and share alike the kid's money.

But Natasha hasn't had enough trouble so she takes to hanging out in an Armenian restaurant. There she meets Mr. X. He's a nice, kindly Jew who has a surprising amount of money and this time it's a real marriage which all goes to show that my people—so, O.K., for the fiftieth time don't tell me you're half Jewish—do not wish to corrupt women the way many of your mother's people so often do. A few years and two children later, over beyond the Urals, strange rumblings are heard in the land. They grow and grow until the storm reveals that Mr. X is one of the bosses of a syndicate, operating, often in caves, with stolen government material to make private light machinery. Scandal, arrest, execution of Mr. X. (Do you remember the story in the *New York Times?*)

Now you can say that Natasha ain't the best luck for a boy, but that kind of talk won't get anybody anything. Anyway, there's always Mummie, and after the two of them have had a good cry, what's there to do but wait, knowing that God has been on their side before.

Now, in time, comes a delegation, half from America, half from Israel to investigate charges of anti-Semitism in the Soviet Union. Our two cozies hot-foot it over to the delegation to tell the story of Mr. X, a fine fellow, an excellent husband, innocent of all knavery, persecuted only because he was a Jew. This saddens the hearts and

confirms the opinions of the visitors, and after several
meetings with Natasha, private or public, I couldn't find
out, the American delegation begs to be allowed to send a
monthly contribution for the support of Mr. X's children.
The Israelis cannot afford money, but certainly they are
sympathetic.

I have a friend here—I first met him during the war—
who is a doctor. Last summer my friend went to the
country to visit his brother. Three A.M. and the brother is
awakened by a man who says his wife is dying down the
road, would the doctor come immediately? The dying
lady—she does not die, she is still down the road—is
Madame Gigglewitz. During the long hours before a Moscow ambulance arrives she occasionally confuses my
friend, the doctor, for a priest, and the tale I've told you is
told to him. The house is filled with pictures of the pretty
Natasha—she offers one to the doctor—and enormous
baskets of fresh and dried fruits. From time to lucid time
Madame Gigglewitz raises her voice above a whisper:
"Have a piece of fruit, Doctor, it comes regularly from
some dirty Jews in Israel."

Around the envelope of my letter was folded a piece of
paper that was the beginning, obviously, of a letter Dottie
never finished. It said, "Come home soon, Lilly, and bring
Natasha on a leash. She'd be such a nice companion for
C'est Tout. I—"

C'est Tout, a very small poodle, was with her when she
died. I was never to see Dottie again, but even now I
don't think of her as dead, and only a few weeks ago,
when Peter Feibleman told me a story I had not heard
before, I had a nice minute of wanting to reach for the
telephone. The story is all of her as age put aside the
deceits of youth, as time solidified the courage she didn't
want to admit was there.

Feibleman was with her when Alan Campbell's body

was taken to the coroner's car. (No charge of suicide was ever made.) Among the friends who stood with Dottie on those California steps was Mrs. Jones, a woman who had liked Alan, had pretended to like Dottie, and who had always loved all forms of meddling in other people's troubles. Mrs. Jones said, "Dottie, tell me, dear, what I can do for you."

Dottie said, "Get me a new husband."

There was a silence, but before those who would have laughed could laugh, Mrs. Jones said, "I think that is the most callous and disgusting remark I ever heard in my life."

Dottie turned to look at her, sighed, and said gently, "So sorry. Then run down to the corner and get me a ham and cheese on rye and tell them to hold the mayo."

15

HELEN

IN many places I have spent many days on small boats. Beginning with the gutters of New Orleans, I have been excited about what lives in water and lies along its edges. In the last twenty years, the waters have been the bays, ponds and ocean of Martha's Vineyard, and autumn, when most people have left the island, is the best time for beaching the boat on a long day's picnic by myself—other people on a boat often change the day into something strained, a trip with a purpose—when I fish, read, wade in and out, and save the afternoon for digging and mucking about on the edge of the shore. I have seldom found much: I like to look at periwinkles and mussels, driftwood, shells, horseshoe crabs, gull feathers, the small fry of bass and blues, the remarkable skin of a dead sand shark, the shining life in rockweed.

One night about six months ago, when I was teaching at Harvard, it occurred to me that these childish, aimless pleasures—my knowledge of the sea has grown very little

with time, and what interested me as a child still does—
which have sometimes shamed me and often caused self-
mocking, might have something to do with the digging
about that occasionally happens when I am asleep. It is
then that I awake, feeling that my head is made of sand
and that a pole has just been pulled from it with the end
of the pole carrying a card on which there is an answer
to a long-forgotten problem, clearly solved and set out as
if it had been arranged for me on a night table.

On that night I was living in a rickety Cambridge house
and went running down the steps at the sound of a crash.
A heavy rainstorm had broken the cheap piece of modern-
ity that had been lighting the ceiling and, as I stood
looking at the pieces on the floor, I thought: Of course, one
has been dead three years this month, one has been dead
for over thirty, but they were one person to you, these two
black women you loved more than you ever loved any
other women, Sophronia from childhood, Helen so many
years later, and it was all there for you to know two
months ago when, poking about the beach, a long distance
from the house Helen and I had lived in, I found a
mangled watch, wondered where I had seen it, and knew
a few hours later that it was the watch I had bought in the
Zurich airport and that had disappeared a short time after
I gave it to Helen. The answer now was easy. She never
walked much because her legs hurt. Sam had brought it
down to the beach and she didn't want to tell me that my
dog, who loved her but didn't love me, could have done
anything for which he could be blamed.

From the night of that rainstorm in Cambridge, for
weeks later, and even now, once in a while, I have
dreamed of Sophronia and Helen, waking up sometimes
so pleased that I try to go on with a dream that denies
their death, at other times saddened by the dream because
it seems a deep time-warning of my own age and death.
When that happens, in argument with myself, I feel guilty
because I did not know about Sophronia's death for two

years after it happened, and had not forced Helen into the hospital that might have saved her. In fact, I had only been angry at her stubborn refusal to go. How often Helen had made me angry, but with Sophronia nothing had ever been bad ... But the answer there is easy: Sophronia was the anchor for a little girl, the beloved of a young woman, but by the time I had met the other, years had brought acid to a nature that hadn't begun that way—or is that a lie?—and in any case, what excuse did that give for irritation with a woman almost twenty years older than I, swollen in the legs and feet, marrow-weary with the struggle to live, bewildered, resentful, sometimes irrational in a changing world where the old, real-pretend love for white people forced her now into open recognition of the hate and contempt she had brought with her from South Carolina. She had not, could not have, guessed this conflict would ever come to more than the sad talk of black people over collard greens and potlikker, but now here it was on Harlem streets, in newspapers and churches, and how did you handle what you didn't understand except with the same martyr discipline that made you work when you were sick, made you try to forgive what you really never forgave, made you take a harsh nature and force it into words of piety that, in time, became almost true piety. Why had these two women come together as one for me? Sophronia had not been like that.

I don't know what year Helen came to work for me. We never agreed about the time, although when we felt most affectionate or tired we would argue about it. But it was, certainly, a long time ago. The first months had been veiled and edgy: her severe face, her oppressive silences made me think she was angry, and my nature, alternating from vagueness to rigid demands, made her unhappy, she told me years later. (She did not say it that way: she said, "It takes a searching wind to find the tree you sit in.")

Then one day, at the end of the first umcomfortable months, she said she was grateful, most deeply. I didn't know what she meant, didn't pay much attention, except that I knew she had grown affectionate toward me, even indulgent. Shortly after, she brought me three hundred dollars done up in tissue paper with a weary former Christmas ribbon. I asked her what it was, she said please to count it, I asked her what it was, she said please to count it, I counted it, handed it back, she handed it back to me and said it was the return of the loan for her daughter. I said I didn't know what she was talking about. Her face changed to angry sternness as she said, "I want no charity. I pay my just debts, Miss Hellman. Mr. Hammett must have told you I said that to him."

Hammett hadn't told me she said anything, but it turned out that one night when he had come from the country to have dinner with me, and found he was too tired to return to the country—it was the early period of emphysema—he decided to spend the night in the library. He had been reading at about three in the morning when the phone rang and a frightened voice said there was an emergency, was it possible to call Helen? He had climbed four flights of steps to fetch her, and when she had finished with the phone she said her niece or her daughter or somebody-or-other had had a terrible accident and she would have to go immediately. He asked her if she needed money and, after the long wait she always took when pride was involved, she asked him for taxi money.

Hammett had said, "What about money for the hospital?"

She had said, "Black people don't have it easy in a hospital."

He had said, "I know. So a check won't do you any good. You'd better have cash."

I said to Hammett, "But what's this got to do with me?"

He said, "It's your money she's returning. I took it out of the safe."

He told me how disturbed she had been when he had

opened my safe and so he had said, "Don't worry. It's O.K. There's no sense waking Miss Hellman because she can't learn how to open the safe and that makes her angry."

For many years after, whenever I tried to open the safe, she would come as close to mirth as ever I saw her, saying always that I wasn't to get disturbed, she thought my fingers were too thin for such work, and then always reminding me of the night Hammett gave her the money, "before he even knew me, that is a Christian man."

I said to him, "Helen thinks you're a Christian man."

"Sure. She's a convert to my ex-church. We teach 'em to talk like that."

"I won't tell her that. She might not like you."

"I won't find that too tough."

"But I'm worried that she might think you don't like her."

"I don't like her."

He didn't like her and he was the only person I ever met who didn't. Sometimes he would say it was because she spoke rudely to me. (He was right: when she didn't feel well, she often did.) Sometimes he would say he couldn't stand Catholic converts, or overbig women, or he would complain that she was the only Negro in America who couldn't carry a tune. Even through the last four and a half years of his life, when he had come to live in the house and when she, a woman older than he by a number of years I never knew, would climb the steps with endless trays or mail or books or just to ask if there was anything he wanted, he never said anything more to her than "Good morning," or "Thank you," or, on special occasions, "It looks like a pleasant day." I think it is possible that the two of them, obsessed with pride and dignity, one of the more acceptable forms of self-love, but self-love nevertheless, had come face to face with a reflection and one of them didn't like what he saw in the mirror.

Other people always came, in time, to like her and

admire her, although her first impression on them was not always pleasant. The enormous figure, the stern face, the few, crisp words did not seem welcoming as she opened a door or offered a drink, but the greatest clod among them came to understand the instinctive good taste, the high-bred manners that once they flowered gave off so much true courtesy. And, in this period of nobody grows older or fatter, your mummie looks like your girl, there may be a need in many of us for the large, strong woman who takes us back to what most of us always wanted and few of us ever had.

It is difficult to date anything between people when they have lived together long enough, and so I can't remember when I knew, forgot, knew, doubted, and finally understood that her feelings for white people and black people were too complex to follow, because what had been said on one day would be denied on the next. In the early years, when she told me of the white family in whose house she had been raised in Charleston, her mother having been the cook there, I would dislike the Uncle-Tomism of the memories, and often when the newspapers carried a new indignity from the South we would both cluck about it, but she would turn away from my anger with talk about good and bad among white people, and she had only known the good. During the University of Mississippi mess, I asked her what she meant by good whites, good to her?

She said, "There's too much hate in this world."

I said, "Depends on where you carry the hate, doesn't it, what it's made of, how you use it?"

She shrugged. "I ain't ever hated."

I said, too fast, "Yes, you have. You just don't know it—" and stopped right before I said, You often hate me, I've known it for years and let you have it as a debt I wouldn't pay anybody else but Sophronia.

Oh, Sophronia, it's you I want back always. It's by you I still so often measure, guess, transmute, translate and act. What strange process made a little girl strain so hard to hear the few words that ever came, made the image of you, true or false, last a lifetime? I think my father knew about that very early, because five or six years after I was separated from Sophronia by our move to New York, when I saw her only during our yearly visits to New Orleans, he shouted at me one night, "To hell with Sophronia. I don't want to hear about her anymore."

That night started in Montgomery, Alabama, although why or how we got to Montgomery I no longer remember. My father had, among other eccentricities, an inability to travel from one place to another in a conventional line; if it was possible to change trains or make a detour, he arranged it. And since we traveled a great deal between New York and New Orleans, stopping for business or for friends, we were often to be found in railroad stations waiting for a train that would take us out of our way.

I had been sleeping on a bench that night in Montgomery, Alabama, so I don't know when I first saw the three figures—a young, very thin Negro girl, and two white men. The men were drunk, my father said later, and maybe that accounted for the awkward, shaggy movements, their sudden twists and turns. The girl would move to a bench, sit, rise as the men came toward her, move to a wall, rest, slide along it as the men came near, try for another bench, circle it, and move fast when they moved fast. She was trying to stay within the station lights and, as the train came in, she ran down the platform toward it. But she miscalculated and ran outside the lights. I saw one of the men light matches and move in the darkness. When he caught the girl he put the lighted matches to her arm before he kissed her. The girl dropped her valise and there was the noise of glass breaking. I have no clear memory of the next few minutes until I heard my father say, "Let the girl alone." Then he hit the man and the other man hit my father, but he didn't seem hurt because he picked the girl up and shoved her up the steps of the

train, came running back for me, shoved me up the steps
of the train, got in himself and suddenly began to yell,
"My God, where is your mother?" My mother was on the
ground repacking the girl's valise. The two men were
running toward her but she smiled and waved at my father
and put up her hand in a gesture to quiet him. She had
trouble with the lock of the valise but she seemed unhur-
ried about fixing it. My father was halfway down the train
steps when she rose, faced the two men and said, "Now
you just step aside, boys, and take yourselves on home." I
don't know whether it was the snobbery of the word
"boys" or the accents of her native Alabama, but they
made no motion as she came aboard the train.

The girl was invited to share our basket supper and she
and my mother spent the next few hours speaking about
the nature of men. I went into the corridor to find my
bored father.

Like most other children, I had learned you usually got
further by pretending innocence. "What did those men
want to do with the girl?"

When he didn't answer, I said, "Rape, that's what.
You're a hero. Sophronia will be pleased."

His voice was loud and angry. "To hell with Sophronia.
I don't want to hear about her anymore."

A few days later, sitting on a bench in Audubon Park,
while the two small boys she now nursed played near us, I
told Sophronia the story. When she didn't speak, I said,
"Papa was brave, wasn't he?"

"Yep."

"What's the matter?"

"Things not going to get themselves fixed by one white
man being nice to one nigger girl."

I thought hard and long about that, as I thought about
everything she said, and by the next year's visit to New
Orleans I had decided on a course for myself. Sophronia
and I had gone to the movies and were returning home on
a streetcar. We had always moved back to sit in the Negro

section of the car, but this time I sat in the front directly behind the driver and pulled her down next to me. She whispered to me, I whispered back, she half rose, I pulled her down, and she sat still for a minute waiting for me to grow quiet. The conductor had evidently been watching us, because he turned his head.

"Back."

I held so tight to her arm that she couldn't move.

He said, "Get back in the car. You know better than this."

I said, my voice high with fright, "We won't. We won't move. This lady is better than you are——"

And the car came to a sudden jolt in the middle of the street. People rose and an old woman moved toward us. The conductor opened the doors.

Sophronia got to her feet and I screamed, "Come back, Sophronia, don't you dare move. You're better than anybody, anybody——" and the old lady slapped me as the conductor took my arm. I was carrying a book bag and I threw it at him, turned to push the old lady, turned back to find Sophronia. She had moved between me and the conductor, who looked more surprised than angry. Now she grabbed my arm and pulled me into the street.

I said, "Let's run."

She said, "You run. I'm past the runnin' age."

So we stood together, staring up at the streetcar, waiting for what we did not know. Then the car started up and moved away from us. I was crying as we walked together toward my aunts' house.

After a while she said, "Crybaby."

"I did wrong?"

It was an old question and she had always had a song for it:

> *Right is wrong and wrong is right*
> *And who can tell it all by sight?*

I said, "Sophronia, I want to go away with you for always, right now. I've thought a lot about it all year and I've made up my mind. I want to live with you the rest of my life. I won't live with white people anymore—"

She put her hand over my mouth. When she took it away, I knew she was very angry. She said, "I got something to tell you, missy. There are too many niggers who like white people. Then there are too many white people think they like niggers. You just be careful."

She crossed the street and was gone before I could move. Sleepless that night and miserable the next day, I went on the second day to find her in Audubon Park.

I said, "Aren't you going to see me anymore?"

She said, "I got a no good daughter and a no good son."

I had heard this from my mother, but I didn't know then, and I don't know now, what no good meant to her, and so I waited. We sat without speaking on the park bench watching one little red-haired brother push the other off a tricycle.

She called out, "Stanley. Hugh," and the fight stopped immediately.

After a while, I said, "Aren't you going to see me anymore?"

"You're growing up, a few years away. Time's approachin' to straighten things out."

"You mean I'm no good, either?"

She turned her head and looked at me as if she were puzzled. "I mean you got to straighten things out in your own head. Then maybe you goin' to be some good and pleasure me. But if they keep on pilin' in silly and gushin' out worse, you goin' to be trouble, and you ain't goin' to pleasure me and nobody else."

Many years later, I came to understand that all she meant was that I might blow up my life with impulsiveness or anger or jealousy or all the other things that she thought made a mess, but that day, in my thirteenth year, I shivered at the contempt with which she spoke. (And there I was not wrong. I came to know as she grew older and I did, too, that she did feel a kind of contempt for the world she lived in and for almost everybody, black or white, she had ever met, but that day I thought it was only for me.)

I got up from the bench in maybe the kind of pain you feel when a lover has told you that not only does the love not exist anymore, but that it possibly never existed at all.

I said, "You mean I am no good and you don't want to see me anymore. Well, I won't hang around and bother you—"

She got slowly to her feet. "You all I got, baby, all I'm goin' to have."

Then she leaned down and kissed me. She hadn't kissed me, I think, since I was three or four years old. Certainly I have had happier minutes since, but not up to then. We shook hands and I went back to the park bench the next day.

There has always been a picture of Sophronia in my house, all of them taken with me as a young child. Some years after Helen came to work for me, I came into the library to find her with one of the pictures in her hand.

I said, "My nurse, my friend. Handsome woman, wasn't she?"

"You look like a nice little girl."

"Maybe I was, but nobody thought so. I was trouble."

"She didn't think so."

I took the picture from Helen and, for the first time in the forty years since it had been taken, saw the affection the woman had for the child she stood behind.

I said, "It takes me too long to know things."

"What?"

"Nothing. I hadn't seen her for two years before she died."

"You didn't go to the funeral?"

"I didn't know she died. Her daughter didn't tell me."

"She was a light-skinned woman?"

I know about that question, I've known about it all my life.

"Yes, very. But she didn't use it, if that's what you mean."

"How old was she?"

"In the picture? I don't know. I—my God. She couldn't have been thirty. I can't believe it, but—"

"Black women get old fast."

"Yes," I said, "watching white women stay young."

"White women never been bad to me."

I was in a sudden bad humor, maybe because she wasn't Sophronia. I said, "Colored women who cook as well as you do never had a bad time. Not even in slavery. You were the darlings of every house. What about the others who weren't?"

She said, "You mean the good house nigger is king, boy."

I said, "I mean a house nigger pay no mind to a field hand."

She laughed at the words we had both grown up on. A half hour later I went down to the kitchen for a cup of coffee. She was using an electric beater and so neither of us tried to talk over the noise. Then she turned the beater off and, I think for the first time in her life, raised her voice in a shout.

"You ain't got no right to talk that way. No right at all. Down South, I cook. Nothing else, just cook. For you, I slave. You made a slave of me and you treat me like a slave."

I said, "Helen! Helen!"

"A slave. An old, broken slave."

"You're a liar," I said, "just a plain God-damned liar."

"God will punish you for those words."

"He is, right now."

She took a check from her apron pocket—her share of

212

the last royalties from *Toys in the Attic*—tore it up, and held out the pieces to me.

"There. Take it. You think money and presents can buy me, you're wrong."

I said, "I'm going up to Katonah. That will give you a few days to move out."

That night, sitting on a pile of books that had become the only place one could sit in the depressing little cottage filled with furniture broken by the weight of phonograph records and books, ashtrays toppling on the edges of manuscripts, a giant desk loaded with unopened mail that had arrived that day or five years ago, facing a window that had been splintered by the gun of somebody who didn't like his politics, I told Hammett about the afternoon.

He said, "Why do you talk to her about the South?"

"I didn't think she hated me."

"She doesn't. She likes you very much and that scares her, because she hates white people. Every morning some priest or other tells her that's not Christian charity, and she goes home more mixed up than ever."

"I guess so. But I don't care about what she hates or doesn't. I care about what I said to her. I'll wait until she has left and then I'll write and say I'm sorry I screamed liar."

He stared at me and went back to reading. After a while he said, "You should have screamed at her years ago. But of course you never lose your temper at the right time. Then you feel guilty and are sure to apologize. I've always counted on that, it's never failed."

I said, "All these years, waiting to catch me out."

"Yep. And shall I tell you something else that goes hand in hand, kind of?"

"I am, as you know, grateful for all high-class revelations."

"Well," he said, "when you start out being angry, you're almost always right. But anybody with a small

213

amount of sense learns fast that if they let you go on talking you come around to being wrong. So after you've slammed the door, or taken a plane, or whatever caper you're up to, that fine, upright, liberal little old sense of justice begins to operate and you'll apologize not only for the nonsense part of what you've said but for the true and sensible part as well. It's an easy game—just a matter of patience."

I thanked him and went back to New York. It has long been my habit to enter the house on the bedroom floor, and on that day I did not wish to see the kitchen without Helen, did not wish to face a life without her, so it was four or five hours before I went downstairs. Helen was sitting in a chair, her Bible on the table.

She said, "Good evening. Your hair is wet."

"Yes," I said, "I'm trying to curl it."

We did learn something that day, maybe how much we needed each other, although knowing that often makes relations even more difficult. Our bad times came almost always on the theme of Negroes and whites. The white liberal attitude is, mostly, a well-intentioned fake, and black people should and do think it a sell. But mine was bred, literally, from Sophronia's milk, and thus I thought it exempt from such judgments except when I made the jokes about myself. But our bad times did not spring from such conclusions by Helen—they were too advanced, too unkind for her. They came, I think, because she did not think white people capable of dealing with trouble. I was, thus, an intruder, and in the autumn of 1963 she told me so.

I had gone down to Washington to write a magazine piece about the Washington March. Through Negro friends, through former Harvard students, through a disciple of Malcolm X, I had arranged to meet the delegations from Louisiana and Alabama. Sophronia's grandson, whom I had never seen, was to arrive with the Alabama delegation. Many years before, I had had letters from his older sister, a teacher at Tuskegee. Now, when I wrote to ask if they would like to come to Washington, she had written back that they could not make the trip. Immediately after, I had a letter from Orin saying that he wanted to come if I would send the bus fare, but please not to tell his sister, because she did not approve. I had sent the money and, as far as I knew, he was on his way.

At seven o'clock on the morning of the March, I was sitting on the steps of the Lincoln Memorial waiting for Orin, wondering if he looked like Sophronia, if he had brought me the photographs I had asked for, if his mother had ever told him much about her. At nine o'clock I went to look for the Alabama delegation. They had been in Washington for six hours, but nobody had heard of Orin and they were sure he had never been on the bus, never signed up to come.

It was, of course, a remarkable day. Two hundred thousand people come to ask only what they thought had been promised, still calm, pleasant and gay in the face of the one-hundred-year-old refusal. But as the day wore on, I felt as if a respectable Madison Avenue funeral had gone on too long. When Martin Luther King rose to speak—and there was no question of the pride the audience felt in the man, no question that he represented all that was gentle and kind in this kindest of people—I remembered too many Negro preachers from my childhood and grew impatient with "I have a dream."

I wandered off looking for something to eat. I dropped my pocketbook, spilled the contents, and was helped by a small colored boy who, when I thanked him, said, "O.K., lady, courtesy of the Commonwealth." I laughed and found that his companion, a tall young Negro, was laughing, too.

I said, "What's that mean, courtesy of the Commonwealth?"

"Nothing," said the young man. "Old George tries to

learn a new word every day. We were up around Boston last night so today it will be 'Commonwealth.' "

Old George turned out to be fourteen years old, small for his age, and the young man's name was Gene Carondelet.

I said, "That's the name of a street in New Orleans."

He said, "Yep. That's why I took it."

Old George weaved in and out of the crowd, bringing frankfurters and then coffee, while Carondelet told me he had been in jail seven times for trying to register Negroes in Greenwood, Mississippi, and for leading a march in Baton Rouge. He said he had never seen old George before McComb, Mississippi, where a policeman had hit George over the head and George's mother had hit the policeman. The next day George's mother said, "Take the boy with you. He's in danger here. Take him and teach him."

"He's been with me for eight months. That George can do, learn anything. Makes a mighty fine speech. Make a speech for the lady."

George rose. "You folks better take your black behinds down to vote your way to freedom. The first correlative to freedom—" At the word "correlative" George grinned at me and sat down, saying he didn't feel too well, he had his headache back again. Carondelet explained that in a few days they were coming to New York to see a doctor about the headaches George had been having since he got hit over the head by the policeman.

About a week later, I came in the house to find Carondelet, George, and a gangly popeyed man of about twenty-four sitting in the living room with Helen. Carondelet said they'd been waiting for an hour and now they had to go because George was on his way to the doctor's. As I took them to the elevator, I did not notice that the strange man was still in the living room until George said, "You wanted him, you got him."

"Who?"

"That Orin something."

Carondelet said, "He's silly stuff."

Orin was, indeed, a dull young man, sleepy, overpolite, as anxious as I was to get the visit over with. He had been born long after Sophronia's death, had no memory of his mother's ever having talked about her. What about his uncle, Sophronia's son? Never heard of him. Where was his mother? She'd skipped long ago, maybe dead, maybe still turning a trick. Why hadn't he come to Washington with the Alabama delegation? They weren't his kind. He'd come to New York, been robbed, lost my address, hadn't eaten, where was the men's room? I pointed toward the kitchen, waited a long time, puzzled and sad that this man should be Sophronia's grandson. When he did come back, I said I had to go to work, and rose to shake his hand. He suddenly began to talk in a more animated way, although the words were now slurred. I had become Miss Hellmar of, more often, "man" in puzzling sentences like "Man, this is some town and they can take me to it any time they got enough, man," and "Man, where them two finkies I come here with, and where is here, just where is here at?" After a while I said I'd get him some money for the trip back home if he wanted to make it, and he began to laugh as I went into the hall to find Helen standing by the door.

She said, "He took a shot in the toilet."

"What do you mean?"

"A no good punkie-junkie. Maybe heroin."

The words were so modern, so unlike her, that I stared, amused and puzzled that there was a side of her I didn't know.

"I don't think so. He's just stupid, and uncomfortable with me."

When I came back down the steps, the phonograph was playing very loudly and Orin was moving around the room. I couldn't hear what Helen said, but his voice was very loud.

"Lady man, I'm stayin' right where I fall, see?"

Helen said, "You a sick boy. You going for a cure, or you going to hell."

"Lady man, hell's my place and you my girl, tired and old. Maybe even have to send you on a little errand soon—"

She crossed to him, pulled his arms behind his back, and stepped to one side as he tried to kick her. She held him easily, gracefully, as she pulled him toward a chair.

She said to me, "Go for a walk," and closed and locked the door.

The following morning she said, "You see, things happen to people."

I didn't answer her, and after an hour or so she appeared again—an old habit, conversation without prelude, in space, from hours or days or months before—"I locked the door 'cause I wanted you out of trouble."

"No," I said. "You just didn't think I'd be any good at it."

"Time I told you what I ain't told you. My daughter, same way, same thing."

After a while I said, "That shouldn't have happened to you."

"No good for colored people to come North, no good," she said. "Live like a slummy, die like one. South got its points, no matter what you think. Even if just trees."

I was never to see or hear from Orin again, but when George got out of the hospital he came to stay with us several times, appearing and disappearing without explanation. There was something odd about his relations with Helen, something teasing on his side, cautious on hers.

The next summer he came to stay with us for a few days on the Vineyard. He was romping with the poodle on the lawn outside her window, while I read on the porch above their heads.

He said to her, "Hey, Mrs. Jackson, your poodle got fleas."

"Lot of people got fleas," she said.

After a long pause, George called out, "I've been thinking about what you said, and I'm God-damned if I understand it."

"You been sleepin' here, Miss Hellman been sleepin' here. That's all I got to say."

George screamed with laughter. "You mean *we* give the dog the fleas? You some far-out lady, Mrs. Jackson." And a door slammed.

At dinner, a few weeks later, he said to Helen, "Could I have a piece of your cornbread?"

"Where you see cornbread?"

"Why you hide it where you do?"

It had long been her habit to hide any food that was fattening on the pretense that she ate very little and thus had inherited her "fat glands." Now she opened the stove, reached far back into the oven, and slammed down on the table a giant cornbread cake and a pot of greens and fatback.

"Can I have some," I said, knowing he had made a bad mistake,—"nothing in the world like potlikker and corn—"

She said to George, "What you do all day, besides snoopin'? You know more about this island than we ever find out, or want to."

"Sure do," said George, "that my job. Got to find out before you organize. You, for example. Find out all about you being like crazy with your money. You got so much money, give it to SNCC instead of wasting it on that no good Almira family down in town."

Helen said, softly, "Eat your dinner, son."

George said to me, "Old man Almira leave his family for a fourteen-year-old girl, and Mrs. Jackson here, that makes her sad, so she send money all year round, *all year round,* to the wife and kiddies—"

Helen said, "No good men, that's what you all are."

George said, "And no good kiddies. You some fine picker, Mrs. Jackson. The Almira boy was the one set the fire last week and the girl whores all over the Cape."

"You lie, boy, and you a mighty dirty talker about your own people."

"First," said George, "they ain't my people 'cause they ain't all black, they part Portuguese. Two, bums is bums, forget the color. Three, a revolutionary got no right to defend the baddies even of his own color, kind or faith. Otherwise it comes about—"

I said, "Oh, shut up, George," and Helen hit me on the arm, an old sign of affectionate approval.

George came to visit us the next summer for a few days but I did not see him at all in 1965, until the cold autumn day of Helen's funeral. That night, quite late, he rang the bell, a small suitcase in his hand.

He said, "I wouldn't have come like this, but I'm going back to Atlanta, and I wanted to— Well, I don't know."

We talked for a while about what he'd been doing, where he'd been, and then he said, "You're worried, Miss Hellman."

"Yes," I said, "if that's the word."

"About the funeral. They didn't come to you?"

"I guess that's part of it, but not much. No, they didn't come to me, although they telephoned, the two nieces, and the daughter I'd never heard from before. They asked me what kind of funeral I wanted, but I didn't like to intrude, or maybe—I don't know."

"Stinking funeral."

I said, "It's hard to know what strong people would want. I've been there before. You think they're trying to tell you something, forbid you something, but you don't know—"

"Ah," he said, "the one thing they knew for sure was she didn't want that coffin, all done up for a bishop, with brass. Seventeen hundred dollars."

"My God, I didn't know that. What fools— Well, at least I talked them into burying her in South Carolina. That I know she wanted."

"It's my birthday," George said, so we had two drinks.

When he got up to leave he said, "Don't worry about the funeral or the coffin. It's done, done."

"That's not what's worrying me. She got sick on Monday. I wanted her to go to the hospital. She wanted to go home. I was annoyed with her and went for a walk. When I came back she was gone. I phoned the next day and she said she was better, but might not be able to work for a while, and then as if she wanted to tell me something. The next morning she was dead."

"She did want to tell you something. She was getting ready to die."

I said, "You know too much, George, too much you're sure of. I don't believe she knew she was going to die. I won't believe it. And how do you know how much the coffin cost?"

"They told me," he said. "On Tuesday morning, Mrs. Jackson asked me to come round."

"She asked you, she didn't ask me. I'm jealous, George."

"She had things for me to do, errands."

I said, "She always had people doing secret errands. I didn't know you saw each other."

"Oh, sure, whenever I came up North, and then I always wrote to her. My second operation, I stayed in her place till I was better."

"You didn't tell me you had a second operation."

He smiled. "Anyway, there I am on Tuesday. She shows me two Savings Bank things and says they're for her grandchildren. Then she give me orders to pack her clothes and take 'em to the post office, all of them except one dress and shoes."

"Where did you send them?"

"Somebody in Augusta, Georgia. Then I take around the TV radio set and I sell that for her. When I come back, she asked me to make her a lemonade and said she wanted to sleep. I said I'd be back at night, but she said not to come, she wanted rest. Then she gave me one

hundred dollars. Eighty-five for me, she said, or whereve
I wanted to give it. Fifteen for Orin when I found him."

"Orin? Orin?"

"He's still hanging around. She always gave him a littl
money. But he ain't going to get this fifteen, 'cause I ain'
going to find him. She was some far-out lady, Mrs. Jack
son. Some far-out Christian lady."

"Sure was," I said.

"I hope you feel better," he said. "Next time I'm here
I'll come see you."

But he never has come to see me again.

16

DASHIELL HAMMETT

For years we made jokes about the day I would write about him. In the early years, I would say, "Tell me more about the girl in San Francisco. The silly one who lived across the hall in Pine Street."

And he would laugh and say, "She lived across the hall in Pine Street and was silly."

"Tell more than that. How much did you like her and how—?"

He would yawn. "Finish your drink and go to sleep."

But days later, maybe even that night, if I was on the find-out kick, and I was, most of the years, I would say, "O.K., be stubborn about the girls. So tell me about your grandmother and what you looked like as a baby."

"I was a very fat baby. My grandmother went to the movies every afternoon. She was very fond of a movie star called Wallace Reid and I've told you all this before."

I would say I wanted to get everything straight for the days after his death when I would write his biography and he would say that I was not to bother writing his biogra-

223

phy because it would turn out to be the history of Lillian Hellman with an occasional reference to a friend called Hammett.

The day of his death came on January 10, 1961. I will never write that biography because I cannot write about my closest, my most beloved friend. And maybe, too, because all those questions through all the thirty-one on and off years, and the sometime answers, got muddled, and life changed for both of us and the questions and answers became one in the end, flowing together from the days when I was young to the days when I was middle-aged. And so this will be no attempt at a biography of Samuel Dashiell Hammett, born in St. Mary's County, Maryland, on May 27, 1894. Nor will it be a critical appraisal of his work. In 1966 I edited and published a collection of his stories. There was a day when I thought all of them very good. But all of them are not good, though most of them, I think, are very good. It is only right to say immediately that by publishing them at all I did what Hammett did not want to do: he turned down all offers to republish the stories, although I never knew the reason and never asked. I did know, from what he said about "Tulip," the unfinished novel that I included in the book, that he meant to start a new literary life and maybe didn't want the old work to get in the way. But sometimes I think he was just too ill to care, too worn out to listen to plans or read contracts. The fact of breathing, just breathing, took up all the days and nights.

In the First World War, in camp, influenza led to tuberculosis and Hammett was to spend years after in army hospitals. He came out of the Second World War with emphysema, but how he ever got into the Second World War at the age of forty-eight still bewilders me. He telephoned me the day the army accepted him to say it was the happiest day of his life, and before I could finish saying it wasn't the happiest day of mine and what about the old scars on his lungs, he laughed and hung up. His death was caused by cancer of the lungs, discovered only two months before he died. It was not operable—I doubt that he would have agreed to an operation even if it had been—and so I decided not to tell him about the cancer. The doctor said that when the pain came, it would come in the right chest and arm, but that the pain might never come. The doctor was wrong: only a few hours after he told me, the pain did come. Hammett had had self-diagnosed rheumatism in the right arm and had always said that was why he had given up hunting. On the day I heard about the cancer, he said his gun shoulder hurt him again, would I rub it for him. I remember sitting behind him, rubbing the shoulder and hoping he would always think it was rheumatism and remember only the autumn hunting days. But the pain never came again, or if it did he never mentioned it, or maybe death was so close that the shoulder pain faded into other pains.

He did not wish to die and I like to think he didn't know he was dying. But I keep from myself even now the possible meaning of a night, very late, a short time before his death. I came into his room, and for the only time in the years I knew him there were tears in his eyes and the book was lying unread. I sat down beside him and waited a long time before I could say, "Do you want to talk about it?"

He said, almost with anger, "No. My only chance is not to talk about it."

And he never did. He had patience, courage, dignity in those last, awful months. It was as if all that makes a man's life had come together to prove itself: suffering was a private matter and there was to be no invasion of it. He would seldom even ask for anything he needed, and so the most we did—my secretary and Helen, who were devoted to him, as most women always had been—was to carry up the meals he barely touched, the books he now could hardly read, the afternoon coffee, and the martini that I insisted upon before the dinner that wasn't eaten.

One night of that last year, a bad night, I said, "Have another martini. It will make you feel better."

"No," he said, "I don't want it."

I said, "O.K., but I bet you never thought I'd urge you to have another drink."

He laughed for the first time that day. "Nope. And I never thought I'd turn it down."

Because on the night we had first met he was getting over a five-day drunk and he was to drink very heavily for the next eighteen years, and then one day, warned by a doctor, he said he would never have another drink and he kept his word except for the last year of the one martini, and that was my idea.

We met when I was twenty-four years old and he was thirty-six in a restaurant in Hollywood. The five-day drunk had left the wonderful face looking rumpled, and the very tall thin figure was tired and sagged. We talked of T.S. Eliot, although I no longer remember what we said, and then went and sat in his car and talked at each other and over each other until it was daylight. We were to meet again a few weeks later and, after that, on and sometimes off again for the rest of his life and thirty years of mine.

Thirty years is a long time, I guess, and yet as I come now to write about them the memories skip about and make no pattern and I know only certain of them are to be trusted. I know about that first meeting and the next, and there are many other pictures and sounds, but they are out of order and out of time, and I don't seem to want to put them into place. (I could have done a research job, I have on other people, but I didn't want to do one on Hammett, or to be a bookkeeper of my own life.) I don't want modesty for either of us, but I ask myself now if it can mean much to anybody but me that my second sharpest memory is of a day when we were living on a small island off the coast of Connecticut. It was six years after we had first met: six full, happy, unhappy years during which I had, with help from Hammett, written *The Chil-*

dren's Hour, which was a success, and *Days to Come,* which was not. I was returning from the mainland in a catboat filled with marketing and Hammett had come down to the dock to tie me up. He had been sick that summer—the first of the sicknesses—and he was even thinner than usual. The white hair, the white pants, the white shirt made a straight, flat surface in the late sun. I thought: Maybe that's the handsomest sight I ever saw, that line of a man, the knife for a nose, and the sheet went out of my hand and the wind went out of the sail. Hammett laughed as I struggled to get back the sail. I don't know why, but I yelled angrily, "So you're a Dostoevsky sinner-saint. So you are." The laughter stopped, and when I finally came in to the dock we didn't speak as we carried up the packages and didn't speak through dinner.

Later that night, he said, "What did you say that for? What does it mean?"

I said I didn't know why I had said it and I didn't know what it meant.

Years later, when his life had changed, I did know what I had meant that day: I had seen the sinner—whatever is a sinner—and sensed the change before it came. When I told him that, Hammett said he didn't know what I was talking about, it was all too religious for him. But he did know what I was talking about and he was pleased.

But the fat, loose, wild years were over by the time we talked that way. When I first met Dash he had written four of the five novels and was the hottest thing in Hollywood and New York. It is not remarkable to be the hottest thing in either city—the hottest kid changes for each winter season—but in his case it was of extra interest to those who collect people that the ex-detective who had bad cuts on his legs and an indentation in his head from being scrappy with criminals was gentle in manner, well educated, elegant to look at, born of early settlers, was eccentric, witty, and spent so much money on women that they would have liked him even if he had been none of the good things. But as the years passed from 1930 to 1948, he wrote only one novel and a few short stories. By 1945, the drinking was no longer gay, the drinking bouts were longer and the moods darker. I was there off and on for most of those years, but in 1948 I didn't want to see the drinking anymore. I hadn't seen or spoken to Hammett for two months until the day when his devoted cleaning lady called to say she thought I had better come down to his apartment. I said I wouldn't, and then I did. She and I dressed a man who could barely lift an arm or a leg and brought him to my house, and that night I watched delirium tremens, although I didn't know what I was watching until the doctor told me the next day at the hospital. The doctor was an old friend. He said, "I'm going to tell Hammett that if he goes on drinking he'll be dead in a few months. It's my duty to say it, but it won't do any good." In a few minutes he came out of Dash's room and said, "I told him. Dash said O.K., he'd go on the wagon forever, but he can't and he won't."

But he could and he did. Five or six years later, I told Hammett that the doctor had said he wouldn't stay on the wagon.

Dash looked puzzled. "But I gave my word that day."

I said, "Have you always kept your word?"

"Most of the time," he said, "maybe because I've so seldom given it."

He had made up honor early in his life and stuck with his rules, fierce in the protection of them. In 1951 he went to jail because he and two other trustees of the bail bond fund of the Civil Rights Congress refused to reveal the names of the contributors to the fund. The truth was that Hammett had never been in the office of the Congress, did not know the name of a single contributor.

The night before he was to appear in court, I said, "Why don't you say that you don't know the names?"

"No," he said, "I can't say that."

"Why?"

"I don't know why. I guess it has something to do with keeping my word, but I don't want to talk about that. Nothing much will happen, although I think we'll go to jail for a while, but you're not to worry because"—and then suddenly I couldn't understand him because the voice had dropped and the words were coming in a most untypical nervous rush. I said I couldn't hear him, and he raised his voice and dropped his head. "I hate this damn kind of talk, but maybe I better tell you that if it were more than jail, if it were my life, I would give it for what I think democracy is, and I don't let cops or judges tell me what I think democracy is." Then he went home to bed, and the next day he went to jail.

July 14, 1965

It is a lovely summer day. Fourteen years ago on another lovely summer day the lawyer Hammett said he didn't need, didn't want, but finally agreed to talk to because it might make me feel better, came back from West Street jail with a message from Hammett that the lawyer had written on the back of an old envelope. "Tell Lilly to go away. Tell her I don't need proof she loves me and don't want it." And so I went to Europe, and wrote a letter almost every day, not knowing that about one letter in ten was given to him, and never getting a letter from him because he wasn't allowed to write to anybody who wasn't related to him. (Hammett had, by this time, been moved to a federal penitentiary in West Virginia.) I had only one message that summer: that his prison job was cleaning bathrooms, and he was cleaning them better than I had ever done.

I came back to New York to meet Hammett the night he came out of jail. Jail had made a thin man thinner, a sick man sicker. The invalid figure was trying to walk proud, but coming down the ramp from the plane he was holding tight to the railing, and before he saw me he stumbled and stopped to rest. I guess that was the first time I knew he would now always be sick. I felt too bad to say hello, and so I ran back into the airport and we lost each other for a few minutes. But in a week, when he had slept and was able to eat small amounts of food, an irritating farce began and was to last for the rest of his life: jail wasn't bad at all. True, the food was awful and sometimes even rotted, but you could always have milk; the moonshiners and car thieves were dopes but their conversation was no sillier than a New York cocktail party; nobody liked cleaning toilets, but in time you came to take a certain pride in the work and an interest in the different cleaning materials; jail homosexuals were nasty-tempered, but no worse than the ones in any bar, and so on. Hammett's form of boasting was always to make fun of trouble or pain. We had once met Howard Fast on the street and he told us about his to-be-served jail sentence. As we moved away, Hammett said, "It will be easier for you, Howard, and you won't catch cold, if you first take off the crown of thorns." So I should have guessed that Hammett would talk about his own time in jail the way many of us talk about college.

I do not wish to avoid the subject of Hammett's political beliefs, but the truth is that I do not know if he was a member of the Communist party and I never asked him. If that seems an odd evasion between two people we did not mean it as an evasion: it was, probably, the product of the time we lived through and a certain unspoken agreement about privacy. Now, in looking back, I think we had rather odd rules about privacy, unlike other peoples' rules. We never, for example, asked each other about money, how much something cost or how much something earned, although each of us gave to the other as, through the years, each of us needed it. It does not matter much to me that I don't know if Hammett was a Communist party member: most certainly he was a Marxist. But he was a ery critical Marxist, often contemptuous of the Soviet Union in the same hick sense that many Americans are contemptuous of foreigners. He was often witty and biting sharp about the American Communist party, but he was, in the end, loyal to them. Once, in an argument with me, he said that of course a great deal about Communism worried him and always had and that when he found something better he intended to change his opinions. And then he said, "Now please don't let's ever argue about it again because we're doing each other harm." And so we did not argue again, and I suppose that itself does a kind of harm or leaves a moat too large for crossing, but it was better than the arguments we had been having—they had started in the 1940's—when he knew that I could not go his way. I think that must have pained him, but he never said so. It pained me, too, but I knew that, unlike many radicals, whatever he believed in, whatever he had arrived at, came from reading and thinking. He took time to find out what he thought, and he had an open mind and a tolerant nature.

Hammett came from a generation of talented writers. The ones I knew were romantic about being writers: it was a good thing to be, a writer, maybe the best, and you made sacrifices for it. I guess they wanted money and praise as much as writers do today, but I don't think the diseased need was as great, nor the poison as strong. You wanted to have money, of course, but you weren't in competition with merchants or bankers, and if you threw your talents around you didn't throw them to the Establishment for catching. When I first met Dash he was throwing himself away on Hollywood parties and New York bars: the throwing away was probably no less damaging but a little more forgivable because those who were there to catch could have stepped from *The Day of the Locust*. But he knew what was happening to him, and after 1948 it was not to happen again. It would be good to say that as his life changed the productivity increased, but

231

it didn't. Perhaps the vigor and the force had been dissipated. But good as it is, productivity is not the only proof of a serious life, and now, more than ever, he sat down to read. He read everything and anything. He didn't like writers very much, he didn't like or dislike most people, but he was without envy of good writers and was tender about all writers, probably because he remembered his own early struggles.

I don't know when Hammett first decided to write, but I know that he started writing after he left army hospital in the 1920's, settling with his wife and daughter—there was to be another daughter—in San Francisco. (He went back to work for Pinkerton for a while, although I am not sure if it was this period or later.) Once, when I asked him why he never wanted to go to Europe, why he never wanted to see another country, he said he had wanted to go to Australia, maybe to stay, but on the day he decided to leave Pinkerton forever he decided to give up the idea of Australia forever. An Australian boat, out of Sydney for San Francisco, carrying two hundred thousand dollars in gold, notified its San Francisco insurance broker that the gold was missing. The insurance company was a client of Pinkerton's, and so Hammett and another operative met the boat as it docked, examined all sailors and officers, searched the boat, but couldn't find the gold. They knew the gold had to be on the boat, and so the agency decided that when the boat sailed home Hammett should sail with it. A happy man, going free where he had always dreamed of going, packed his bags. A few hours before sailing time, the head of the agency suggested they give a last, hopeless search. Hammett climbed a smokestack he had examined several times before, looked down and shouted, "They moved it. It's here." He said that as the words came out of his mouth, he said to himself, "You haven't sense enough even to be a detective. Why couldn't you have discovered the gold one day out to sea?" He fished out the gold, took it back to the Pinkerton office, and resigned that afternoon.

With the resignation came a series of jobs, but I don't remember what he said they were. In a year or so, the tuberculosis started to cut up again and hemorrhages began. He was determined not to go back to army hospitals, and since he thought he had a limited amount of time to live, he decided to spend it on something he wanted to do. He moved away from his wife and children, lived on soup, and began to write. One day the hemorrhages stopped, never to reappear, and sometime in this period he began to earn a small living from pulp magazines and squibs and even poems sold to Mencken's *Smart Set*. I am not clear about this time of Hammett's life, but it always sounded rather nice and free and 1920's Bohemian, and the girl on Pine Street and the other on Grant Street, and good San Francisco food in cheap restaurants, and dago red wine, and fame in the pulp magazine field, then and maybe now a world of its own.

July 18, 1965

This memory of Hammett is being written in the summer. Maybe that's why most of what I remember about him has to do with summer, although like all people who live in the country, we were more closely thrown together in winter. Winter was the time of work for me and I worked better if Hammett was in the room. There he was, is, as I close my eyes and see another house, reading *The Autumn Garden*. I was, of course, nervous as I watched him. He had always been critical, I was used to that and wanted it, but now I sensed something new and was worried. He finished the play, came across the room, put the manuscript in my lap, went back to his chair and began to talk. It was not the usual criticism: it was sharp and angry, snarling. He spoke as if I had betrayed him. I was so shocked, so pained that I would not now remember

233

the scene if it weren't for a diary that I've kept for each play. He said that day, "You started as a serious writer. That's what I liked, that's what I worked for. I don't know what's happened, but tear this up and throw it away. It's worse than bad—it's half good." He sat glaring at me and I ran from the room and went down to New York and didn't come back for a week. When I did come back I had torn up the play, put the scraps in a briefcase, put the briefcase outside his door. We never mentioned the play again until seven months later when I had rewritten it. I was no longer nervous as he read it: I was too tired to care and I went to sleep on the couch. I woke up because Hammett was sitting beside me, patting my hair, grinning at me and nodding.

After he had nodded for a long time, I said, "What's the matter with you?"

"Nice things. Because it's the best play anybody's written in a long time. Maybe longer. It's a good day. A good day."

I was so shocked with the kind of praise I had never heard before that I started out of the door to take a walk.

He said, "Nix. Come on back. There's a speech in the last act went sour. Do it again."

I said I wasn't going to do it again. He said O.K., he'd do it, and he did, working all through the night.

When *The Autumn Garden* was in rehearsal Dash came almost every day, even more disturbed than I was that something was happening to the play, life was going out of it, which can and does happen on the stage and once started can seldom be changed.

Yesterday I read three letters he wrote to a friend about his hopes for the play, the rehearsals and the opening. His concern for me and the play was very great, but in time I came to learn that he was good to all writers who needed help, and that the generosity had less to do with the writer than with writing and the pains of writing. I knew, of course, about the generosity long before, but generosity and profligacy often intertwine and it took me a long time to tell them apart.

A few years after I met Dash the large Hollywood money was gone, given away, spent on me who didn't want it and on others who did. I think Hammett was the only person I ever met who really didn't care about money, made no complaints and had no regrets when it was gone. Maybe money is unreal for most of us, easier to give away than things we want. (But I didn't know that then, maybe confused it with showing off.) Once, years later, Hammett bought himself an expensive crossbow at a time when it meant giving up other things to have it. It had just arrived that day and he was testing it, fiddling with it, liking it very much, when friends arrived with their ten-year-old boy. Dash and the boy spent the afternoon with the crossbow and the child's face was awful when he had to leave it. Hammett opened the back door of the car, put in the crossbow, went hurriedly into the house, refusing all cries of "No, no" and such.

When our friends had gone, I said, "Was that necessary? You wanted it so much."

Hammett said, "The kid wanted it more. Things belong to people who want them most."

And thus it was, certainly, with money, and thus the troubles came, and suddenly there were days of no dinners, rent unpaid and so on; there they were, the lean times, no worse than many other people have had, but the contrast of no dinner on Monday and a wine feast on Tuesday made me a kind of irritable he never understood.

When we were very broke, those first years in New York, Hammett got a modest advance from Knopf and began to write *The Thin Man*. He moved to what was jokingly called the Diplomat's Suite in a hotel run by our friend Nathanael West. It was a new hotel, but Pep West and the depression had managed to run it down immediately. Certainly Hammett's suite had never seen a diplomat, because even the smallest Oriental could not have functioned well in the space. But the rent was cheap, the awful food could be charged, and some part of my idle time could be spent with Pep snooping around the lives of the other rather strange guests. I had known Dash when he was writing short stories, but I had never been around for a long piece of work. Life changed: the drinking stopped, the parties were over. The locking-in time had come and nothing was allowed to disturb it until the book was finished. I had never seen anybody work that way: the care for every word, the pride in the neatness of the typed page itself, the refusal for ten days or two weeks to go out even for a walk for fear something would be lost. It was a good year for me and I learned from it and was, perhaps, frightened by a man who now did not need me. So it was a happy day when I was given half the manuscript to read and was told that I was Nora. It was nice to be Nora, married to Nick Charles, maybe one of the few marriages in modern literature where the man and woman like each other and have a fine time together. But I was soon put back in place—Hammett said I was also the silly girl in the book and the villainess. I don't know if he was joking, but in those days it worried me: I was very anxious that he think well of me. Most people wanted that from him. Years later, Richard Wilbur said that as you came toward Hammett to shake his hand in the first meeting, you wanted him to approve of you. There are such people and Hammett was one of them. I don't know what makes this quality in certain men—something floating around them that hasn't much to do with who they are or what they've done—but maybe it has to do with reserves so deep that we know we cannot touch them with charm or jokes or favors. It comes out as something more than dignity and shows on the face. In jail the guards called Hammett "sir" and out of jail other people came close to it. One night in the last years of his life, we walked into a restaurant, passing a group of young writers that I knew but he didn't. We stopped and I introduced him: these hip young men suddenly turned into deferential schoolboys and their faces became what they must have been at ten years old. It took me years of teasing to force out of Hammett that he knew what effect he had on many people. Then he told me that when he was fourteen years old and had his first job working for the Baltimore and Ohio Railroad, he had come late to work each day for a week. His employer told him he was fired. Hammett said he nodded, walked to the door, and was called back by a puzzled man who said, "If you give me your word it won't happen again, you can keep the job." Hammett said, "Thank you, but I can't do that." After a silence the man said, "O.K., keep the job anyway." Dash said that he didn't know what was right about what he had done, but he did know that it would always be useful.

When *The Thin Man* was sold to a magazine—most of the big slick magazines had turned it down for being too daring, although what they meant by daring was hard to understand—we got out of New York fast. We got drunk for a few weeks in Miami, then moved on to a primitive fishing camp in the Keys where we stayed through the spring and summer, fishing every day, reading every night. It was a fine year: we found out that we got along best without people, in the country. Hammett, like many Southerners, had a deep feeling for isolated places where there were animals, birds, bugs and sounds. He was easy in the woods, an excellent shot, and later when I bought the farm, he would spend the autumn days in the woods, coming back with birds or rabbits, and then, when the shooting season was over, would spend many winter days sitting on a stool in the woods watching squirrels or beavers or deer, or ice fishing in the lake. (He was, as are most sportsmen, obsessively neat with instruments, and obsessively messy with rooms.) The interests of the day would carry into the nights when he would read *Bees: Their Vision and Language* or *German Gunmakers of the Eighteenth Century* or something on how to tie knots, or

inland birds, and then leave such a book for another boo'
on whatever he had decided to learn. It would be impos
sible now for me to remember all that he wanted to learn
but I remember a long year of study on the retina of the
eye; how to play chess in your head: the Icelandic sagas
the history of the snapping turtle; Hegel; would a hearing
aid—he bought a very good one—help in detecting bird
sounds; then from Hegel, of course, to Marx and Engels
straight through; the shore life of the Atlantic; and finally
and for the rest of his life, mathematics. He was more
interested in mathematics than in any other subject except
baseball. Listening to television or the radio, he would
mutter about the plays and the players to me who didn'
know the difference between a ball and a bat. Often I
would ask him to stop it, and then he would shake his
head and say, "All I ever wanted was a docile woman and
look what I got," and we would talk about docility, how
little for a man to want, and he would claim that only vain
or neurotic men needed to have "types" in women—all
other men took what they could get.

The hit and miss reading, the picking up of any book
made for a remarkable mind, neat, accurate, respectful of
fact. He took a strong and lasting dislike to a man who
insisted mackerel were related to herring, and once he left
my living room when a famous writer talked without
much knowledge of existentialism, refusing to come down
to dinner with the writer because, he said, "He's a waste
of time. Liars are bores." A neighbor once rang up to ask
him how to stop a leak in a swimming pool, and he knew;
my farmer's son asked him how to make a pair of snow-
shoes, and he knew; born a Maryland Catholic (but having long ago left the Church), he knew more about
Judaism than I did, and more about New Orleans music,
food and architecture than my father, who had grown up
there. Once I wanted to know about early glassmaking for
windows and was headed for the encyclopedia, but Hammett told me before I got there; he knew a great deal about

birds and insects, and for a month he studied the cross-pollination of corn, and for many, many months tried plasma physics. It was more than reading: it was a man at work. Any book would do, or almost any—he was narrowly impatient when I read letters or criticism and would refer to them as my "carrying" books, good only for balancing yourself as you climbed the stairs to bed. It was always strange to me that he liked books so much and had so little interest in the men who wrote them. (There were, of course, exceptions: he liked Faulkner and we had fine drinking nights together during Faulkner's New York visits in the '30's.) Perhaps it is more accurate to say that he had a good time with writers when they talked about books, but would usually leave them when they talked about anything else. He was deeply moved by painting—he himself tried to paint until the last summer of his life when he could no longer stand at an easel, and the last walk we ever took was down the block to the Metropolitan Museum—and by music. But I never remember his liking a painter or a musician, although I do remember his saying that he thought most of them peacocks. He was never uncharitable toward simple people, he was often too impatient with famous people.

There are, of course, many men who are happy in an army, but up to the Second World War I had never known any and didn't want to. I was, therefore, shocked to find that Hammett was one of them. I do not know why an eccentric man who lived more than most Americans by his own standards found the restrictions, the disciplines, and the hard work of an army enlisted man so pleasant and amusing. Maybe a life ruled over by other people solved some of the problems, allowed a place for a man who by himself could not seek out people, maybe gave him a sense of pride that a man of forty-eight could stand up with those half his age; maybe all that, and maybe simply that he liked his country and felt that this was a just war and had to be fought. Whatever Hammett's reasons, the miseries of the Aleutian Islands were not miseries to him. I have many letters describing their beauty and for years he talked of going back to see them again. He conducted a training program there for a while and edited a good army newspaper: the copy was clean, the news was accurate, the jokes were funny. He became a kind of legend in the Alaska-Aleutian army. I have talked to many men who served with him, and have a letter from one of them: "I was a kid then. We all were. The place was awful but there was Hammett, by the time I got there called Pop by some and Grandpop by others, editor of the paper, with far more influence on us, scaring us more in a way than the colonel, although I think he also scared the colonel. . . . I remember best that we'd come into the hut screaming or complaining and he'd be lying on his bunk reading. He'd look up and smile and we'd all shut up. Nobody would go near the bed or disturb him. When money was needed or help he'd hear about it and there he was. He paid for the leave and marriage of one kid. When another of us ran up a scarey bar bill in Nome, he gave the guy who cleaned the Nome toilets money to pay it and say it was his bill if anybody in the army asked him. . . . A lot of kids did more than complain—they went half to nuts. And why not? We had the worst weather in the most desolate hole, no fighting, constant williwaws when you had to crawl to the latrines because if you stood up the wind would take you to Siberia, and an entertainment program which got mixed up between Olivia de Haviland and recordings of W. H. Auden. But the main worry was women. When you'd been there a year all kinds of rumors went around about what happened to you without them. I remember nightly bull sessions in our hut about the dangers of celibacy. Hammett would listen for a while, smile, go back to reading or when the talk got too loud he'd sigh and go to sleep. (Because of the newspaper his work hours started around two A.M.) One night when the session was extra loud crazy and one kid was yelling, Hammett got off his bunk to go to work. The kid yelled, 'What do you think, Pop? *Say something.*' Hammett said, 'O.K. A woman would be nice, but not getting any doesn't cause your teeth or hair to fall out and if you go nuts you'd have gone anyway and if you kiddies don't stop this stuff I'm going to move into another hut and under my bed is a bottle of Scotch so drink it and go to sleep.' Then he walked out to go to work. We got so scared about losing him that we never said another word like that in front of him."

But, as I have said, the years after the war, from 1945 to 1948, were not good years; the drinking grew wilder and there was a lost, thoughtless quality I had never seen before. I knew then that I had to go my own way. I do not mean that we were separated, I mean only that we saw less of each other, were less close to each other. But even in those years there still were wonderful days on the farm of autumn hunting and squirrel pies and sausage making and all the books he read as I tried to write a play. I can see him now, getting up to put a log on the fire and coming over to shake me. He swore that I would always say, "I haven't been sleeping. I've been thinking." He would laugh and say, "Sure. You've been asleep for an hour, but lots of people think best when they're asleep and you're one of them."

In 1952 I had to sell the farm. I moved to New York and Dash rented a small house in Katonah. I went once a week to see him, he came once a week to New York, and we talked on the phone every day. But he wanted to be alone—or so I thought then, but am now not so sure because I have learned that proud men who can ask for nothing may be fine characters, but they are difficult to live with or to understand. In any case, as the years went on he became a hermit, and the ugly little country cottage grew uglier with books piled on every chair and no place to sit, the desk a foot high with unanswered mail. The signs of sickness were all around: now the phonograph was unplayed, the typewriter untouched, the beloved, foolish gadgets unopened in their packages. When I went for my weekly visits we didn't talk much and when he came for his weekly visits to me he was worn out from the short journey.

Perhaps it took me too long to realize that he couldn't live alone anymore, and even after I realized it I didn't know how to say it. One day, immediately after he had made me promise to stop reading "L'il Abner," and I was laughing at his vehemence about it, he suddenly looked embarrassed—he always looked embarrassed when he had something emotional to say—and he said, "I can't live alone anymore. I've been falling. I'm going to a Veterans Hospital. It will be O.K., we'll see each other all the time, and I don't want any tears from you." But there were tears from me, two days of tears, and finally he consented to come and live in my apartment. (Even now, as I write this, I am still angry and amused that he always had to have things on his own terms: a few minutes ago I got up from the typewriter and railed against him for it, as if he could still hear me. I know as little about the nature of romantic love as I knew when I was eighteen, but I do know about the deep pleasure of continuing interest, the excitement of wanting to know what somebody else thinks, will do, will not do, the tricks played and un-played, the short cord that the years make into rope and, in my case, is there, hanging loose, long after death. I am not sure what Hammett would feel about the rest of these notes about him, but I am sure that he would be pleased that I am angry with him today.) And so he lived with me for the last four years of his life. Not all of that time was easy, indeed some of it was very bad, but it was an unspoken pleasure that having come together so many years before, ruined so much, and repaired a little, we had endured. Sometimes I would resent the understated or seldom stated side of us and, guessing death wasn't too far away, I would try for something to have afterwards. One day I said, "We've done fine, haven't we?"

He said, "Fine's too big a word for me. Why don't we just say we've done better than most people?"

On New Year's Eve, 1960, I left Hammett in the care of a pleasant practical nurse and went to spend a few hours with friends. I left their house at twelve-thirty, not knowing that the nurse began telephoning for me a few minutes later. As I came into Hammett's room, he was sitting at his desk, his face as eager and excited as it had been in the drinking days. In his lap was the heavy book of Japanese prints that he had bought and liked many years before. He was pointing to a print and saying to the nurse, "Look at it, darling, it's wonderful." As I came toward him, the nurse moved away, but he caught her hand and kissed it, in the same charming, flirtatious way of the early days, looking up to wink at me. The book was lying upside down and so the nurse didn't need to mumble the word "irrational." From then on—we took him to the hospital the next morning—I never knew and will now not ever know what irrational means. Hammett refused all medication, all aid from nurses and doctors in some kind of mysterious wariness. Before the night of the upside-down book our plan had been to move to Cambridge because I was to teach a seminar at Harvard. An upside-down book should have told me the end had come, but I didn't want to think that way, and so I flew to Cambridge, found a nursing home for Dash, and flew back that night to tell him about it. He said, "But how are we going to get to Boston?" I said we'd take an ambulance and I guess for the first time in his life he said, "That will cost too much." I said, "If it does, then we'll take a covered wagon." He smiled and said, "Maybe that's the way we should have gone places anyway."

And so I felt better that night, sure of a postponement. I was wrong. Before six o'clock the next morning the hospital called me. Hammett had gone into a coma. As I ran across the room toward his bed there was a last sign of life: his eyes opened in shocked surprise and he tried to raise his head. He was never to think again and he died two days later.

But I do not wish to end this book on an elegiac note. It is true that I miss Hammett, and that is as it should be. He was the most interesting man I've ever met. I laugh at what he did say, amuse myself with what he might say, and even this many years later speak to him, often angry that he still interferes with me, still dictates the rules.

But I am not yet old enough to like the past better than the present, although there are nights when I have a passing sadness for the unnecessary pains, the self-made foolishness that was, is, and will be. I do regret that I have spent too much of my life trying to find what I called "truth," trying to find what I called "sense." I never knew what I meant by truth, never made the sense I hoped for. All I mean is that I left too much of me unfinished because I wasted too much time. However.

READ THE WOMEN
WHO TAKE STANDS
AND ACT ON THEM

THE NAMES THAT SPELL
GREAT LITERATURE

Choose from today's most renowned world authors—every or
an important addition to your personal library.

Hermann Hesse

☐	2906	KNULP	$1.
☐	11916	MAGISTER LUDI	$2.
☐	12024	DEMIAN	$1.
☐	10060	GERTRUDE	$1.
☐	11978	THE JOURNEY TO THE EAST	$1.
☐	12529	SIDDHARTHA	$2.2
☐	10352	BENEATH THE WHEEL	$1.9
☐	12509	NARCISSUS AND GOLDMUND	$2.
☐	11289	STEPPENWOLF	$1.
☐	11510	ROSSHALDE	$1.9

Alexander Solzhenitsyn

☐	10111	THE FIRST CIRCLE	$2.5
☐	12677	ONE DAY IN THE LIFE OF IVAN DENISOVICH	$2.2
☐	2997	AUGUST 1914	$2.5
☐	11300	CANCER WARD	$2.5
☐	12079	LENIN IN ZURICH	$2.9

Jerzy Kosinski

☐	12465	STEPS	$2.2
☐	12460	THE PAINTED BIRD	$2.2
☐	2613	COCKPIT	$2.2

Doris Lessing

☐	11870	THE SUMMER BEFORE THE DARK	$2.2
☐	10425	THE GOLDEN NOTEBOOK	$2.2
☐	12461	THE FOUR-GATED CITY	$2.9
☐	11717	BRIEFING FOR A DESCENT INTO HELL	$2.2

André Schwarz-Bart

☐	12510	THE LAST OF THE JUST	$2.9

Buy them at your local bookstore or use this handy coupon for ordering

DISCOVER
THE DRAMA OF LIFE
IN THE LIFE OF DRAMA

11880	**CYRANO DE BERGERAC** Rostand	$1.50
12204	**FOUR GREAT PLAYS** Ibsen	$1.95
11881	**COMP. PLAYS SOPHOCLES**	$2.25
11936	**FOUR GREAT PLAYS BY CHEKHOV** Anton Chekhov	$1.75
7853	**THE CITIZEN KANE BOOK** Pauline Kael, Herman J. Mankiewicz, and Orson Welles	$2.95
10036	**THE NIGHT THOREAU SPENT IN JAIL** Jerome Lawrence and Robert E. Lee	$1.50
12832	**THE PRICE** Arthur Miller	$1.95
12358	**BRIAN'S SONG** Blinn	$1.75
12548	**THE EFFECTS OF GAMMA RAYS ON MAN-IN-THE-MOON MARIGOLDS** Paul Zindel	$1.95
12711	**50 GREAT SCENES FOR STUDENT ACTORS** Lewy Oltson, ed.	$1.95
11996	**INHERIT THE WIND** Lawrence & Lee	$1.50
10758	**LOOK BACK IN ANGER** John Osborne	$1.50
11508	**TEN PLAYS BY EURIPIDES** Hadas	$1.95
12418	**THE CRUCIBLE** Arthur Miller	$1.95
12214	**THE MIRACLE WORKER** Gibson	$1.75
11777	**AFTER THE FALL** Arthur Miller	$1.95

Buy them at your local bookstore or use this handy coupon for ordering:

Bantam Books, Inc., Dept. EDH, 414 East Golf Road, Des Plaines, Ill. 60016

Please send me the books I have checked above. I am enclosing $_____
(please add 75¢ to cover postage and handling). Send check or money order
—no cash or C.O.D.'s please.

Mr/Mrs/Miss_____

Address_____

City_____State/Zip_____

EDH—1/79

Please allow four weeks for delivery. This offer expires 7/79.

Bantam Book Catalog

Here's your up-to-the-minute listing of over 1,400 titles by your favorite authors.

This illustrated, large format catalog gives a description of each title. For your convenience it is divided into categories in fiction and non fiction—gothics, science fiction, westerns, mysteries, cookbooks, mysticism and occult, biographies, history, family living, health, psychology art.

So don't delay—take advantage of this special opportunity to increase your reading pleasure

Just send us your name and address and 50¢ (to help defray postage and handling costs).